My chefs joke that 'did you add the lemon' should be inscribed on my tombstone. It is the question I consistently ask as plates leave the kitchen. Sometimes, a few drops is all a dish really needs to sing.

US-born Danielle Alvarez is head chef at Sydney restaurant Fred's, where her mission is to serve food that tastes like the best kind of home cooking. The recipes shared here channel Fred's much-admired flair for honest, seasonal food, but they are also the recipes that Danielle cooks at home whenever she can.

Always Add Lemon
Danielle Alvarez

Hardie Grant

BOOKS

For my mom – thank you for being the
woman that you are. The feeling of love and
warmth your cooking exudes is what I have
tried to chase through these recipes.

For my beloved brother Manny – not
a day goes by without you in my heart.
I hope you would be proud.

Introduction 4

I. Kitchen staples 8

1   Equipment and tools 10
2   Seasoning and more 10
3   Essentials 12

II. Recipes 18

1   Salads 20
2   Fruits and vegetables 48
3   Pasta, grains and legumes 94
4   Seafood 134
5   Poultry and meat 164
6   Dessert 198

III. Projects 224

1   Pastry 226
2   Bread 230
3   Dairy 236
4   Meat 240
5   Pickles 246

What to cook 248
Index 250
Thank you 256

Introduction

Cooking was never what I set out to do in life. I had a lucky but pretty normal upbringing: middle class in Miami, FL, two amazing parents, siblings, a good education and not too many worries. The maybe not-so-normal part was the focus on food and cooking. My family is Cuban. Maybe this means nothing to you, but let me explain ... Everything was centred around what meal was being made when, and even before one meal was finished, the next was simmering away. Ours was the kind of family that would spend an entire day roasting a suckling pig only to start talking about how to use the leftovers before it had even been served! This was not 'eat to live', it was a 'live to eat' childhood. It was only after I grew up, moved away and travelled a bit that I realised that all the food I connected with was from cultures that also lived this way: Italian, French, Spanish, Japanese, Mexican, Lebanese ... They value good food and good eating and, crucially, the gathering of family and friends around a table. They all know that you must start with quality, seasonal ingredients. The way a cook puts those ingredients together is the learned skill. And, sometimes, it's not that easy. It doesn't have to be difficult, but it does take practice and time.

I realised that it wasn't the simplified, from a tin, 15-minute meal that made me fall in love with food and cooking. It was the all-day, overnight, sourced from the farmers' market, made-from-scratch kind of cooking that enchanted me. I love the suspense and transformation and, ultimately, the reward when you braise a piece of meat in the oven for hours, or you mix bread dough and check on it every 30 minutes.

But what I probably love most is cooking for others. The look of happiness on people's faces when they taste something delicious is an indescribable feeling. Food can make us happy and it can also be the great unifier. It stops us in our tracks and forces us to pause, no matter our culture, background, religion or history – we all need this. It is my hope that, over a delicious plate of food, we can draw our attention to each other, have discussions about important issues or simply enjoy each other's company. Cooking and sharing a meal with people you love is, for me, one of the greatest luxuries in life. It was this love for food and what it can do that led me to pursue a career in cooking.

I probably have one of the most charmed professional cooking stories out there. From the moment I decided I wanted to cook, life just seemed to conspire to make it happen. I moved to California after landing an internship at The French Laundry, then moved to San Francisco and worked for the incredible Amaryll Schwertner and her utterly chic and charming Ferry Building restaurant, Boulettes Larder. My next big move had the most impact on my personal and professional view of food.

The previous restaurants opened my eyes to the great ingredients and bounty of the Bay Area, but Chez Panisse really taught me how to put them together. To quote British food writer Diana Henry, Chez Panisse is making food that a very good and thoughtful home cook would make. It wasn't restaurant-y, which is what I loved. The menus changed daily. They were ambitious, perfectly seasonal, always well constructed, and made with a lot of care. I never cooked the same thing twice. Over four years, I saw and did more than many cooks will do in double that time. It was a daily dive into tradition, culture, beauty and food for pleasure. Of course, this kind of cooking, especially as a fairly green chef, is exhilarating and terrifying. For the first two years, every day was filled with something I hadn't done before. Guests arrive at 5.30 pm, and they don't care how challenging your day was filleting the salmon. I made many mistakes, but I learned from them. I learned to have faith in myself, to observe others, to listen to my palate and to exist in that place that is always slightly on the edge.

It was a dream job, but I was determined to seek new challenges. When an opportunity in Sydney came up, I took it. I was hired to be head chef of Fred's in inner-city Paddington. It's a busy, lively restaurant where we try to capture the essence of good home cooking. Ultimately, though, a restaurant is not your home, no matter how much you try. It's a fast-paced environment with teams of people and demanding guests. It's a different feeling to that of lingering in the home kitchen all day, pottering around the house while the beans simmer or the cake bakes. Maybe it is the frantic pace of life that makes me crave a day in the kitchen when time doesn't matter. Even if it's just for myself; I need that sometimes.

This is my first step into writing, and I find myself back in this place that is slightly closer to the edge. Cooking is familiar and comforting, and I am learning how to translate what has taken years to discover into words on a page. What I hope to convey is that food and cooking should be big parts of our lives, and time should be made for them. We are all busy, and the thought of spending all day in the kitchen is not for everyone, but I'm not speaking to that person; I'm speaking to the home cooks and even professional cooks who want to be in the kitchen all day and use cooking as a way to discover new cultures, new ingredients, new and old ways of doing things. I want to share some of what I've learned through a lot of trial and a lot of error.

I also want to share a few cooking projects. The kind that produce something that you might easily buy at the shop, but without the satisfaction of making it yourself. I am talking about bread, pastry, fresh cheese, yoghurt, terrines and pickles. These recipes are more step-by-step than the others and should be followed accordingly. I have included them for the younger me, who searched for this information in one place in endless books. For the other recipes, once you know the basic technique and flavour, please adjust to your taste, use different ingredients – I won't be offended.

Now, the last bit I want to say before you progress to the recipes: I believe in the power of food and cooking and the joy it can bring to our lives. In the words of Michael Pollan, eating is a political act and the way we grow our food, the way we buy what we eat, dictates the kind of society we live in. Please pass your love of cooking and the traditions you create on to your children – they are our future.

On the following page, I share a few strong beliefs about cooking (rules, if you will; allow me that terminology) that I believe will deliver the best and tastiest results.

1   Cook with the seasons.

2   Support your local farmers.

3   Don't freak out when things
go wrong.

4   Read the full recipe before
you start.

5   Find your favourite wooden spoon.
Keep it.

6   Taste, taste, taste.
At every step of the way.

7   Invite people over for a meal.
But don't overthink it.

8   A little bit of lemon will
change everything.

1   This is not a new idea, and I imagine if you're reading this you know it already, but nuances of specific seasons in different locations can be tricky. It's more about taking the time to understand what's happening in nature (and if you follow rule #2, this will be especially relevant) and you will be better able to select the best ingredients for that moment. This may also mean substitutions in recipes, which you shouldn't be afraid of! The point is, go to the shop or market first and decide what to make later; the recipe can be your guide, but every ingredient doesn't need to be exactly as I've stated (with the exception of baking and dessert).

2   I realise not every community is as lucky as Sydney or northern California or towns in Europe to have beautiful abundant produce growing within a radius of a few hours, but in that case keeping it local might mean keeping it domestic. If you are lucky to live in a food basket, appreciate it and buy from your local farmers. Your community and your food will be better for it.

3   As someone who has probably made every mistake possible (in food and, sometimes, life), I also know how to recover from them and how to make it seem like nothing went wrong. I'll try to point out some common pitfalls along the way so you can avoid the mistakes I made. In case you've hit a snag, asses if something is not salvageable at all or if you just need to scrape a bit of the burn off. If there is no saving it and you're entertaining, just fess up and order a pizza. Even the greatest chefs in the world have had enormous kitchen disasters.

4   Twice, actually.

5   I don't know what it is about wooden spoons, but I adore them. Maybe it's how they feel in my hand, smooth and soft, or perhaps it is because they often look a bit old and worn, and I can imagine all the pots they have stirred and they make me feel like there is history and love there. Everyone should keep a favourite in their kitchen.

6   Eventually you will figure out what you're tasting for.

7   You don't need a big house built for entertaining. Some of the best times I have had have been in small apartments eating on a blanket on the floor. You just need to know what is achievable in the space you have – entertaining needn't be filled with anxiety. It should be enjoyable and fun. My number one tip is to make sure you have a cocktail or a wine and simple snack ready when guests arrive; it takes the edge off for everyone. That, and a great playlist, will ensure good times no matter what.

8   My chefs joke that, 'Did you add the lemon?' should be inscribed on my tombstone. It is the question I consistently ask as plates leave the kitchen. Sometimes, a few drops is all a dish needs to really sing.

I.
Kitchen staples

1	Equipment and tools	10
2	Seasoning and more	10
3	Essentials	12

1 Equipment and tools

Every kitchen should have a few things that enable you to make virtually anything. I am not a fan of single-purpose appliances, but some things are necessary, such as an ice-cream machine if you want to make ice cream at home, or a pasta machine if you want to make your own pasta. But, as you'll see throughout this book, I also like the idea of doing everything by hand, so I've made a few suggestions on how to avoid using a machine, if possible, in the recipes.

My essential kitchen tools are:

wide, cast-iron frying pan

enamel-lined Dutch oven

wide, stainless steel sauté pan

soup or stockpot with lid

commercial-style 45×33×2.5 cm (18×13×1 in) baking tray (sheet)

pizza stone

rolling pin

pasta machine

assorted sizes of mixing bowls

wooden spoon

whisk

rubber spatula

large stone mortar and pestle

round cake tins

fluted tart mould

blender

ice-cream machine

large wooden chopping board

sharp chef's knife

small and large serrated knives

small paring knife

measuring spoons

good set of scales

baking paper

terracotta or glass baking dishes

bamboo steamer baskets

I certainly have more than this in my kitchen, but I could happily cook with just these items and be ready to make almost anything.

2 Seasoning and more

Salt I almost exclusively use flaky sea salt unless I specify fine sea salt. Keep your salt in a salt cellar and pick it up with your fingertips unless you are adding measured spoonfuls to something. Do not pour it directly out of the packaging onto or into foods. I like the fact that with flaky salt I can feel how much I'm adding, and it allows me more control, whereas fine sea salt tends to slip out of my fingers without me noticing how much I've just added. If you use only fine salt, reduce the salt measurements by half and taste as you go.

Fine sea salt is perfect for sprinkling on fried items, as it sticks to whatever you are sprinkling it on. I also use it to season pasta water or blanching water since both require so much of it and flaky salt is often more expensive.

Salts in fact have distinct flavours and densities and I recommend tasting them to choose what you like.

Butter   Always, always use unsalted butter for cooking. The only time I opt for salted butter is if I am serving it with bread. Unsalted allows you better control over the seasoning, and I also just prefer its sweet flavour.

Cream   I use thick (double/heavy) cream in all my recipes – not to be confused with thickened (whipping) cream (which I don't recommend). It is the purest, and is easily pourable. Some creams also contain gelatine and other stabilisers, which I avoid. Crème fraîche is a cultured cream that thickens as it cultures. I love this too and have included a recipe (see page 239) so you can try it at home.

Ovens   Most ovens are wildly imprecise with temperature. I'm sure if you have a fancy oven you can be confident of its reliability, but otherwise, I recommend a small oven thermometer to hang inside the oven. You would be surprised at how much the temperature can differ. This is most important for baking recipes and the projects. Otherwise, if your home oven is like mine, I use it more in the categories of low, medium and hot. Low is anything 170°C (340°F) or below, medium is 170–200°C (340–400°F), and anything over that is hot. Get to know your oven so you can navigate temperature differences.

And as for fan-forced or convection ovens, reduce the oven temperatures by about 20°C (70°F) to mimic conventional oven temperatures I give in this book. Convection, fan-forced and fan-assisted ovens are great for rapid browning, evenness and more rapid cooking, but can dry things out if you don't use them for the right items.

Measurements   This book uses 250 ml (8½ fl oz) cups and 15 ml (½ fl oz) tablespoons.

3
Essentials

Everyday roasted chicken and broth

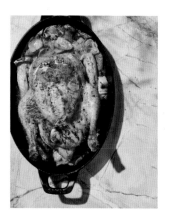

I get it: chicken broth is one of those things that seems easier to buy than bother making at home. If a recipe calls for chicken stock, you're hardly going to make chicken broth first and then get on with the rest of the prep. Madness! But the boxed stuff? Really? Look, I've used it too, but I can always taste the difference. That's why it is so important to keep some homemade stock in the fridge or freezer. Whenever I cook a roast chicken, I use it as an opportunity to get as much out of that bird as possible. Making stock from the frame of a roasted bird is not how I would do it at the restaurant. Instead, we would carefully sauté wings in the bottom of a pot, build up the 'fond', aka the brown bits on the bottom, sweat the mirepoix in the same pot and add beautifully caramelised bones that we have been turning and roasting in the oven. We cover the whole thing with cold water and simmer for 6–8 hours. But this would take the joy out of home cooking. So, what I suggest is much simpler. It also involves roasting a chicken to eat for dinner first – you're welcome. Also, this is how my mom roasts a chicken and it remains the simplest, best way I have ever had it.

Serves 4/Makes 1.5 litres (51 fl oz/6 cups)

1×2–2.5 kg (4 lb 6 oz–5½ lb) whole organic chicken
4 thyme sprigs
1 bay leaf
1 lemon, halved
1 large onion
1 large carrot
2 celery stalks
1 bulb fennel
1 garlic bulb (split in half through the equator)
30 g (1 oz) soft butter

Season your bird liberally with salt, inside the cavity and all the way around. Crack some pepper on top. Put the thyme, bay leaf and lemon inside the cavity. Set aside.

Preheat the oven to 200°C (400°F).

Roughly cut your vegetables into large pieces (I don't bother peeling the carrots) and arrange in the bottom of a shallow roasting tin, along with the garlic. Avoid tins with deep sides; you won't get enough colour on the vegetables. The other important thing here is that you want everything to fit snugly, in one even layer. Too spread out and everything will burn, piled high and everything will just steam. Sprinkle the vegetables with salt. Place your chicken, breast side up, on top of the mirepoix and rub the butter over the bird.

Place the tin in the centre of the oven and roast for at least 40 minutes. Turn the tin halfway through roasting. The bird is done when the juices between the leg and breast run clear when pierced with a knife and a cooking thermometer inserted in the thickest part of the meat reaches 68–72°C (154–162°F). If the bird hasn't got a nice brown colour, I let it sit under the grill (broiler) for a minute or two to get golden, but I warn you, do not walk away from anything under the grill; your hard work can be ruined in the space of a minute.

Pull it out of the oven and leave to rest in the tin for at least 20–30 minutes. Then carve away! I pull the meat off the bones from the legs and save the bones for the stock. Maybe not ideal if you're entertaining, but if you're just at home with family I doubt anyone will mind. I serve some of the roasted vegetables but keep at least half for the stock. That evening, I gather all the bones (lemon and thyme removed and discarded, but keep the bay leaf), vegetables and resting juices and scrape them into a pot. I cover it and put this in the fridge to make stock the next morning. Feel free to make it the same day, I just tend to be too tired to stay up babysitting stock.

When ready, add enough cold water to the bones and mirepoix to just cover the chicken. How much depends on the size of the pot. Again, choose something where everything fits snugly and your chicken isn't floating; this would dilute the stock too much. Place it on your stove and bring to a full simmer over a high heat. Immediately drop this down to a low simmer and let it gently bubble away for 1 hour. Skim off any foamy scum that rises to the top. After that time, strain the stock, discard the bones and allow the liquid to cool to just above room temperature. Divide between smaller freezer-safe containers so you can use only a little if a recipe calls for it. Freeze and use as needed or keep in the fridge for up to 3 days.

Rich poultry broth

So, while my roasted chicken broth is great for everyday use, some recipes really require a rich, sweet and deeply golden-brown stock. Pasta in brodo is one that springs to mind. My poached chicken recipe (see page 170) would also be wonderful cooked in this broth. Alice Waters used to call this 'the life-giving broth', and any time we made it at Chez Panisse she would take a jar to drop off at a sick friend's house or take it home for herself.

The key to this broth is to seek out some older birds from your butcher. Whether they be squab, turkey, guinea fowl or chicken, those older birds that perhaps have stopped laying eggs are perfect to make a rich and flavourful broth. Their flesh is darker, meatier and too tough for any other use, and their fat more yellow, which produces a beautiful colour and flavour. The only exception to this is duck. Use duck bones here, but the skin is just too fatty to produce a clean broth. I know this mixture of bones is not something readily available at your local shop, but frozen is fine and, with a little notice, any good butcher should be able to source them for you.

The other key is to spend a lot of time browning the bones and meat. It takes longer than you think, and it requires you to flip and turn things around to get them browned on all sides. Feel free to add more bones, but always use a mixture of meat and bones – you really need the meat to add sweetness.

Makes 2 litres (68 fl oz/8 cups) broth

2 kg (4 lb 6 oz) mixed poultry frames (bones) or whole older birds
1 tablespoon extra-virgin olive oil
2 onions, sliced
2 carrots, sliced
2 celery stalks, sliced
8 garlic cloves, crushed
200 ml (7 fl oz) dry Madeira or sherry
2 bay leaves
1 tablespoon black peppercorns
½ bunch thyme
1 tablespoon salt

Preheat the oven to 220°C (430°F).

Cut the wings and legs off the birds and cut the rest of the bodies into a few pieces. You can also ask your butcher to do this for you. Heat a very large stockpot over a high heat and add the olive oil. When it's hot, add enough of the poultry pieces to cover the bottom of the pot without overcrowding it. Place the rest of the poultry on a baking tray and roast in the oven until browned all over.

When the meat in the pot is nicely coloured, remove it, leaving the fat behind, then add all your vegetables and sauté them until they are just starting to turn golden brown. At this stage, add all the browned meat from the oven and the pot back in. Add your Madeira and, maintaining a high heat, let that cook out for 2 minutes. Then add your bay leaves, peppercorns and thyme, along with 3 litres (101 fl oz/ 12 cups) cold water. Add the salt and bring this up to a simmer. Don't ever boil it, as the fatty foam that rises to the surface will emulsify into the stock, giving you a cloudy appearance and murky flavour. Simmer gently, uncovered, for 2 hours. Skim off and discard any foam or excess oil that floats to the top. Strain and reserve the broth. It can be used straight away or frozen.

Breadcrumbs

Breadcrumbs ... ah, breadcrumbs. The joy! The usefulness! That delicious crunch! But also ... the frustration. When I first started leading a kitchen, making breadcrumbs was the job that people got wrong the most. It was also the job that made me realise I had better start being extremely clear on every detail if I wanted the result I was looking for. There are just SO MANY WAYS to make breadcrumbs. None are really wrong per se, but without using my method I watched people do the most interesting things: leave the crust on, take the crust off, dry out before processing into crumbs or process while fresh, toast dry, toast with oil, toast in a low oven, toast in a hot oven, or even on the stove. The possibilities were endless and therefore I experienced a lot of dry, uneven, chewy and not perfect breadcrumbs. Here is my favourite way to produce a crunchy but delicate, oily breadcrumb that makes the perfect pasta topping.

Firstly, the type of bread you select is important; you want a loaf with some integrity and a good amount of crumb compared to crust, like a sourdough or miche, or Italian loaf. A baguette or sandwich bread would not work with this method.

Preheat the oven to 180°C (350°F).

Take a loaf of at least one-day-old bread – a few days older is also fine, just as long as it hasn't gone completely hard. Using a serrated knife, carefully cut off all the crusts and discard them. Tear the bread into chunks, place in a food processor and process until everything is completely crumbly. Transfer those crumbs to a mixing bowl and pour a lot of extra-virgin olive oil on them. How much? Again, this depends on how much crumb you have but, as a starting ratio, I would say for every 200 g (7 oz) crumbs, 75 ml (2½ fl oz) olive oil should suffice. Season the crumbs with a good pinch of salt and lay them on a baking tray lined with baking paper. Spread them out so they are snug, but in a pretty flat layer.

Bake, checking and mixing them around every 5 minutes, until they are done (this is the most annoying part of this process, but I promise they are worth it). You don't have to do it as much in the beginning, but once they start to colour, you need to be near the oven. A metal spatula is a good tool for mixing up the crumbs as they toast. If you don't take the time to do this you will end up with a ring of burned crumbs around the edges and wet, soggy crumbs in the centre. When they are golden brown all over, you can remove the tray from the oven and allow the crumbs to cool on the tray, remembering though that they will keep deepening in colour for a few minutes after you remove them. Once cooled, store in an airtight container and they will keep for up to 1 week in your cupboard.

Aioli

Aioli is a dish whose name has been misappropriated. It is made with garlic, salt and olive oil, and usually egg yolks, though not always. And that's it. Sure, some add vinegar, some add lemon, some add mustard but, in my opinion, it then becomes something else: a garlic mayonnaise, for example, but not aioli. David Tanis, my head chef at Chez Panisse, taught me this and it stuck with me because I felt so misinformed until that moment. I am all for a bit of fusion, but you must also know how to honour the traditions you are taking from. Part of the beauty of learning about traditions not my own is figuring out how they fit with what I like to cook. The other beautiful thing is the learning itself, and the teaching that should come with that; only then can you tell the full story of a dish and, I think, cook the best food.

Aioli, for example, is comprised of two Provençal words: ai, meaning garlic, and oli being oil. It is both a sauce and a dish, and one of my favourite summertime dishes at that. The 'dish' of aioli is simply a generous bowl (or mortar) of the sauce served with boiled and raw summer vegetables, such as tomatoes, capsicums (bell peppers), potatoes, fennel, zucchini (courgettes), carrots and beans. A 'grand aioli' usually includes some sort of added protein, like salt cod, octopus, or boiled eggs or meats. It's best in summer because garlic is at its best then. A French chef once told me a good aioli should warm you with the essence of garlic.

Serves 6–8

1 large or 2–3 small-medium
    garlic cloves
½ teaspoon salt
4 egg yolks
350 ml (12 fl oz) extra-virgin
    olive oil

The olive oil you choose here is important. It should be at the softer, fruitier end of the spectrum. You don't want pepperiness or bitterness, or anything too green, or the result will be too harsh. Also, importantly, everything should be at room temperature. If your eggs or oil are too cold or too warm, too different in temperature, it will split. You will probably split an aioli once or twice when you start attempting it, but don't let this stop you. Once you know what to look for, you won't make the same mistake again. The good news is you can also take the broken aioli and gently drip that into a clean bowl with a couple of fresh egg yolks and start from scratch without wasting it. To save yourself some frustration, though, just follow the recipe and you'll be fine.

Crush the garlic in a mortar and pestle with a pinch of salt until it is smooth, then scoop into a flat-bottomed bowl. Add the egg yolks and gently whisk with another pinch of salt to incorporate. I find adding the salt at this stage is the only way to get the seasoning to distribute evenly; adding it at the end doesn't achieve that.

Now, while whisking gently in one continuous direction, slowly drip in the oil in one thin stream. You'll notice the emulsion will thicken and, at this stage, it's important to add a few drops of tepid water, as this will relax the mix just enough so that it can take on more oil without splitting. Continue whisking and pouring in a thin stream, but once the emulsion looks like it is well established, you can pour in a quicker stream. If ever it feels too thick, like thick mashed potatoes, add another few drops of water and it should rebound. Too much water though and you will end up with something too thin. The result should be spoonable without being runny, and should be thick enough to dip in without dripping. The end result is creamy and luxurious, redolent with garlic but balanced with beautiful olive oil. If it's a very hot summer day, place it, covered, in the fridge until ready to serve. It cannot be made more than a few hours in advance and cannot be kept overnight.

Chardonnay and honey vinaigrette, and how to dress a salad

This is probably the recipe that I get asked about the most at the restaurant and I am proud of that. Made well, it is a lesson in balance. It is so simple and yet so difficult to get right. There are so many variables: choice of different vinegars, oils, emulsified or not? And even if you get the vinaigrette right, you still need to dress the leaves properly. Do not despair though, a perfectly dressed salad is not out of reach. Maybe only true salad connoisseurs like my former boss Alice Waters could pick up on the subtleties, but I think we've all had salads that weren't quite right; perhaps heavy or oily, or not enough acidity. Whatever the case, the vinaigrette often gets forgotten or we rely too heavily on ratios like 3:1 or 4:1 and assume that's good enough. Well, it's not. Not if you want the deep satisfaction of a delicious salad.

I remember working in a kitchen before Chez Panisse and Alice Waters came in for lunch. She ordered a leafy salad (as she always does), which had some shaved persimmon in it. I overheard her telling the head chef after the meal that her salad was perfect. I ran over to the girl who had made the salad and asked her to mix some dressing up for me. I wanted to know what 'perfect' in the eyes of Alice Waters tasted like. I made a mental note, and have tried to emulate it since. Please do add this version to your repertoire, it will be helpful in just about any salad situation.

Serves 6–8

1 teaspoon salt
70 ml (2¼ fl oz) chardonnay vinegar (or Champagne vinegar)
1 tablespoon sherry vinegar
2 tablespoons finely diced shallot
2 teaspoons honey
150 ml (5 fl oz) olive oil

In a bowl, combine the salt, vinegars and shallot. Mix well and allow to marinate for at least 15 minutes. It's important to add the salt at this stage to draw out the flavour from the shallot. Next, add the honey and, using a whisk, slowly drizzle in the olive oil. You are not trying to emulsify here, because the vinegar and oil will split, but if you don't take the time to do this part slowly, for some reason I can't explain, the dressing ends up feeling disjointed, like there is oil and there is vinegar but they aren't holding hands. This gentle, slow mixing helps them become acquainted, so that even after they separate, when you mix them together again to finally dress your salad, their bond feels that little bit stronger. Because of the shallot, this dressing is only good for one day. You can strain out the shallot and reserve the leftover vinaigrette, but it's really never as good as when it's fresh.

To dress the salad, add your leaves to a large bowl – much larger than you think you need. You absolutely must use your (just-washed) hands for this. Do not even think about using tongs or putting on gloves; you need to be able to feel the dressing coating the leaves. Shake the jar really well to vigorously mix the dressing from bottom to top, then ladle in the dressing a little at a time. Sprinkle in some sea salt and mix gently. Taste. Does it need more dressing? Can you taste the leaves? Maybe a pinch more salt? Don't add too much dressing early on; as you've heard before, you can always add more but you can't take it away.

Important to note is that different leaves require different amounts of the dressing and different sharpness. Romaine (cos) or gem leaves, which can often be a bit bitter, will require extra dressing to balance them – maybe a bit more honey or a bit more vinegar. If I realise this after I've made the dressing, I just splash the vinegar or drizzle the honey directly on the leaves. Leaves like this also want you to gently rub the dressing onto them. Don't be afraid; they like it. True bitter leaves like radicchio or treviso require even more dressing, more salt, more acidity to balance them, and they also have enough backbone to hold up to it. A delicate spring mix or herb salad wants the smallest amount of dressing and a gentle touch to just coat it.

Salsa verde

When my creativity is a little low and I need a sauce to go on fish, meat or vegetables, or even eggs, salsa verde is my go-to, and it's why I regard it as one of my most important staple recipes. Unlike vinaigrettes or even aioli, I'm less specific about what goes in it. You should use what's on hand and whatever herbs are at their best.

Salsa verde has its origins in Italy, Spain and France. At its core, it's a piquant green, herbaceous condiment made punchy by either vinegar, mustard or lemon juice. Almost all versions include flat-leaf (Italian) parsley, but, after that, all bets are off. The French often include chopped cornichons and perhaps a bit of dijon; Italian versions can have capers, maybe anchovies and a bit of soaked bread, while Spanish versions would surely include lots of fresh garlic. Basically, you can't really go wrong if you know what purpose you want it to serve. If I am serving it with fish, I want something delicate, so I would probably omit bread or mustard, opting instead for a thinner version with more olive oil and herbs such as chervil and chives, and perhaps lemon instead of vinegar. If I am serving it with boiled beef short ribs, I would definitely add mustard, some freshly grated horseradish and perhaps some crunchy breadcrumbs for texture. The results are different, but the goal is the same: to heighten the flavour of whatever I am serving it with. I'll leave it to you to experiment, but here is a good all-around version that works with almost everything.

Serves 8–10

2 tablespoons finely
    chopped shallots
    (approx. 1 small shallot)
3 tablespoons red-wine
    vinegar or lemon juice
1 teaspoon salt
1 bunch flat-leaf
    (Italian) parsley (approx.
    30 g/1 oz leaves)
1 bunch chervil (5–10 g/
    ⅛–¼ oz leaves)
100 ml (3½ fl oz) extra-virgin
    olive oil
3 anchovy fillets,
    finely chopped
2½ tablespoons salt-packed
    capers, rinsed
    then chopped

This recipe starts the same way as a vinaigrette: soak the shallots in the vinegar and salt. Set aside.

Wash and pick the leaves from the parsley and chervil and dry completely. Don't be too fussy about the stems, thin and fine stems are perfectly fine to go in the salsa. Chop quite finely – you need a sharp knife for this; a dull knife will bruise the herbs and muddy their bright, verdant flavour. I also am opposed to making salsa verde in a blender; hand-chopped produces the cleanest flavour and the extra effort is worth it.

Add the olive oil, anchovies and capers to the herbs, then add the shallot vinegar. Mix well and set aside for at least 1 hour. This allows the flavours to meld and become cohesive. This sauce can be saved for the following day, but it will discolour due to the acid being in contact with the herbs, so it's best served the day it is made.

Variations

For poached chicken, the anchovies are optional, use vinegar and add 2 tablespoons minced cornichons.

For a light springtime version, remove the capers and the anchovies and cut the acidic element down to 2 tablespoons, but add 3 g (⅛ oz) chopped tarragon leaves, 5 g (⅛ oz) chopped dill and 8 g (¼ oz) snipped chives.

For a punchy version to serve with poached beef short ribs or rich meats, add 2 tablespoons prepared or freshly grated horseradish, 3 tablespoons chopped watercress and 2 teaspoons dijon mustard.

For a Spanish type, use sherry vinegar, omit the capers, but add 1 tablespoon good-quality smoked paprika and 1 large garlic clove, either crushed in a mortar and pestle or microplaned.

For pasta or to mix with a grain salad, remove the capers and anchovies, but add 2 teaspoons finely minced fresh, de-seeded red chilli.

II.
Recipes

1   Salads 20
2   Fruits and vegetables 48
3   Pasta, grains and legumes 94
4   Seafood 134
5   Poultry and meat 164
6   Dessert 198

Salads

Beetroot and persimmon salad with feta, honey, pistachio and Aleppo 25

Fig and goat's curd salad with smoky paprika vinaigrette 27

Tomato salad with sumac onions, tahini yoghurt and wild fennel 27

Tomato and fried crouton salad with tonnato and capers 28

Cucumbers with mustard vinaigrette and dill 30

Zucchini with mint, lemon and bottarga 30

Baba ghanoush with roasted spring onions, beetroot and green olive 33

Radicchio with bagna cauda and walnut oil 34

Iceberg with dried oregano dressing and creamy sheep's milk cheese 34

Castelfranco with warm chestnut, thyme and prosciutto 37

Celeriac, walnut, pear and bresaola 38

Persimmon, witlof, pomegranate and gorgonzola dolce 38

Grilled chicory with celery, anchovy parmesan dressing and breadcrumbs 39

Citrus with Meyer lemon dressing and shaved fennel 40

Wilted spinach with fennel, apple and pistachio butter 42

Radish with preserved lemon, feta, mint and sesame 45

Roasted fennel and Jerusalem artichoke with hazelnuts and grapefruit 45

Side note:
Farmers' markets and what to know before you start cooking 46

Salads

For most of my life, a salad included some form of lettuce as a base, be it romaine (cos), iceberg, or perhaps an exotic spring mix of leaves. It possibly contained some kind of substandard, partly green tomato, maybe a dried-out cucumber and, quite usually, some fibrous carrot shavings. Mostly, it acted as a side dish or accompaniment to some piece of protein. I can remember this dark time in my life so vividly, it's no wonder that I never really appreciated the possibilities of salads. Like so many of my food revelations, this all changed when I arrived in California. Here, my eyes were opened to the idea of any vegetable or fruit – or protein, for that matter – being highlighted as the star of a salad. And wait, salads could also be served at different temperatures? Cold, warm, room temperature – what? My mind was blown.

I became enamoured with bitter salad greens such as puntarelle, which makes an appearance in the dreary winter months. A member of the chicory family, this particularly curious green forms a head or crown a few years after first being planted. This crown, which forms at the base, with the leaves extending outwards, is the part you thinly slice and use as the main body of the salad. It is delightfully bitter but, when picked during a cold snap, that bitterness turns to sweetness. Dressed with piquant and salty anchovy and lemon vinaigrette, maybe with a grating of good parmesan cheese, it is without a doubt my favourite salad.

It taught me to appreciate all members of the bitter leaf crew, and I have spent much of my career trying to persuade other people to love them like I do. Along with citrus, they are the best parts of winter. Their hearty, crunchy texture is what makes them so versatile; bitter leaves love to be grilled as part of a warm salad, they love to be served cold, they love lots of juicy dressing and even when they go a little soft in the bowl, they somehow get even better. Can iceberg say the same thing? I don't think so. Now don't get me wrong, I love iceberg. A proper American wedge salad with blue cheese dressing and bacon or a good green goddess dressing is one of the greatest pleasures (if done well, of course). But the problem is, most people don't pay as much attention as they should to iceberg lettuce. It isn't as versatile or forgiving as a chicory. It should always be ice cold, and it needs to be cut just before serving. To get the best out of it, you need to first coat the leaves in a vinaigretty dressing before drizzling with something creamy. You see what I mean? It's about figuring out all the little tricks to bring out the best characteristics of something and not try to make it something it's not.

I digress, though, as my point here is that salad is more than just lettuce! Assorted citrus, peeled and thinly sliced, scattered with sliced raw onion and black olives, generously drizzled with fresh, new-season olive oil is also a revelation, and so much more than the sum of its parts. Seriously, try it. Shaved persimmon or Asian pear tossed with toasted nuts, a simple vinaigrette and perhaps some fresh curd or blue cheese is another realisation of the potential of salad.

To summarise, can we all agree to abandon the sad side salad and learn to expect more from our salads? I think so.

Beetroot and persimmon salad with feta, honey, pistachio and Aleppo

This is such a pretty salad. I would never sacrifice substance for looks but in this case, you get both. Aleppo is a perfect sprinkle chilli. Originally from Aleppo in Syria, but now most likely coming from Turkey, it has a good amount of heat but is not powdery when ground, so you can use less and still see the pretty red flecks. And use sweet fuyu persimmons: the variety you slice thinly and eat before they have fully ripened; the hachiya variety, which have to completely soften before you can eat (due to tannins), are beautiful scooped on a cheese plate or for baking.

The trickiest part of this salad is cooking the beetroot. I recommend this method as it intensifies their flavour in the best way, but the trick is in maintaining the texture. Almost all beetroot will cook at different times depending on type and size, so it's important to know what you're looking for. You want the beetroot skin to slip off quite easily, but when you stick a knife in there should be a slight resistance, as if you are piercing into wet sand – otherwise it's overcooked and mushy. It's not the end of the world, and you almost have to overcook some before you can understand the difference, but in my opinion a beetroot with some texture is far superior.

Serves 4

Beetroot

6 medium-sized golden or multi-coloured beetroot, washed
2 tablespoons olive oil
1 teaspoon salt

Salad

1 small shallot, diced
3 teaspoons chardonnay or Champagne vinegar
100 g (3½ oz) creamy cow's or sheep's milk feta, or something similar to Bulgarian, Danish or French feta, which tends to be creamier
1 fuyu persimmon
1½ tablespoons extra-virgin olive oil
1 teaspoon honey
60 g (2 oz) toasted pistachio nuts
2 tablespoons pomegranate seeds
20 mint leaves
½ teaspoon Aleppo chilli flakes

Preheat the oven to 200°C (400°F).

Remove the beetroot greens and save for another dish. Place the beetroot in a baking dish and drizzle with the olive oil, salt and 3 tablespoons water. Cover tightly with aluminium foil and bake for at least 20 minutes before you check their doneness. Medium-sized beetroot will probably take closer to 40 minutes to cook. Once cooked, remove the foil and allow them to cool. When cooled, peel the skins – they should slip right off. Set aside.

Soak your shallot in the vinegar with a pinch of salt and set aside.

To assemble, spread the feta on the bottom of a serving plate or platter. Thinly slice the beetroot and persimmon using a mandoline and arrange the slices in a pretty pattern over the feta. Sprinkle over the vinegar-soaked shallot, a pinch of salt and the olive oil, and drizzle with the honey. Toss the pistachios, pomegranate seeds and mint on top, then finally sprinkle the chilli flakes over the whole thing. Serve immediately.

Fig and goat's curd salad with smoky paprika vinaigrette

Figs with a bit of olive oil and salt are pretty perfect on their own, but if you wanted to go one step further, the combination of sweet figs and smoky dressing is an excellent one. I suggest using good pimentón de La Vera for this. This is a smoked paprika from the La Vera valley in Spain, and you simply can't find better. It has AOC distinction, meaning you can't call it pimentón de La Vera if it's not from that region in Spain. You'll find three varieties: dulce, which is sweet and smoky, agridulce, which is just a little bit bitter, and picante, which is spicy. All have their own best uses, but for vinaigrettes I like the dulce.

Make this salad in autumn when the long hot days of summer have made the figs super ripe and bursting with sweetness. This recipe makes a bit more dressing than you need, but some crusty bread dipped into it would be a delicious addition.

Serves 4

8 ripe figs
12 large rocket (arugula) leaves
150 g (5½ oz) fresh goat's curd
70 g (2½ oz) toasted almonds

Vinaigrette

20 ml (¾ fl oz) sherry vinegar
20 ml (¾ fl oz) agrodolce-style white-wine vinegar
½ garlic clove
1½ teaspoons pimentón de La Vera dulce
100 ml (3½ fl oz) extra-virgin olive oil

To make your dressing, combine the vinegars in a jar and grate in the garlic. Add a pinch of salt and the pimentón and shake to combine. Next, add the olive oil and shake again. This can be made ahead of time, but no more than a few hours as the raw garlic tends to change over time and becomes stronger and sweeter.

Tear open your figs at the centre and arrange them on a platter with the rocket and goat's curd crumbled around. Shake your vinaigrette just before pouring it right over everything. Use only enough to drizzle; you don't want to drown out the other ingredients. Finally, scatter your toasted almonds over the top and finish with a good sprinkle of salt. Serve immediately.

Tomato salad with sumac onions, tahini yoghurt and wild fennel

It is a universally acknowledged fact that we eat with our eyes, and this salad, bright with colour, is one that people gravitate towards. Middle Eastern cuisine does this so brilliantly, with its vibrant produce, multi-coloured spices, chilli powders, seeds, sumac, pomegranate and fresh herbs. It's a feast for the senses, and the dishes, prepared with skill, never disappoint. By borrowing a few ingredients from the Middle East, you can adapt fresh produce you have on hand to create something that is beautiful to look at and to eat. This is a fabulous summer salad and goes well with other salads and grilled meats.

Sumac, if you don't know it, is a small fruit that is dried and ground into a powder, used for its tart acidity. It replaces other acidic ingredients, such as lemon or vinegar, in this salad entirely. Wild fennel grows in many places in the summer, when tomatoes are also at their peak. If you don't live somewhere you can find it, swap it for a smaller amount of dried fennel pollen or use fresh herbs such as basil or mint instead.

Serves 4

2 garlic cloves
150 g (5½ oz) Yoghurt (page 237)
50 g (1¾ oz) unhulled tahini
1 small red onion, thinly sliced
2 teaspoons powdered sumac
500 g (1 lb 2 oz) mixed heirloom tomatoes, cut into large chunks
2 tablespoons olive oil
red-wine vinegar, to taste
2 teaspoons wild fennel flowers

First, crush your garlic in a mortar and pestle or grate it using a microplane. Mix with the yoghurt and tahini and spread that mixture on the base of a platter. You may need to add a splash or two of cold water to get a spreadable consistency.

To make your sumac onions, sprinkle the onion with a good few pinches of salt and toss together. Allow the salted onion to sit for at least 10 minutes, then rinse under cold water. Try to squeeze out as much excess liquid as you can. Mix the sumac with the onion and set aside.

Top the yoghurt and tahini mixture with the tomatoes, then sprinkle with the olive oil, some red-wine vinegar, flaky sea salt and black pepper. Finally, sprinkle the fennel flowers and sumac onions on top.

See image on page 29.

Tomato and fried crouton salad with tonnato and capers

Tonnato is an Italian dressing made thick like mayonnaise, but with tinned tuna as its base. It is typically served over thin slices of poached veal in a classic dish known as vitello tonnato. I've taken a bit of creative licence with the sauce, adding some soy sauce and Worcestershire for a bit of extra savouriness. It's certainly not Italian, but that's OK sometimes. It would also be delicious served as a dip for crudités, or with some raw chopped tuna on top of some grilled Romano beans, or slathered on some crusty bread as part of a sandwich. Or you could even turn this salad into a crostini by slathering the tonnato on the bread and topping with the tomatoes. It has a wonderful umami taste, is creamy and totally craveable.

It's pretty important to make this in a food processor or blender, as doing it by hand, although not impossible, never produces the smoothest texture.

Serves 6

Salad

2 tablespoons olive oil, plus extra if needed
2 tablespoons salt-packed capers,
    rinsed and dried
½ country sourdough loaf, crust removed
800 g (1 lb 12 oz) mixed heirloom tomatoes
1 bunch basil, leaves picked

Tonnato

100 g (3½ oz) good-quality olive oil-packed
    tinned tuna
3 anchovy fillets
1 tablespoon salt-packed capers, rinsed
1 egg yolk
90 ml (3 fl oz) extra-virgin olive oil
2 teaspoons soy sauce
2 tablespoons lemon juice
1 teaspoon Worcestershire sauce
3 tablespoons cream

To make the tonnato, add your tuna, anchovies, capers and egg yolk to a food processor. Put the lid on and process. Once it looks like everything is broken up a little, begin to stream in the olive oil. When it starts to thicken, add the soy sauce, lemon juice and Worcestershire, then the remaining olive oil. Finish with the cream and a bit of water to loosen it to a thick but drizzly consistency. Add a few cracks of fresh black pepper and check and adjust the seasoning. Refrigerate until ready to use.

For the salad, heat the olive oil in a small sauté pan over a high heat and add the dry capers. Ensure they are as dry as you can make them to avoid too much splatter. Allow the capers to sizzle a little and, when they have almost finished sizzling (meaning most of the water has evaporated), scoop them out and dry them on a piece of paper towel. Reserve the oil.

Tear your bread into rough pieces and add it to the pan. Use the caper oil and some more olive oil, if needed, to shallow-fry the croutons over a medium heat. You want to fry the bread on a couple of sides, but you don't want it to be completely crispy. You want a bit of soft chew with a crusty exterior. Try to do this in one layer so that you don't overcrowd the pan. This might mean you need to do it in a couple of batches. Season the croutons with salt and pepper when they come out of the pan.

Spread the tonnato on the plate first, then cut up the tomatoes into thick slices and arrange them on top. Sprinkle with salt and black pepper. Scatter the croutons over the top. Finish with the fried capers and some fresh picked basil leaves. Serve immediately.

Top   Tomato and fried crouton salad with tonnato and capers (opposite)
Bottom Tomato salad with sumac onions, tahini yoghurt and wild fennel (page 27)

Cucumbers with mustard vinaigrette and dill

Zucchini with mint, lemon and bottarga

This is one of those dishes that has stuck in my mind since childhood. My best friend was a girl named Ashley. Her mom, Marie Therese, was French and she was a great cook. For a girl who only ate Cuban food at that age, dining at my friend's house was a total deviation from the norm. I recognise now how impactful those early food memories have been on my life, how they sparked my curiosity for the larger world, and I can still remember my experience eating this simple salad for the first time. It was sweet and bright with vinegar, but you could still taste the delicate, thinly shaved cucumbers. I never actually got the recipe from Ashley's mom (I'm sure it's just something she threw together), but I have tried to recreate it based on that memory and some research. Turns out, it's a pretty classic picnic food or lunch side dish that many French people associate with their childhood. Funny how some things make such an impression, isn't it? I hope you like this salad as much as I do.

Serves 4

1 large seedless cucumber, thinly sliced on a mandoline
2 teaspoons salt
1 tablespoon caster (superfine) sugar
2 teaspoons dijon mustard
4 tablespoons white-wine vinegar
1 medium shallot, thinly sliced
1½ tablespoons chopped dill (approx. ½ bunch)
olive oil, for drizzling

In a bowl, toss the cucumber with the salt and sugar and set aside for 10 minutes. Mix the dijon, vinegar and shallot in a small bow, then pour over the cucumber.

At the last minute before serving, toss in the dill so that the colour stays bright and drizzle with some nice delicate olive oil.

Note

The cucumber can be left with its skin on if it is a thin-skinned variety, otherwise it should be peeled.

I love summer produce but I hate to 'cook' in summer; it's too hot to be cooped up in a kitchen. This is when I turn to salads. Next to some grilled fish or poached prawns, this salad is perfect, and so simple that it's not even a recipe so much as an idea.

Zucchini (courgette) and summer squash are so ubiquitous that I think we forget their peak season is summer, and they are at their best picked straight from the garden. They are crisp and sweet, hearty yet delicate. As soon as they are picked, they start to diminish. This is when cooking them is the only option. If you're lucky to find some firm and crunchy zucchini and squash, try this salad. It will become a part of your repertoire.

As for bottarga, that's the salted and dried roe of the mullet fish. Its origins are in Sicily, but it is used throughout Italy and Greece. It is commonly grated over pasta for a briny, oceanic hit. If you like flavours of the ocean, you'll find lots of uses for it. Wrapped up tightly it keeps for a while in the fridge, so use it here but try it over some simple spaghetti with garlic and olive oil for a summery change from parmesan cheese.

Serves 4

2–4 large fresh green or yellow zucchini (courgettes),
    or any mixture of fresh summer squash
juice of 1 lemon
1 bunch picked mint leaves
extra-virgin olive oil, for drizzling
bottarga, for grating

Shave your zucchini thinly on a mandoline, lengthways or into rounds – whatever you prefer. Place it in a large bowl and squeeze over the juice of half a lemon. Sprinkle with salt and pepper and give it a taste. If the zucchini tastes well seasoned and has the brightness of the lemon, it is ready to serve. If it's a bit dull, add a little more salt and lemon juice.

Arrange the zucchini on a plate or platter. Add the picked mint leaves and drizzle liberally with good olive oil. Grate the bottarga over the top and add one last squeeze of lemon and a crack of black pepper. Taste and adjust the seasoning if needed, but bear in mind that the salty bottarga is part of your seasoning.

Baba ghanoush with roasted spring onions, beetroot and green olive

The best way to cook eggplant is over an outdoor grill over charcoal or wood embers. It's my feeling that grilling over the flames of a gas burner does nothing good for the flavour. Instead of subtle smokiness and char, you end up with an acrid, burnt flavour. You want the eggplant to taste as if it has been just kissed by smoke, not like a piece of charcoal. Some charring on the outside is OK, just don't aim to blacken it like you would a capsicum; it just needs to get soft. I like to serve this a bit like a salad, with some flatbreads on the side for dipping.

Serves 6

1 bunch baby beetroot (beets) of any colour, leaves trimmed and reserved for another use
olive oil, for drizzling
3 tablespoons white-wine vinegar
4–5 new-season spring onions (scallions)
50 ml (1¾ fl oz) verjus or white wine
24 whole green olives
extra-virgin olive oil and flatbreads, to serve

Baba ghanoush

700–800 g (1 lb 9 oz–1 lb 12 oz/approx. 2 large) purple eggplant (aubergine)
6 tablespoons unhulled tahini
2 garlic cloves, crushed in a mortar and pestle
juice of ½ lemon
1 tablespoon olive oil

To make the baba ghanoush, prick the eggplants a few times with a knife to allow steam to escape as they cook, then roast on an outdoor grill over a medium heat. Alternatively, you can cook them under the grill (broiler) of the oven or in a grill pan, but know that you won't get the same smoky flavour that is typical in baba ghanoush. You want the eggplant to be completely soft and collapsing in the middle. Once cooked, place in a bowl and cover with aluminium foil to allow them to continue softening. When cool enough to handle, peel off any black skin and finely chop the flesh. Drain the eggplant for about 15 minutes in a sieve to eliminate most of the water. Place the strained flesh in a bowl and add the tahini, garlic, lemon juice, olive oil and some salt. Check for seasoning, then set aside.

Preheat the oven to 200°C (400°F).

Place the beetroot in a baking dish, drizzle with olive oil and sprinkle with salt. Add a splash of water, then cover with aluminium foil and bake for 30–40 minutes, depending on their size. You should be able to pierce the beetroot all the way through with slight resistance when they're done. Leave to cool, then peel and cut into slices or wedges. Mix with the vinegar and set aside.

While the beetroot is cooking you can roast your onions. Halve your spring onions lengthways and lay them in a baking dish, cut side up. Drizzle with olive oil and sprinkle with salt, then pour the verjus into the dish. Cover with foil and bake for about 15 minutes, then remove the foil and cook for another 8–10 minutes until completely soft and lightly golden on one side. If the dish is looking very dry at the end, add a splash of water to the onions so they don't completely dry out. Remove and set aside. Wrap the olives loosely in a tea towel (dish towel) and crush them lightly with the bottom of a frying pan to remove the pits. Set aside the pitted olives for plating.

To serve, spread the baba ghanoush on the bottom of a platter and top with the beetroot, onion and olives. Drizzle with good-quality extra-virgin olive oil. Serve with warm flatbreads.

Radicchio with bagna cauda and walnut oil

Bagna cauda, in Italian dialect, translates as 'warm bath' but it is also used to describe a warm sauce for dipping crudités. I say it all the time, but I could drink this bagna cauda. There is really nothing better in my mind than a delicious plate of raw vegetables and this sauce. Perhaps one thing might be better, and that's using the radicchio leaves like little cups to spoon more of the sauce into my mouth. It's just that good. I can also confirm that this sauce is great on pasta, on eggs, in a sandwich, on a piece of fish – you name it. Get the highest quality anchovies you can buy (Ortiz are my favourite. They cost a bit more than your standard everyday ones, but they are essential for making an insanely delicious bagna cauda versus one that is just OK).

Serves 4

40 g (1½ oz) best-quality anchovy fillets
2 large garlic cloves
75 g (2¾ oz) butter
25 ml (¾ fl oz) walnut oil (see Tip)
50 ml (1¾ fl oz) olive oil
2 teaspoons lemon juice, plus extra to serve
1 teaspoon grated lemon zest
1 head radicchio, leaves roughly torn

Crush the anchovies and garlic in a mortar and pestle until they form a paste. Add to a small saucepan with the butter and oils and cook over a low heat for 4 minutes. Do not let it sizzle.

Transfer the mixture to a blender and blend with the lemon juice and zest, then return the sauce to the pot and cook for an additional 3 minutes over a low heat while gently whisking. Spoon the warm sauce onto the radicchio leaves and top with an extra squeeze of lemon juice and some cracked black pepper. Check for seasoning and add salt if needed. Store any remaining bagna cauda in the fridge in an airtight container for 2–3 days, then reheat to serve.

Tip

Keep your walnut oil in the fridge as nut oil can go rancid pretty quickly.

Iceberg with dried oregano dressing and creamy sheep's milk cheese

This salad is nostalgic for me in a lot of ways. Iceberg was the lettuce of choice in my house growing up, and I can remember the bottle of 'Italian' dressing poured over it. Of course, now I find those bottled dressings terrible, but there is something really good about crunchy lettuce and a bright shallot dressing filled with the flavour of dried oregano. The creamy feta is a perfect counterpoint to this. I love this salad alongside grilled or roasted meats, or sometimes I'll add some chickpeas or shaved zucchini (courgette) for a more substantial salad.

I prefer to dress iceberg by pouring the dressing over it as opposed to tossing it together with the dressing in a bowl. This is because iceberg tends to stay in wedges or chunks without the layers separating into leaves. Pouring the dressing on allows you to dress the leaves while retaining their crunchy layers. Always keep your iceberg super cold right up until serving, as this will give you the best crunch – which is, after all, its biggest appeal.

Serves 6–8

2 heads iceberg lettuce, outer leaves removed
1 bunch chives, snipped
½ bunch dill, fronds picked
50–70 g (1¾ oz–2½ oz) creamy sheep's milk feta
    (Bulgarian sheep's milk feta works, or even
    a Danish cow's milk feta would be good too)

Dressing

30 g (1 oz) thinly sliced shallot
50 ml (1¾ fl oz) agrodolce-style white-wine vinegar
    (if you can't find that, add 2 teaspoons honey to
    regular white-wine vinegar)
1 teaspoon salt
1½ teaspoons dried oregano
120 ml (4 fl oz) extra-virgin olive oil

First, make your vinaigrette. In a small bowl or jar with a lid, combine the shallot, vinegar and salt. Leave to macerate for about 15 minutes. Next, add the oregano and olive oil and mix or shake to combine.

Cut your iceberg into thin, long wedges and arrange on a platter. Shake the dressing up just before pouring it over the lettuce. Sprinkle a bit of salt on top, followed by the chives and dill, then shave slices of cheese over the whole thing, or simply crumble it in. Serve immediately.

Castelfranco with warm chestnut, thyme and prosciutto

A chestnut can feel like a pretty luxurious thing. Number one, they aren't that cheap and number two, they take a little while to prepare, but when they are fresh and perfect in autumn you really must seize the opportunity to use them. This elegant salad highlights them beautifully. The first chestnuts of the season are usually the easiest to peel and don't take as long to cook.

Serves 4

15 chestnuts
250 ml (8½ fl oz/1 cup) extra-virgin olive oil
10 lemon thyme sprigs (use regular thyme if lemon is unavailable)
1 head fresh, firm castelfranco or treviso radicchio or other beautiful winter chicory
120 g (4½ oz) good-quality ricotta
100 ml (3½ fl oz) Chardonnay and honey vinaigrette (page 16)
2 teaspoons good-quality aged balsamic vinegar
8 slices prosciutto

Begin by peeling your chestnuts. Using a small paring knife, score a small 'x' on the flat side of each chestnut. Add to a saucepan and cover with 3–4 cm (1¼–1½ in) water. Simmer for 10–12 minutes (this loosens the skins). Using a slotted spoon, remove the chestnuts and place in a bowl covered with a tea towel (dish towel). The trick is to keep them warm while you peel them. If they go cold, drop them back into the simmering water for a minute or two to warm up again. Using the knife, peel away the thick outer skin, then gently peel away the thinner, more papery skin from around the chestnut. Set the peeled chestnuts aside.

In a small saucepan, warm the olive oil then add six thyme sprigs. The oil should only just be warm; you should still be able to touch it and the thyme shouldn't sizzle when you add it. Add the chestnuts to the oil and leave to poach and soften the starches over a low heat. This could take 20 minutes or up to 1 hour depending on the chestnuts. The later the season, the starchier they get and the more cooking they require. Taste them. If they are dry and starchy, they need longer, but if they're soft and creamy, they're done.

Cut the base core off the castelfranco, which should allow you to separate the leaves. Wash and set aside, covered with a damp cloth, until you're ready to serve.

To assemble, divide the ricotta evenly between four plates, or you can serve it on one big platter. Toss your radicchio leaves with some dressing and a good pinch of salt. How much vinaigrette you use depends on how you like your salad. I would add a little at first, then just taste until it is to your liking. You don't want the leaves to be too acidic; the savouriness of the chestnuts and prosciutto needs to shine through. Drop the leaves onto the ricotta, then place your warm chestnuts in and around the leaves. Drizzle the balsamic over the whole thing and sprinkle over a good pinch of crunchy salt and a few twists of black pepper. Finish with slices of prosciutto and a sprinkle of fresh thyme leaves.

Strain the olive oil through a fine-mesh sieve and store in an airtight container in the fridge to make this dish again, or to add to dressings.

Celeriac, walnut, pear and bresaola

Good bresaola (carefully salted and air-dried beef) paired with juicy, new season pears and celeriac makes a really, really good combination.

A really good-quality bresaola with a lot of fat in it is worth the splurge. It will start to oxidise as soon as it is sliced, but there is no way around that unless you happen to have a meat slicer in your house and can slice it just before serving? I didn't think so, so don't worry too much about it.

Serves 4

1 small celeriac
15 ml (½ fl oz) lemon juice (approx. ½ lemon)
1 heaped tablespoon Crème fraîche (page 239)
2 of the juiciest, sweetest pears you can find
    (my favourites would be a good nashi or beurre bosc)
3 tablespoons olive oil
4 large sage leaves
12 slices good-quality bresaola
90 g (3 oz) toasted walnuts

Peel and carefully slice the celeriac as thinly as possible on a mandoline while still maintaining nice rounds. You want roughly 4–6 slices per portion. Place the celeriac in a bowl and add the lemon juice. Sprinkle with salt and a few cracks of fresh pepper, and toss to combine. Add the crème fraîche and mix again. The salt will soften the celeriac and the liquid will become your dressing.

Just before you serve, cut your pears into quarters – remove the cores, but leave the skin on. Slice thinly using the mandoline, then set aside.

I like to assemble this salad with the pear and the celeriac underneath and the striking beautiful bresaola on top, unless the oxidation has turned the bresaola a bit too brown and, in that case, I would place it on the bottom. Place the dressed celeriac on the bottom of your plate or platter and disperse the sliced pear over that. Drizzle with 2 tablespoons olive oil and gently tear the sage leaves over the top. Sprinkle with salt and pepper, then delicately lay the slices of bresaola over everything. Drizzle with the remaining olive oil and scatter over the toasted walnuts. Serve immediately.

Persimmon, witlof, pomegranate and gorgonzola dolce

This is another beautiful example of an autumnal salad. The colours are gorgeous, and the sweet and salty combination of fruit and cheese wins out again, this time with creamy and piquant gorgonzola dolce paired with crisp, honey-sweet fuyu persimmon and pomegranate seeds. I would serve this at the beginning or end of an autumnal meal, like a cheese course. Keep your witlof in a dark bag until you are ready to use it; exposure to light will begin to turn it green, which makes it more bitter.

Serves 4

4 tablespoons pomegranate seeds
2 fuyu persimmons
2 witlof heads
3–4 tablespoons Chardonnay and honey
    vinaigrette (page 16)
80 g (2¾ oz) gorgonzola dolce

To get the seeds out of a pomegranate, I find it is best to stick a small paring knife into the crown end of the pomegranate, just wedging it inside enough so that you can twist and split it open where it naturally wants to split. Then, using the back of a wooden spoon over a large bowl of water, tap the pomegranate skin so that the seeds drop out into the bowl beneath. If you know there are more seeds inside, but nothing comes out while tapping, break it apart using your hands to find those pockets of seeds and try again. This can be a little messy, so make sure you're doing it on a bench you can easily wipe clean. The water allows the seeds to drop to the bottom of the bowl and any white skin pieces will float to the top. You won't use all the seeds from one pomegranate for this recipe, but take them all out at once and use any leftover seeds in salads for the next couple of days.

Using a vegetable peeler, peel the persimmons and thinly slice on a mandoline. Set aside.

Cut the base from the witlofs and separate the leaves. Toss those in a bowl with a few tablespoons of the vinaigrette, then sprinkle with salt and taste. Assemble the leaves on the base of your serving plate, then arrange the fuyu slices and pomegranate seeds on top. I like to fold the fuyu up to create pretty little wavy pockets to catch some dressing. Next, crumble the gorgonzola on top. Sprinkle a pinch more salt and drizzle a little extra dressing over everything and serve straight away.

Grilled chicory with celery, anchovy parmesan dressing and breadcrumbs

Anchovy and parmesan dressing is absolutely one of my favourite things. It is savoury in a way that makes me salivate just thinking about it. Combine that with the rich smokiness of the grilled greens and the fresh crunch of the celery and breadcrumbs, and this salad definitely delivers in a big way. Grill your greens ahead of time and serve the salad at room temperature alongside other room temperature vegetable salads or with a good steak. Also, use the dressing on any other hearty lettuce leaf like cos (romaine) or radicchio. I even use it as a crudité dip sometimes.

Serves 4–6

Dressing

1 small garlic clove (or ½ large clove)
20 g (¾ oz) anchovy fillets (either oil- or salt-packed, but if salt-packed, rinse well before using)
40 ml (1¼ fl oz) lemon juice
25 g (1 oz) grated parmesan
20 g (¾ oz) dijon mustard
2 teaspoons Worcestershire sauce
120 ml (4 fl oz) extra-virgin olive oil

Salad

400 g (14 oz) chicory or dandelion greens (see Note)
30 ml (1 fl oz) olive oil
2 celery stalks
30 g (1 oz) Breadcrumbs (page 14)

To make your dressing, crush the garlic in a mortar and pestle with a pinch of salt. Add the anchovies and crush them into a paste as well. Scoop this out into a bowl and whisk in the lemon juice, parmesan, mustard and the Worcestershire sauce. It should be salty enough at this stage that you don't need to add any more seasoning. Slowly drizzle in the olive oil and mix to combine. Add a few cracks of black pepper and set aside until ready to assemble the salad.

Set up your charcoal grill and get it quite hot, but ensure all the coals have turned white or grey to give the cleanest flavour. If you're cooking inside, heat a chargrill pan over a very high heat, then prep everything. Split the chicory in half lengthways and wash. If using cos or treviso, split the head through the length and leave the core intact to make grilling easier. Toss with the olive oil and some salt and leave to sit for 5 minutes. Place the chicory halves on the hot grill or into the pan. Because of the water and oil dripping off the greens, it may flame up so do your best to manage this by smothering those small fires. Cook for about 5 minutes in total, flipping halfway through. It's a delicious textural contrast if some areas are still a bit raw and others are well charred (if using dandelion greens, reduce the cooking time to 1–2 minutes). Set on a serving platter and immediately drizzle with half of the dressing. Toss together and allow to cool to room temperature.

Peel the back, ribbed side of the celery stalks with a vegetable peeler, then slice thinly on the bias. Blanch for 10 seconds in well-salted boiling water, then immediately plunge into iced water. Drain, then set aside.

To assemble, spread the celery on top of the greens, then drizzle a bit more dressing over the top. Taste everything. Does it need more dressing? Is that enough? As I said, this is not a delicate salad, so lots of juicy, salty and savoury dressing is what you want, but you can go too far. Finish by sprinkling the toasted breadcrumbs over the top and serve immediately.

Note

Chicory, also known as dandelion, is good here, but you could also use treviso, radicchio or even cos or gem lettuce in its place.

Citrus with Meyer lemon dressing and shaved fennel

The dressing for this salad was another Chez Panisse lesson on one of my first days. Whole Meyer lemons, zest and pith, get diced up and mixed with shallots, their juices and olive oil to make the most heavenly winter salad dressing. I had never used lemons in this way before and it was, again, one of those lightbulb moments that just changed how I saw every ingredient. This dressing is great on a raw fish crudo or winter chicory salad as well. Look for different kinds of citrus at the farmers' market and use everything from kumquats to grapefruits to oranges. Although we use Meyer lemons in the dressing, stay away from lemons and limes for slicing into the salad as they can be too tart.

Serves 4

1 red-fleshed navel orange (cara cara)
1 blood orange
1 grapefruit
1 navel orange
1 tangelo
3 kumquats
1 fennel bulb, thinly sliced on a mandoline

Dressing

30 g (1 oz) diced shallot
1 whole Meyer lemon, cut into tiny dice,
    seeds removed and juice from the lemon
    core squeezed over the lemon dice
1 teaspoon salt
40 ml (1¼ fl oz) extra-virgin olive oil

Using a sharp knife, carefully cut the very tops and bottoms from the citrus and lay them flat on your chopping board. Cut from top to bottom, following the natural curve of the citrus, to remove all the white pith, but do it slowly and carefully so you end up with nice round clean citrus. Do this for everything except the kumquats, which you eat whole, skin and all. Slice all the citrus about 8 mm (¼ in) thick, but the kumquat as thin as you can. If your citrus is particularly large, it's best to cut that into segments. There shouldn't be too many seeds in anything in the winter, but if there are, or it's late in the season, just gently pick them out. Try to slice the citrus close to serving time.

To make your dressing, mix the shallot and Meyer lemon bits and juice with the salt, then set aside to macerate for 15 minutes. Whisk in the olive oil and set aside. This should be made the day you want to serve it.

To assemble, first cover the bottom of the plate with the citrus, fanning the rest out on top so you see all the colours. Sprinkle the top with the sliced fennel and a good pinch of salt, then drizzle the dressing over the top of everything. Serve immediately.

Wilted spinach with fennel, apple and pistachio butter

I love mixing textures of cooked and raw vegetables in salads. In this case, soft wilted spinach with shaved fennel and apple that add sweetness and crunch, while the pistachio butter adds nutty creaminess. I also throw a few crushed, deeply toasted fennel seeds in to add a bit more interest.

If you're lucky enough to find beautiful spinach clusters with the roots attached, leave those on as they look so beautiful on the plate.

Serves 4

2 large bunches English spinach, large stems trimmed (leave whole if using baby spinach with the roots attached)
1 large fennel bulb
1 large sweet apple
2 teaspoons darkly toasted fennel seeds
grated zest of ½ lemon
2 tablespoons extra-virgin olive oil
juice of 1 lemon

Pistachio butter

50 g (1¾ oz/⅓ cup) toasted pistachios
20 ml (¾ fl oz) olive oil

First, wash the spinach really well as it can be quite sandy. Heat a wide frying pan over a medium heat, add the spinach with a pinch of salt, cover with a lid and sauté for 1 minute. The water that clings to the leaves will steam the spinach without the need to add anything else. When just wilted, remove from the pan and set aside to cool. Once cool, squeeze gently to remove any excess moisture.

To make the pistachio butter, crush the toasted pistachios in a mortar and pestle until they begin to form a paste. Add the olive oil with a pinch of salt and mix to combine. Set aside.

Cut the core from the fennel and remove any tough, browned outer leaves. Cut the fennel down the middle and slice very thinly on a mandoline or using a knife if it's good and sharp. Slice the apple the same way, being careful to stop when you begin to hit the core. Toss these shavings in a bowl with the spinach. Add the fennel seeds, lemon zest, olive oil, salt and pepper and enough lemon juice to brighten everything.

Assemble on your plate so that everything is layered and gently stacked. Drizzle the top with the pistachio butter and serve. If your pistachio butter is very thick, mix with a small amount of boiling water to loosen.

Radish with preserved lemon, feta, mint and sesame

This salad is so vibrant it's just guaranteed to garner oohs and aahs. No longer relegated to being just the colourful add-on to a lettuce salad, here, the radish is centre stage, and yet, everything else has purpose. This is a lovely accompaniment to grilled meats or fish, or serve it alongside some hummus, a poached egg and flatbreads.

Serves 4

½ preserved lemon (rinsed and pith scooped
    out and discarded)
juice of 1 lemon
80 ml (2½ fl oz/⅓ cup) olive oil
6 round pink or red radishes, washed
3 medium watermelon radishes, peeled and washed
2 medium purple daikon, peeled and washed
60 ml (2 fl oz/¼ cup) Crème fraîche (page 239), loosened
    with a splash of water or cream for drizzling
2 teaspoons unhulled sesame seeds
1 bunch mint, leaves picked
1 tablespoon snipped chives

First, chop your preserved lemon very finely, almost to a paste, and place in a jar or bowl with the lemon juice and olive oil. Mix and set aside.

Slice your radishes and daikon fairly thin on a mandoline, then arrange them on a plate or platter. Pour the dressing over the radishes, then drizzle with the crème fraîche and scatter over the sesame seeds, mint and chives. Season with salt and a bit of black pepper and serve immediately.

Roasted fennel and Jerusalem artichoke with hazelnuts and grapefruit

This winter recipe combines roasted and raw elements, which produce the most wonderful and surprising mixture of sweet and bright flavours and creamy texture. Jerusalem artichokes, or sunchokes as they are also known, start appearing in early to mid autumn and have a unique and nutty flavour.

Serves 4

1 large fennel bulb, fronds reserved
3 tablespoons olive oil
300 g (10½ oz) Jerusalem artichokes
1 large grapefruit
20 g (¾ oz) grated ricotta salata
50 g (1¾ oz) hazelnuts, toasted and outer skins
    rubbed off, nuts crushed
juice of ½ lemon
extra-virgin olive oil, for drizzling
½ bunch chives, cut into batons

Preheat the oven to 200°C (400°F).

Trim the base of your fennel and remove any outer layers that look tough. Cut the fennel into 8–10 wedges and toss with the olive oil, some salt and pepper, then lay on a tray. Next, cut the Jerusalem artichokes into fairly large pieces and toss them with olive oil, salt and pepper, then place alongside the fennel. Add 300 ml (10 fl oz) water to the tray. This will steam the veggies as they cook. Roast until everything is golden brown and tender. The fennel will take about 20–25 minutes and the artichokes will take closer to 30–35 minutes, so just be prepared to pull the fennel off the tray using tongs and allow the Jerusalem artichokes to continue roasting. Remove from the oven and leave to cool.

Arrange your vegetables on a serving platter. Peel and segment the grapefruit and toss the segments in among the vegetables. Sprinkle over the ricotta salata and crushed hazelnuts, then top the whole thing with the lemon juice. Drizzle with extra-virgin olive oil and give a final sprinkling of salt and pepper, finishing with the chives and reserved fennel fronds.

Farmers' markets and what to know before you start cooking

If you're lucky enough to live in a place with farmers' markets, or you have access to fresh, organic produce (through something like produce boxes) for much of the year, then you really must take advantage of that. It is a luxury, but having good, nutritious food is also a right. Fresh, quality food has the power to make us healthier and more productive members of society, which in turn can lead us to solving the really big issues in the world. And there is no better place to start this journey than at your local farmers' market. It is also the first step to good cooking.

I do the same thing as many of you sometimes: I decide I want to make X, then run off to the market to find all the little bits needed to make it. But when I get to the market and Z looks better, I either change my plan or, sadly, stick to my original plan, always wondering what might have been. Recipes and cookbooks are great inspiration for ideas, but once you learn a few techniques such as seasoning, layering flavours and mastering heat, you really should only use them for support. I've tried to include as many recipes as possible using the lesser-known fruits and vegetables that you can really only find through small local farms simply to help show you one way of enjoying them. Hopefully that little bit of inspiration will give you the confidence to buy something you may not have used before. Speak to the farmers or those tending the market stands; they have incredible insight and usually love a little bit of a chat.

More than even the produce though, my favourite thing about markets is the sense of community. Where else can you slow down, have a coffee, a conversation, maybe a pastry and mull over the fresh bounty of the day? Farmers' markets, like great restaurants that promote good, organic produce, are like the modern bastions holding firm against fast-food culture. The more we support them, the better we will all be.

Fruits and vegetables

Celeriac schnitzel with
salsa verde 53

Greens and onion galette
with crème fraîche and
Comté 55

Celeriac and Jerusalem
artichoke soup with kale
and chilli garlic oil 57

Whole roasted pumpkin
stuffed with wild mushrooms
and gruyère 59

Pencil leeks with hazelnut
picada and citrus zest 60

Grilled escarole with
prosciutto, balsamic
and hazelnuts 60

Slow-roasted, crispy
sweet potatoes 61

Roasted brussels sprouts
with sour cream and
kumquat and chilli relish 61

Cauliflower and smoked
cheese gratin 64

Potato, green garlic
and sorrel gratin 67

Witlof tarte tatin 68

White wine–braised
artichokes, carrots and
green garlic 70

Tomato, red capsicum and
carrot soup with squash
blossoms and basil 73

Corn and soffrito with
fish sauce 73

Asparagus with brown butter,
egg yolk, lemon and young
pecorino 74

Charred Romano beans
with buttermilk herb dressing
and crispy shallots 75

Peas and broad beans
with tarragon, mustard
and horseradish 78

Steamed eggplant with
chilli and pork mince 79

Grilled broccoli shoots
with anchovy butter and
salsa verde 81

Warm camembert with
oven-roasted mushrooms
and spring onions 81

Carrot and beetroot curry 82

Greens with garlic,
turmeric, fenugreek and
breadcrumbs 85

A very green soup 86

Tomato, onion and
cheddar tart 88

Fennel braised in
chicken fat 91

Verjus-roasted quince
with gorgonzola dolce
and fresh walnuts 91

Side note:
Cooking like my Cuban
grandma Aida 93

Fruits and vegetables

This is my favourite topic. If I could achieve one thing in this book, it would be to teach you to love and appreciate fruits and vegetables. It was, again (sorry Mom!), not something I had much of growing up. Or, let's just say fruit and veg was there but it was forgettable. Like, so forgettable that I would have happily forgotten it on the plate and prayed the dog would eat it. My mother was a wonderful cook. She knew how to make a delicious pork braise or roasted chicken, and her black beans were to die for. Vegetables, for Mom, were things like onions, capsicums (bell peppers), potatoes, pumpkin and yucca (or cassava) – all staples of her home country of Cuba (a country not known for its variety of produce, so I don't blame her). She cooked what she knew and what was available, and she did it well, but it was mainly protein, legumes and starchy vegetables. And they were delicious. But my discovery of the joy of fresh, seasonal produce meant the possibilities of healthy, delicious cooking were suddenly multiplied by the thousands of varieties of fruits and vegetables out there.

Roasted brassicas, fresh, young, tender string beans, asparagus, artichokes, broad beans, radishes, turnips, so many different onions and capsicums, zucchini (courgette), pumpkin, fresh peas, fresh-shelling beans, leafy greens – you name it, I was hooked. Almost always at the restaurant, it is the fruit and vegetables that drive the menu. Once I know what is coming from the farms, I can write something cohesive that makes the most out of that moment in time. And waiting for the farm to tell me what's ready means I get tastier produce than if I just order whatever I want from our veg supplier. Just because it's available, it doesn't mean it's good. Maybe the limits of seasonality help me to contain my thoughts. I can't think of anything more overwhelming than having anything and everything at my disposal. The challenge of what to make for dinner becomes altogether too hard, but tell me that Romanesco cauliflower and onions are sweet and delicious, and I'll say, 'pasta Paolina!'

Maybe it's also about living in the moment. The best things at the farmers' market only come around once a year, and we need to be ready to embrace them and then also let them go when that lifecycle has ended. European cultures do this much better than we do in Australia or even the US. There are onion, wine, apple and truffle festivals throughout the European continent at different times of year. They are joyous events that celebrate seasonality through community and food. I'm not an idealist, but give me a world that celebrates that more and I think we would all be in a better place.

The best fat and juicy asparagus of the season, or the perfect moment for figs, when their insides are literally jam, or the first wild mushrooms, or late-summer tomatoes, sweet and bursting! It takes skill to recognise true seasonality and ripeness. I remember this was the most daunting lesson to me as a young cook. There is really no way to teach this skill other than to just be around the ingredients and to taste as much as possible and, without shame, I can say that it took me years. I don't mean this to deter anyone from cooking and going to farmers' markets, but more to help you be OK with the not knowing and to help you realise that not many people really know either, but I can help. Your farmers can too.

Get to know the farmers at your local markets. They will tell you what's good and give you a sample that you can taste and file away in your flavour memory bank. Then, next time around, you can say things like, 'Last year's tomatoes were better' or 'These mulberries are the best I've had in the market' or 'Oh my God, have you had Annabelle's chicories?' These are the phrases I overheard as a young chef visiting farmers' markets in the Bay Area and I just thought, 'How will I ever know?' But then, like magic, I started saying the same things. I knew I had graduated from the not knowing, and that is a big step in good cooking.

Celeriac schnitzel
with salsa verde

Anytime I can produce a recipe that swaps out meat for a vegetable but gives equal satisfaction, I feel I have achieved something. Although I am not a vegetarian, I don't want to eat meat every day, and with such abundance of fresh fruits and vegetables where I live, I like to take advantage of it. Also, it just makes you feel good to eat a lot of vegetables. Even if they are crumbed and fried in clarified butter. This could be served with so many things, but I would probably opt for a nice radicchio or rocket (arugula) salad.

Serves 4

1 large celeriac, peeled
30 g (1 oz) butter
4 thyme sprigs
50 g (1¾ oz/⅓ cup) plain (all-purpose) flour
2 eggs, beaten
100 g (3½ oz/1⅔ cup) panko (Japanese) breadcrumbs
200 ml (7 fl oz) clarified butter or ghee, for frying

To serve

Salsa verde with capers (see page 17)
lemon wedges
salad greens

Preheat the oven to 180°C (350°F).

Cut the celeriac into 1.5 cm (½ in) thick slices. You should get four nice slices from one large celeriac, but if yours is a bit smaller, just use two and serve two slices per portion. Place the celeriac in a baking dish and season with salt and pepper. Add the butter, thyme and 100 ml (3½ fl oz) water and cover with aluminium foil. Bake for 30 minutes, or until a knife can be inserted with ease. Remove from the dish and allow to cool.

Set up a crumbing station. Add the flour to one dish, the egg to another, and the breadcrumbs to a third. Since you are only crumbing one side, you want to make sure that the dish with the eggs in it is shallow so that the egg just barely goes up the sides of the celeriac. Dredge the slices first in the flour, then the egg, making sure the egg really sticks, and then, finally, in the breadcrumbs. Set aside.

Heat a wide sauté or cast-iron pan over a medium heat and allow it to get hot before adding the clarified butter. You want enough butter to go up the side of the celeriac, but not submerge it, so you may need to add more or less depending on the size of your pan. You can also cook these in batches if you only have a small pan.

When the butter is good and hot, place a slice of celeriac, crumbed side down, in the pan and cook until it is golden brown. You want this to happen over the course of 4 or so minutes. If it happens too quickly, your pan is too hot and you won't get that crisp exterior. Once brown, flip the celeriac over and cook for a minute or so just to make sure it's warmed through. Season liberally with salt and pepper as soon as it comes out of the butter.

Once fried, serve on a warm plate or platter with salsa verde and lemon wedges.

Greens and onion galette with crème fraîche and Comté

I am a sucker for a savoury galette. I also love greens and always have too many in my fridge. I realise that topping a buttery crust with loads of greens doesn't make this a health food, but I can pretend can't I? I do, however, know that even if we are talking about a pie, if you're able to get loads of nutrient-dense greens into it and make it into something delicious that you can share with friends and family then it is still waaaaaay better for you than anything processed. I like to imagine children would really enjoy this because it also almost looks like pizza, and I know from having a niece and nephew that getting greens into them is a tough one. I've not made it for them, but I think they would lap it up.

If you're making it for adults, serve alongside a shaved radish, fennel and black olive salad with some lemon and olive oil and it's a perfect vegetarian lunch or dinner.

You will need a baking stone for making galettes at home. They are readily available from kitchen supply stores, and I think they're essential for achieving a crispy base on galettes and pizzas.

Serves 6–8

1 quantity Flaky dough (page 227)
flour, for dusting

Filling

400–500 g (14 oz–1 lb 2 oz) mixed green leaves with thick stems removed (any combination of spinach, silverbeet/Swiss chard, beetroot/beet tops, sorrel, kale, etc.), roughly chopped
2 tablespoons olive oil
170 g (6 oz) onion, sliced
2 teaspoons salt
20 g (¾ oz) flat-leaf (Italian) parsley leaves, chopped
15 g (½ oz) grated parmesan
⅛ teaspoon freshly grated nutmeg
100 ml (3½ fl oz) Crème fraîche (page 239)
50 g (1¾ oz) grated Comté cheese

Egg wash

1 egg
splash of milk or cream

First, make the dough according to the instructions on page 227. Refrigerate to rest for at least 30 minutes while you gather the rest of the ingredients. You can also make the dough ahead of time and freeze it. You'll just need to thaw it in the fridge overnight.

For the filling, wash and drain all your greens but keep them damp. There's no need to excessively dry them, as some moisture helps with the cooking process. To a large frying pan, add the olive oil, onion and 1 teaspoon of the salt. Place over a medium heat and sweat until the onion is soft and just lightly golden. Add the parsley and sizzle for 1 minute, then add all the greens and remaining salt. Put a lid on the pan to speed up the wilting process. Once everything has started to cook, remove the lid and continue cooking until the greens are fairly soft, about 10 minutes. You can add your greens in batches if they don't all fit in the pan at once. Drain the greens over a colander to remove any excess liquid. Allow to cool completely, then mix in the grated parmesan and nutmeg.

Preheat the oven to 230°C (445°F). Place your baking stone on the middle rack of the oven.

Remove your dough from the fridge and place on a well-floured work surface. Dust the top of the dough with some more flour and roll it out as evenly as you can in all directions until it is 2–3 mm (¼ in) thick. Don't worry if the edges aren't smooth, and if you get a crack just patch it up. Once it's rolled out, try to slide a piece of baking paper under the dough. This will make it easier to move around and to place on the stone.

Continued >

Make the egg wash by beating the egg with the splash of milk.

To assemble, dust the base of the dough with a good pinch of flour, then spread your cooled greens on top, leaving a 3 cm (1¼ in) edge. Fold the edges of the galette up in as rustic or pretty a shape as you'd like, leaving the middle of the filling exposed. Brush the folded edge with egg wash, then use the baking paper to pick up the galette and place it on the pre-heated baking stone. If you have a fan-forced oven, turn on the fan, otherwise just add 5–10 minutes on to the baking time. Bake first for 15 minutes, then turn it around to ensure it bakes evenly on all sides. After another 15 minutes, slide the galette off the baking stone and onto an upturned baking tray.

Drizzle the crème fraîche onto the greens (not on the crust). It doesn't have to be perfectly covered or even as it will melt. Also add your Comté on top of the crème fraîche. Slide the galette back onto the baking stone and continue baking for another 20 minutes. Once everything is golden and beautiful and your cheese is just starting to brown, remove the galette from the oven and pull it onto a cooling rack using the baking paper. Serve warm or at room temperature.

Celeriac and Jerusalem artichoke soup with kale and chilli garlic oil

I haven't encountered too many of them, but there are people out there who don't like puréed soups. To me, however, it is the purest expression of an ingredient's flavour. My trick for excellent puréed soups is to sauté the main vegetable for a while with the onions and butter or olive oil and a good pinch of salt. Most recipes tell you to sauté the onions first, then add stock or water and throw in your vegetables. I say sauté the vegetables first, get them a bit tender and juicy before adding the stock or water. It will coax out their natural flavour and sweetness.

Specific to this soup are Jerusalem artichokes. I love their flavour, and the best thing is that you don't need to bother peeling them. Thin slices fried into chips are the most delicious thing and another perfect garnish for this soup. They can be so sweet though that, on their own, their flavour can get a bit overpowering. For this reason, I'm adding celeriac to balance and lengthen the flavour. They're the perfect pair.

Serves 4

40 g (1½ oz) butter
2 tablespoons olive oil
150 g (5½ oz) thinly sliced onion
350 g (12½ oz) Jerusalem artichokes, well washed and cut into 2 cm (¾ in) pieces
350 g (12½ oz) celeriac, peeled and cut into 2 cm (¾ in) cubes
1.3 litres (44 fl oz) light chicken stock (page 12, or use store-bought), or water
1 bunch cavolo nero (Tuscan kale) or curly kale, stems removed, leaves washed and cut into long, thin strips
extra-virgin olive oil, for tossing

Chilli garlic oil (optional; see Note)

3 garlic cloves, thinly sliced
75 ml (2½ fl oz) olive oil
4 g (⅛ oz) dried chilli flakes (Aleppo preferred, but whatever you have)

Set a large stockpot over a medium heat. Add half the butter and the olive oil and let the butter melt. Next, add your sliced onion and a pinch of salt and sauté gently for 8–10 minutes until the onion is super soft but hasn't taken on any colour. Next, add the Jerusalem artichokes, celeriac and another pinch of salt. Drop your heat to low and sweat the vegetables for approximately 10–15 minutes. When they're just starting to soften, add your stock, bring the whole mix up to a simmer and cook for 15 minutes. Taste the liquid: is it seasoned enough? It's important to add salt at this stage of cooking so that the seasoning penetrates the veggies.

While that simmers, put together your chilli oil. This is optional but recommended, and any extra can be stored in a jar. Place your garlic and the oil in a small saucepan and slowly increase the heat until the garlic is sizzling. You want to do this gently, but it should only take about 5 minutes. Next, strain out the garlic, reserving the oil. Immediately add the chilli to the hot oil and leave to infuse in a warm place for 10–15 minutes. Set aside until ready to use. You can store this at room temperature or in the fridge.

Preheat the oven to 200°C (400°F).

When the vegetables are tender, purée them in a high-speed blender until silky smooth. You probably want to do this in two batches. With the motor still running, add the remaining butter. This helps to emulsify the soup and create a velvety texture. If you need to add a splash of water to loosen it to the right consistency, do that while the machine is running as well. Check for seasoning.

Toss the kale in extra-virgin olive oil, then place on a baking sheet and roast for 10 minutes until wilted and crunchy in some places.

Divide the hot soup between four serving bowls and garnish with the chilli garlic oil and a handful of roasted kale.

Note

If you swap the chilli and garlic oil for some freshly grated black truffle, you're in for a great treat (if you are up for the splurge).

Whole roasted pumpkin stuffed with wild mushrooms and gruyère

I first made this pumpkin for a last-minute booking a friend made at the restaurant. Normally, we go to the trouble of ordering something special for our regulars and friends, but since they booked last minute, we had to use what we had. And what we had was a gorgeous pumpkin that looked like it belonged in a fairytale. I knew we had to serve it whole and it was then that I recalled a version of this recipe in an old French cookbook. I got to work early and began on this pumpkin because I knew it would take at least 2 hours to cook. You can imagine how disappointed I was when my friend cancelled at the last minute. It worked out well for the rest of the guests in the room though, as I went around and scooped out a little bit for everyone. The big roasted pumpkin was not the only beautiful sight to see that day; the delight in the guests' eyes when we popped the lid off and scooped out the glorious mix of mushrooms, cheese and pumpkin was something to behold. I think this would be a winner for an autumn or winter holiday menu, as a side dish or the main event.

If you use a bigger pumpkin just be aware that you need to scale up the amount of filling and allow for exponentially longer cooking times as the heat takes longer to reach the centre.

Serves 6–8

20 g (¾ oz) butter
2 onions, thinly sliced
200 g (7 oz) wild mushrooms, such as chanterelle, porcini and slippery jack, cleaned and sliced
50 ml (1¾ fl oz) white wine
6 thyme sprigs, leaves picked and roughly chopped
170 g (6 oz) stale bread, sliced
1.8 kg (4 lb) your favourite heirloom-variety pumpkin (winter squash)
100 ml (3½ fl oz) cream
100 ml (3½ fl oz) mushroom, vegetable or chicken stock (see page 12)
60 g (2 oz) grated gruyère
cayenne pepper, for sprinkling
1 tablespoon grated parmesan
olive oil, for rubbing

Start by cooking your onions. Heat the butter in a sauté pan over a medium–low heat. Add the onions with a pinch of salt and pepper and cook them gently and slowly until they are well on their way to being caramelised. This takes about 15–20 minutes. Next, add the mushrooms and wine with another pinch of salt and sauté for another 5–7 minutes until the mushrooms release their juices, are cooked and the liquid has reduced to almost dry. Next, add the thyme and, finally, check for seasoning before setting aside.

Toast your bread until lightly golden in colour, or just a bit crisp. Set aside.

Cut around the stem to make a hole in the top of your pumpkin roughly the same size as the palm of your hand (you need to be able to reach in and scoop out the flesh). Pull the top off gently, then scrape out the seeds and pulp on the inside and discard. Season the inside of the pumpkin with salt and pepper.

Preheat the oven to 220°C (430°F).

Next, combine the cream and stock in a saucepan and heat until just below simmering point. Begin layering the mushroom and onion mixture, bread, cheese, and cream and stock into the pumpkin. I like to add a little salt and pepper on top of the bread as well as a tiny sprinkling of cayenne pepper. Repeat until all ingredients have been used and the pumpkin is filled generously. You don't want it exploding though, so don't push down too much on the filling to get more in. If it doesn't all fit, then you just have a smaller pumpkin cavity and you'll have a little excess filling. Finish with the grated parmesan and replace the pumpkin top.

Rub the outside of the pumpkin generously with olive oil and roast it on a tray, uncovered, for 2–3 hours or until the outside is darkened, tender to the touch and you see the cream mixture on the inside simmering out of the top. Allow to cool for 10 minutes or so before serving.

Serve by removing the top and scooping a spoonful of the inside (including some pumpkin) onto plates.

Pencil leeks with hazelnut picada and citrus zest

I absolutely adore steamed or blanched leeks. Room temperature, cold or warm, for me, they are a great accompaniment to fish, but they make an excellent standalone salad too. The leeks in this dish are best served just warm, but would be beautiful blanched and then grilled. When blanching leeks, it's important to make sure they are fully cooked. To prevent them from turning a dull green, blanch in a large pot – bigger than you think you need – and salt the water to make it as salty as the ocean. There are two reasons for this: 1) it keeps greens bright, and 2) the salt needs to penetrate through all layers of the leek, which is quite a dense vegetable.

If you have never tried hazelnuts in the autumn, freshly cracked from the shell, it will be a revelation.

Serves 4

1 small garlic clove
80 g (2¾ oz) toasted hazelnuts
15 g (½ oz) Breadcrumbs, toasted (page 14; optional)
6 fresh oregano or marjoram sprigs, leaves picked
1 teaspoon grated lemon zest
2 teaspoons lemon juice
50 ml (1¾ fl oz) extra-virgin olive oil
24 pencil leeks
grated orange zest, to serve

First, make your picada. Crush the garlic in a mortar and pestle, then add 60 g (2 oz) of the hazelnuts and crush those too. Next, add the breadcrumbs, if using, and oregano and crush that all together. Now you can scoop this mixture out into a small bowl. Add the lemon zest, juice, olive oil and a good pinch of salt, then set aside. This can be made up to 3 hours in advance.

Next, blanch your leeks in a saucepan of heavily salted water for about 3–5 minutes, depending on their size, until they are tender. Test them by cutting off a piece and tasting it. If it's still chewy, leave them to boil a little longer. If they are tender without being mushy, they are ready. Pull them out of the water onto a tray to cool and dry off.

Crush the remaining hazelnuts in a mortar and pestle and reserve for garnish.

Plate the leeks on a platter or individual plates and sprinkle the picada and extra hazelnuts on top. Finish with freshly grated orange zest. Serve warm or at room temperature.

See image on page 62.

Grilled escarole with prosciutto, balsamic and hazelnuts

Escarole is another member of my favourite chicory family of greens. It is not as bitter as radicchio and it sort of looks like cos (romaine), but it isn't a lettuce. It makes a delicious salad leaf, but is also great cooked in soups or grilled, or even sautéed. It can be a little bit tricky to find and, I must say, it doesn't really have many close substitutes. You could swap with curly endive, castelfranco or witlof, but if you live near a strong Italian community, I would bet that someone could tell you where to find it. It is an essential ingredient in Italian wedding soup. Here, though, we are serving it like a side dish. This would be a great accompaniment to grilled beef.

Serves 4

1 garlic clove
15 ml (½ fl oz) chardonnay or Champagne vinegar
30 ml (1 fl oz) extra-virgin olive oil
1 large head escarole, tough outer leaves removed, quartered and washed well
8 slices prosciutto
2 teaspoons good-quality aged balsamic vinegar (thick like syrup)
25 g (1 oz) toasted hazelnuts, crushed

First, set your grill (broiler) to high or create a large fire with white coals underneath.

Microplane your garlic into a small bowl and add the vinegar and oil, then mix to combine. If you've just washed your escarole and a bit of water is still clinging to the leaves, that is a good thing as that will create steam and aid in the cooking process. If it's pretty dry, splash it with water. Next, brush the garlic mixture on the outside of the escarole, season with salt and grill quickly for 1–2 minutes on each side. You want to cook the escarole quickly so the outside gets nicely charred, but the inside remains fresh.

Move the escarole to your serving plate or platter. Drape two prosciutto slices over each wedge, then drizzle with the balsamic and scatter over the crushed hazelnuts. Serve warm.

Slow-roasted, crispy sweet potatoes

My dear friend Sean Moran, owner of the legendary Sean's Panaroma in Sydney, served a version of these to me at an exquisite Christmas lunch where my entire team from Fred's was celebrating our Christmas holiday. I remember Sean really turned it on that day and spoilt us beyond our dreams. There was course after course of Sean's signature low-key, super fresh Australian fare. It was perfect. But I must say – and I'm not sure I ever told him this – the thing that stole the show were the sweet potatoes, which were dropped without announcement next to the roast chicken. They had a super crispy exterior and an incredible creamy inside. I never asked him how he made them, but instead, tried to work it out myself. They always steal the show, no matter what I put them next to.

Bake the whole sweet potatoes a day ahead, then just let them roast in the oven the day you want to serve them. It's a long cook time altogether but it's totally worth it.

Serves 2–4

1–2 large sweet potatoes
olive oil, for rubbing and drizzling

Preheat the oven to 200°C (400°F).

Pierce the sweet potatoes with a fork and rub with just enough olive oil to coat them, then sprinkle on some sea salt. Wrap them tightly in aluminium foil and bake until they are completely yielding and soft. This depends on how big they are, but it takes about 1–2 hours.

When they're soft, unwrap the foil and cut each potato into four pieces widthways. Allow to cool, then crush each piece to squash and flatten it. Leave the skin on and try to push any of the 'meat' of the potato back under the skin. This part can be done a day ahead. Just leave the potatoes, uncovered, to dry out in the refrigerator.

Reheat the oven to 200°C (400°F).

Place the potatoes on a baking tray lined with baking paper. Coat each piece with a generous drizzle of olive oil on both sides and a good sprinkle of salt. Roast for another hour, flipping them every 15 minutes, so that both sides get crispy. After an hour, they should have a crispy exterior but still be soft and creamy on the inside. Cook for a little longer if they don't feel super crispy. Drain on paper towel and serve immediately or cool and reheat when ready to serve.

See image on page 63.

Roasted brussels sprouts with sour cream and kumquat and chilli relish

It's funny how brussels sprouts used to have such a bad reputation when I was a child. Now it seems like people can't get enough of them. I love combining their deep earthy flavour with fresh and bright citrus, such as kumquat; it works incredibly well.

As far as kumquats are concerned, I don't think most people know you can eat them whole, like Meyer lemons. They only show up for a few months a year, so take advantage of that moment. In this case they make an excellent relish for these sprouts, but I love to put the same relish on fish, duck, sugar-snap peas or even chicken.

Serves 4

600 g (1 lb 5 oz) brussels sprouts, ends trimmed, halved
olive oil, for rubbing
10 sweet kumquats
1 long red chilli
15 g (½ oz) flat-leaf (Italian) parsley leaves, finely chopped
45 ml (1½ fl oz) extra-virgin olive oil
40 g (1½ oz) sour cream or Crème fraîche (page 239), thinned with some milk or water, to drizzle

Preheat the oven to 200°C (400°F).

Toss the brussels sprouts in enough olive oil to coat them, then sprinkle with salt and pepper. Spread them out on a baking tray lined with baking paper and roast for 25–30 minutes, or until well browned and crispy.

To make your relish, thinly slice the kumquats, removing any seeds as you go. Give them a rough chop. Thinly slice the chilli (removing the seeds if you don't like things too spicy) and combine with the kumquat. Mix that all together with the chopped parsley and the extra-virgin olive oil with a good pinch of salt.

Spread the brussels sprouts on a platter and drizzle with the sour cream. Sprinkle the relish over the top and serve warm or at room temperature.

See image on page 63.

Left   Pencil leeks with hazelnut
          picada and citrus zest
          (page 60)

Top   Slow-roasted, crispy sweet
          potatoes (page 61)

Right   Roasted brussels sprouts with
          sour cream and kumquat and
          chilli relish (page 61)

Cauliflower and smoked cheese gratin

OK, you got me, this is cauliflower and cheese, but really elevated! I am certainly not above a good cheesy gratin and I would suggest that no one else is either. The inspiration for this came from my sister, who admittedly is not someone who loves the kitchen, but once, at a dinner at her home, she served the family a cauliflower and cheese gratin using smoked gouda because that is what she had in the fridge, and it turned out better than she or any of us could have imagined. The smokiness from the cheese really makes this a much better take on regular cauliflower and cheese and it will leave people asking if there is bacon in it.

Serves 6–8

1 kg (2 lb 3 oz) cauliflower (approx. 1 large head)
70 g (2½ oz) butter
50 g (1¾ oz) panko (Japanese) or other fresh breadcrumbs, dried
30 g (1 oz) plain (all-purpose) flour
550 ml (18½ fl oz) cold full-cream (whole) milk
1 bay leaf
1 tablespoon salt
70 g (2½ oz) grated parmesan
1 bunch chives, snipped
pinch of freshly grated nutmeg
100 g (3½ oz) grated smoked gouda or other smoked creamy cheese, like mozzarella

Bring a large saucepan of salted water to the boil. Cut your cauliflower into large but even-sized florets. Boil for 3 minutes, then scoop out of the water and lay them in the gratin dish you will use.

Preheat the oven to 200°C (400°F). Melt 30 g (1 oz) of the butter in a small saucepan and add the breadcrumbs. Mix to combine, then set aside.

Next, make the béchamel sauce. Melt the remaining butter in a small saucepan set over a medium heat. Add the flour and cook for about 2 minutes while mixing with a wooden spoon. Gradually add the milk, then the bay leaf. Switch to a whisk and whisk the mixture together so you don't have many lumps, then go back to a wooden spoon and continuously stir the mixture, making sure to scrape the bottom of the pan so that it doesn't burn. Once the mixture simmers, it's done.

Remove and discard the bay leaf and add the salt, parmesan, chives, nutmeg and a few cracks of black pepper. Mix well and taste. It should be well seasoned. Pour it over the cauliflower and try to spread it out evenly, then sprinkle the smoked cheese over the top. Season with salt and pepper and bake for 15 minutes for a fan-forced oven or 20 minutes for a conventional oven. At this stage, remove it from the oven and sprinkle the breadcrumbs on top. Bake for another 15–20 minutes, or until the topping is golden brown. If it needs more browning beyond this point, put it under the grill (broiler) for a minute or two, but don't walk away from it; it can burn easily! Serve immediately.

Potato, green garlic and sorrel gratin

A good potato gratin should be a part of every cook's repertoire. There are a few important things involved in making a great potato gratin. One is that you must season each layer. Another is that you need to use the right potato. You want a variety that is both waxy and starchy, like a Dutch cream or a Yukon gold. Potatoes that are too starchy, like russets, absorb too much liquid and you end up with mash. Too waxy and not enough starches are released so the layers end up sliding all over one another. If you're not sure which ones are best, ask around at your local farmers' market as there are hundreds and thousands of potato varieties out there.

Unlike many recipes that ask you to cook the potatoes before layering, I think it makes the most sense to bake this directly in the gratin dish from raw. The same goes for the garlic and the sorrel. Sorrel is a lovely soft herb with a sour flavour that works incredibly well at cutting the richness of all that cream.

Serves 8

150 g (5½ oz) sorrel leaves
1 kg (2 lb 3 oz) starchy potatoes, peeled
100 ml (3½ fl oz) full-cream (whole) milk
400 ml (13½ fl oz) cream
10 g (¼ oz) soft butter
100 g (3½ oz) thinly sliced green garlic
    (see Note on page 70)

Stack the sorrel leaves on top of one another and roll them up, then slice them thinly and set aside.

Thinly slice your potatoes on a mandoline to a thickness of 2 mm (⅛ in). Set those aside as well.

Preheat the oven to 180°C (350°F).

Combine the milk and cream in a measuring jug with a spout to make pouring easy. Spread the butter on the bottom and sides of a 30×20 cm (12×8 in) gratin dish, then splash a bit of the cream mixture on the bottom. Cover the bottom of the dish with a layer of overlapping potatoes. Sprinkle with salt and about a one-quarter of the garlic, followed by one-quarter of the sorrel. Pour about one-quarter of the cream and milk mixture on top, then continue layering the ingredients until they have all been used. Cover the whole thing with aluminium foil and place on a tray.

Bake for 30 minutes, then uncover and bake for another 20–30 minutes, or until the top is golden and bubbly. It is best to let this dish rest for a few minutes so that the layers have a chance to cool slightly and stick to each other. Serve while still hot.

Witlof tarte tatin

When presented with this idea, the first question most people ask is, 'Is it sweet?' or 'Is it savoury?' and the answer is, it's both. I would, however, not serve this as a dessert. To me, the sweetness mixed with the slight bitterness of the witlof makes this unquestioningly savoury. I would serve it with a leafy green salad with a sharp mustard vinaigrette, maybe with some cornichons and a piece of soft goat's cheese as a gorgeous lunch. It may look intimidating, but I promise it's pretty easy. Bake this in a good cast-iron pan, something around 28 cm (11 in) in width. Look for witlof that is still pale yellow; exposure to light will turn witlof green and bitter. This is important to note when storing in your fridge too. Keep it wrapped in a brown paper bag so the light won't affect it.

Serves 4–6

1 quantity Flaky dough (page 227)
750 g (1 lb 11 oz) witlof (approx. 5 heads)
40 g (1½ oz) butter
½ tablespoon olive oil
1 egg, beaten with a little water

Caramel

35 g (1¼ oz) caster (superfine) sugar
40 g (1½ oz) butter
1 tablespoon white vinegar

Make your flaky dough, then roll it out thinly. Set it aside in the fridge to keep cold.

Trim the ends off your witlof and split them in half lengthways. Season the cut side with salt. Take a large frying pan and place it on the stove over a medium-high heat. Depending on the size of your pan, you may need to work in two batches. Add the butter and oil and place the witlof in the pan, cut side down. Cook for about 3 minutes, or until caramelised, then flip over and cook on the other side for another 3 minutes. Take the witlof out of the pan and place on a nearby plate.

Next, make the caramel. Place your cast-iron pan on the stove and add the sugar. Warm over a high heat to melt and caramelise the sugar, stirring occasionally only once the sugar starts to take on colour. It might be difficult to see the colour if your pan has a black base, but you can also tell by the smell – it's ready when it smells toasted and caramelised. When the right colour is reached, turn the heat off and add the butter and the vinegar. Mix well. Be careful, as the caramel will want to bubble up.

Preheat the oven to 190°C (375°F) and place a baking stone inside.

Add the witlof, cut side up, to the cast-iron pan, working in concentric circles with the stem end facing out. Discard any of the witlof liquid that was released while resting. Squeeze all of the witlof in, even if it looks packed, as they will continue to shrink as they cook. Place the sheet of dough on top and carefully (the pan will still be hot) tuck the edges in around the inside of the pan. Feel free to make a nice edge, but don't fret too much as you won't see it. Brush the top of the dough with the beaten egg.

Place the pan on the baking stone and bake for 40–50 minutes until the crust is deeply golden and you can see the caramel bubbling up the sides. When finished, remove from the oven and allow to cool for 5 minutes. Place an inverted plate on the pan. Take the pan by the handle, holding the plate firmly against the pan with your other hand. Quickly and carefully flip it over, then lift the pan off. Allow the tarte to rest and cool for 10 minutes, then cut into wedges and serve immediately.

White wine–braised artichokes, carrots and green garlic

Artichokes come around once a year, usually towards the middle or end of winter and into spring. They are one of those vegetables we get so excited for in the restaurant, but we also celebrate when they are finished. Truthfully, artichokes are not that practical to serve because there is a fair bit of labour involved in their preparation, but I don't care. I will drop most things so that I can prep artichokes if my team is furiously busy. It's important that we keep serving the things that are special yet laborious because this is how we show our guests that we care about their experience. But it is also the beauty of cooking at home. In your own kitchen, you don't need to worry about labour expenses or how much you need to charge for an artichoke to make it worth it. You can simply cook and celebrate the fruits of your labour at the table. Take all the time you need; I promise, a good artichoke prepared with love is a revelation. Serve this dish at room temperature either on its own or accompanied by a fresh mozzarella or burrata.

Serves 4

juice of 1 lemon, to prepare artichokes
4 large globe artichokes
100 ml (3½ fl oz) olive oil
4 stems young green garlic,
    cut into 3 cm (1¼ in) lengths (see Note)
½ bunch thyme
1 fresh bay leaf
200 ml (7 fl oz) white wine
1 tablespoon salt
1 teaspoon whole coriander seeds
3 tablespoons white-wine vinegar
8 heirloom carrots, peeled and cut in half

Note

Green garlic is just immature, not fully formed garlic. At the beginning of the season (mid winter and into spring), it is tender and soft and the entire plant is usable. Unlike garlic where you peel and use only the cloves, green garlic can be sliced up and used the same way you would green shallots or spring onions (scallions). As the season progresses, the bulb will begin to form, along with its cloves. Up until this stage, you can still slice and cook the whole thing. Once the cloves have formed, you'll want to peel them back and use them as you would cured garlic, because the other bits will be dried and fibrous by then.

To prepare the artichokes, fill a bowl with water and add the lemon juice, then set aside. Next, start by removing the outer layers of the artichoke until the leaves begin to appear pale green or yellow. The tips might still be green, but as long as most of the leaf is pale in colour, it shouldn't be fibrous. Cut off the top third of the artichoke leaves with a sharp knife. Next, use a small paring knife to cut around the base and remove any jagged green bits so you are left with a smooth, white centre. If you're lucky enough to find artichokes with nice long stems, leave them long, but trim to 8–10 cm (3¼–4 in). Peel the stems until you reach a soft, white centre, then cut the entire artichoke in half lengthways. Using a small teaspoon – and holding the artichoke stem facing up – dig the top of the spoon into the base where the 'hairy' choke begins. Scoop out as much of this as you can while still leaving the outer leaves intact. Remove any leaves that look papery or have pink or purple tips; their texture when cooked is less than desirable. Some young artichokes will not have a choke and won't need to be scraped out. Immediately place the artichoke in the lemon water and prepare the others in the same way.

Combine the olive oil, garlic, thyme and bay leaf in a saucepan over a medium heat and sizzle for about 2 minutes. Add the white wine, salt, coriander seeds, vinegar and 400 ml (13½ fl oz) water and bring to the boil. Boil for about 2 minutes, then add the drained artichokes and carrots. Place a cartouche or sheet of baking paper directly over the vegetables to keep them moist and submerged and reduce the heat to a gentle simmer. Top up the water if necessary to ensure the vegetables are completely covered. Simmer for 5–10 minutes, or until the carrot and artichokes (at the stem) can be pierced easily with a knife. Do not cook them beyond this point, or they will turn mushy. Remove the vegetables from the liquid to cool, but reserve the liquid. Once the liquid and veggies are cool, place the veggies back in the liquid until you are ready to serve. Serve with fresh cheese or as part of a salad.

Tomato, red capsicum and carrot soup with squash blossoms and basil

A good, hot tomato soup is one of my favourite things. I made this soup for a friend towards the end of summer, with few ingredients. It was delicious because everything was so sweet at that time of year. However, even a great tomato can have too much acidity, so I included sweet red pepper, and the flavour was incredible. Look for a variety such as bullhorn or Jimmy Nardellos, which are superior to your standard watery capsicum (bell pepper). The squash blossom leaves are not essential, but add the loveliest texture. And, of course, basil – nothing says summer more than the combination of tomato and basil.

Serves 4

4 large red or yellow heirloom tomatoes
80 ml (2½ fl oz/⅓ cup) olive oil, plus extra for drizzling
1 onion
2 garlic cloves, thinly sliced
2 teaspoons fine sea salt
2 large carrots or 8 small heirloom carrots, peeled and finely chopped
150 g (5½ oz) Jimmy Nardello sweet red peppers (capsicums), cut lengthways, seeds removed, finely chopped
800 ml (27 fl oz) light chicken stock (page 12, or use store-bought), or water
½ bunch basil, plus extra leaves, to garnish
30 g (1 oz) cold butter
8 squash blossoms or zucchini (courgette) flowers, to garnish

Cut the tomatoes through the equator, gently squeeze out the seeds and discard. Dice up the flesh and set aside.

Add half the olive oil to a large stockpot and sauté the onion and garlic with 1 teaspoon of the salt for 10–12 minutes until soft but without any colour. Next, add the carrots, peppers and tomatoes with the remaining salt. Sauté for at least 10 minutes before adding the stock and basil, then bring up to a simmer. Simmer for about 15 minutes until the carrot and pepper are tender. Remove the basil, then transfer to a high-speed blender and blitz until smooth. Add the butter and remaining olive oil while the machine is still running. Check for seasoning and add more salt if needed. Adjust the consistency with water until it is slightly thicker than thick (double/heavy) cream.

Bring back to a simmer. Serve hot with two flowers pulled apart over each bowl (discard the stamen first). Garnish with basil leaves and finish with a drizzle of olive oil.

Corn and soffrito with fish sauce

Soffrito is something I know well. In fact, it is the smell I most remember from my youth. My mom made dinner every night and, in Cuban cuisine, almost every dish starts with a base of soffrito. This mix of onions, garlic, red and green capsicum (bell pepper) with tomato and white wine transports me back to being by my mom's side in the kitchen. It's widely used in Caribbean and Creole cuisines, and it's pretty magical stuff, and although I typically leave the Cuban cooking to my mom (she is much better than I am), I do sometimes crave it. This dish is not Cuban, but since it does include soffrito, I guess it's Cuban-ish to me. It works so well with the corn and chilli, and the fish sauce is there for a salty umami kick. Serve this with some pan-fried scallops or a piece of grilled fish or simply grilled prawns.

Serves 4

1 small onion, finely diced
1 small green capsicum (bell pepper), finely diced
1 small red capsicum (bell pepper), finely diced
1 teaspoon sambal oelek
3 garlic cloves, finely minced
3 tablespoons olive oil
250 g (9 oz) tomato passata (puréed tomatoes)
125 ml (4 fl oz/½ cup) dry white wine
4 ears corn, shucked and kernels cut off the cobs
6 splashes fish sauce
30 g (1 oz) butter
juice of 1 lime

Make the soffrito by gently sautéing the onion, capsicums, sambal oelek and garlic in a sauté pan with a pinch of salt and the olive oil over a medium heat. When those are all soft and translucent, after 5–7 minutes, add the tomato passata and white wine and simmer gently over a low heat for 10–15 minutes until reduced by half.

Add the corn and a good splash of water and continue cooking for another 5 minutes. When the corn is sweet and tender, remove half of the mixture and blend it until smooth. Add that back to the rest and stir to combine. Finish by seasoning with the fish sauce and salt and by melting in the butter and adding the freshly squeezed lime juice. Set aside and reheat when you're ready to serve.

Asparagus with brown butter, egg yolk, lemon and young pecorino

Asparagus may be the ultimate harbinger of spring. Its presence in the local market means you are well and truly getting into the warmer months, and fresh peas and strawberries are near as well. Although people love to do different things with asparagus, I think there is no better way to cook it than simply blanching. Yes, grilled is delicious, but when asparagus is around, I want to eat it every day and who can be bothered to fire up the grill every day? This preparation is a bit rich, but oh so satisfying. You don't necessarily need to coddle the egg, but I think it makes the yolk slightly thicker, which works better here. If your asparagus is thin, you don't need to peel it and it will require only seconds in the boiling water, but if your asparagus is fat, which is preferred, definitely don't skip the peeling; it really adds a bit of finesse to a super simple dish.

Serves 2

10 fat asparagus spears
2 eggs, at room temperature
40 g (1½ oz) butter
1 lemon
15 g (½ oz) young pecorino, or other young
    sheep's milk semi-hard cheese

Snap the woody end off the asparagus where it naturally wants to break, then use a vegetable peeler to peel the bottom third of the spear.

Bring a saucepan of water to the boil. Set a bowl of iced water near the stove. Gently drop the eggs into the boiling water and leave them for exactly 50 seconds. Immediately pull them out and drop into the iced water. Leave for 1 minute, then remove them and set aside. To that same saucepan of water, add a good amount of salt to make the water almost as salty as the sea.

In another small saucepan, melt the butter over a medium heat and simmer until the milk solids turn golden brown, then turn off the heat.

Drop the asparagus into the boiling water and blanch for 1½–3 minutes depending on their size. You want them to still be crunchy when they come out of the water. Put five spears on each plate. Carefully crack open a coddled egg and drop it into the palm of your hand. Allow the white to slip through your fingers, but hang on to the yolk. Place the yolk on top of the asparagus, then drizzle half the brown butter equally over the top. Repeat with the other egg. If you're making more of this for a crowd, don't worry about separating each individual egg yolk – simply drizzle it on with the brown butter. (The egg whites can be reserved and used for an omelette the next day.) Squeeze a little lemon juice over each portion, then shave the pecorino over the top. Finish with a pinch of salt and a couple of cracks of black pepper. Serve immediately while everything is still warm.

See image on page 76.

Charred Romano beans with buttermilk herb dressing and crispy shallots

Romano beans are the wide, flat cousins of the green bean. They're not as widely available as green beans, so feel free to use whatever green beans you can get your hands on. Many Americans, when they think about green beans, think of green bean casserole: the classic Thanksgiving side dish, which usually combines green beans from a tin (awful) with cream of mushroom soup, also from a tin (doubly awful). But! There is a highlight to this dish, and that's the crispy onions that usually garnish the top. This is my much fresher and lighter take on the same idea, best made in summer when green beans are young and tender and haven't yet developed the bean inside, which can make them tough and fibrous.

Serves 4

200 ml (7 fl oz) grapeseed oil, plus extra
    for tossing the beans
4 shallots or 1 small red onion, thinly sliced
300–400 g (10½–14 oz) Romano beans

Dressing

150 ml (5 fl oz) Crème fraîche (page 239)
50 ml (1¾ fl oz) buttermilk, plus extra if needed
15 ml (½ fl oz) lemon juice
1½ teaspoons salt
1 heaped tablespoon chopped dill, plus extra
    fronds to serve
15 g (½ oz) snipped chives
10 g (¼ oz) finely minced flat-leaf (Italian)
    parsley, plus extra leaves to serve
¼ teaspoon Worcestershire sauce
couple of dashes of Tabasco sauce (hot sauce)
1 small garlic clove

Combine the oil and shallots in a small sauté pan and slowly bring the heat up to medium. The shallots are cooked when they stop sizzling, meaning most of the moisture has cooked out. If they start to colour too quickly, you have heated the oil too fast, so reduce the heat a little. It should take about 8–10 minutes for them to get nice and crispy. Lift them out of the oil and spread out on paper towel to drain. Season with fine salt and set aside to completely cool. They can be stored in an airtight container until you are ready to use them.

Bring a large saucepan of heavily salted water to the boil. Trim off the stem ends of the beans. When the water is boiling, dunk the beans for 2–3 minutes. Test 1–2 minutes: if they're still crunchy but soft enough not to feel raw, quickly pull them out of the water and spread them onto a wide tray to steam and cool.

Next, make your dressing. Combine all the ingredients except the garlic in a bowl. Use a microplane to finely shave the garlic into the dressing. Lots of black pepper is good here too. Whisk to combine. Add a bit more buttermilk if you want it thinner. The dressing should be a bit thicker than the consistency of thick (double/heavy) cream. Give it a taste and adjust the dressing as needed, then refrigerate until ready to use.

To char your beans, toss them in a small amount of olive oil and set them over a hot grill or in a hot chargrill pan. Cook quickly until they start to caramelise and blacken in a few spots. You don't want to overdo this; you just want to get that smoky flavour without killing the bean.

To serve, toss your warm or room temperature beans on a platter, drizzle with the dressing and sprinkle over the crispy shallots. Crush a bit more black pepper over the top and garnish with the remaining dill and parsley.

See image on page 77.

Fruits and vegetables

Left   Asparagus with brown butter, egg yolk, lemon and young pecorino
     (page 74)
Top left Charred Romano beans with buttermilk herb dressing and crispy shallots
     (page 75)
Top right Peas and broad beans with tarragon, mustard and horseradish (page 78)

Peas and broad beans with tarragon, mustard and horseradish

This is a really lovely spring salad that pairs beautifully with grilled fish or a roasted chicken. Feel free to add any kind of snow pea (mangetout) or English peas into this mixture. Look for firm and crunchy sugar-snap peas; if they have gone soft and limp, you won't get a nice flavour or texture from them. A super quick 1-minute blanch is all you need, followed by a good dunking in iced water to lock in sweetness and colour. If you don't, the vegetables will turn grey and wrinkly. To double-peel your broad beans, first remove them from the pod, blanch them, drop them into iced water, then peel off the second light green layer from around the beans. If they are super teeny and soft, these green skins will be quite tender, so you can skip the second peeling stage.

Serves 4

150 g (5½ oz) snow peas (mangetout)
150 g (5½ oz) sugar-snap peas
80 g (2¾ oz) podded peas
50 g (1¾ oz) double-peeled broad beans
2–3 cm (¾–1¼ in) piece fresh horseradish, peeled (you won't need it all, but you need a big enough piece to hold on to while grating)
3 tablespoons Crème fraîche (page 239)
8 tarragon sprigs, leaves picked
chopped fresh chervil, to garnish

Vinaigrette

½ teaspoon wholegrain dijon mustard
2 teaspoons honey
2 teaspoons diced shallot
1 teaspoon salt
1 tablespoon agrodolce-style white-wine vinegar
3 tablespoons extra-virgin olive oil

Bring a saucepan of water to the boil. Add enough salt to make it almost as salty as the sea. Prepare a bowl of iced water. Snap the stems off the snow peas and snap peas, pulling downwards to remove any 'strings' that run down the sides. Repeat on the other end of the peas as well. Dunk the snap and snow peas in the boiling water for 1 minute, then remove with a slotted spoon and immediately plunge them into iced water. Do the same with the peas and broad beans, but keep in mind that they may take longer than 1 minute to blanch depending on their starchiness. After 1 minute, taste and see if they need another 30 seconds to 1 minute longer.

Make the vinaigrette by combining all the ingredients in a small jar, then shaking to combine. Set aside.

Grate 5 g (⅛ oz) of the horseradish directly into the crème fraîche and add a pinch of salt. Mix well, then set aside.

To assemble, spread your peas on a platter and drizzle with the horseradish cream, then the vinaigrette. Shave some of the remaining horseradish over the top and, finally, garnish with the tarragon leaves, chervil and black pepper.

See image on page 77.

Steamed eggplant with chilli and pork mince

You can't live in Australia and not be influenced by Asian cuisine. Thai and Chinese restaurants are dotted around the country and the locals know what they like and who does it best. It's all quite new to me. I'm not saying there aren't excellent Chinese and Thai restaurants in the US, but it's not so much a part of the culture. It was actually one of my reasons for moving to Australia: to see what I could learn about these cuisines by dining out. The answer is, a fair bit. I have also discovered (and I should have known) that they are far more complex than I imagined. I don't attempt too many Asian dishes at home, but there is one that continues to call to me because of its simplicity – Hunan-style eggplant. All I need is a pan and a steamer basket. Hunan cuisine, known for its use of fresh and dried chillies, shallots and garlic, is all about heat. Some people don't like the slippery texture of steamed eggplant, but I love it. It's lighter than you might think. Although this is typically a vegetarian dish, I have added some minced pork. Feel free to leave it out. Served with steamed rice, it's an excellent Chinese-style dinner. A few ingredients require a visit to Chinatown or ordering online, but once you have them, you'll find many ways to use them.

Serves 2

400 g (14 oz) Chinese or Japanese eggplant (aubergine), or use regular eggplant
2 tablespoons grapeseed or other neutral oil
15 g (½ oz) fresh ginger, peeled and minced
2 garlic cloves, minced
2 teaspoons unhulled sesame seeds
2 long red chillies, sliced
2 green shallots or spring onions (scallions), sliced
1 tablespoon Chinese sesame paste or unhulled tahini
¼ teaspoon roasted sesame oil
1 tablespoon fermented black beans
200 g (7 oz) minced (ground) pork
2 tablespoons Chilli oil (see below)
1 tablespoon soy sauce
1 tablespoon black vinegar
1 teaspoon caster (superfine) sugar

Chilli oil

350 ml (12 fl oz) grapeseed or other neutral oil
2 tablespoons sesame seeds
2 tablespoons Sichuan peppercorns
5 cm (2 in) piece cinnamon stick
2 teaspoons Chinese five-spice
2 star anise
2 bay leaves
75 g (2¾ oz) Chinese chilli flakes (or Aleppo chilli flakes)

Start by making your chilli oil. Heat the oil in a small saucepan over a medium heat, then carefully add all the other ingredients, except the chilli flakes. Reduce the heat to low and allow the oil to sizzle and infuse until the sesame seeds are golden, about 3–4 minutes. If they are colouring quickly, your oil might be too hot and it will take much less time, so keep an eye on them and don't let them burn. Strain through a small sieve directly into a bowl with the chillis. Mix and allow the oil and chillis to sit together until they are cooled, at which point this can be stored away.

Cut the stems off your eggplants and discard, then cut the eggplants into 7–8 cm (2¾–3¼ in) lengths, then into wedges. Fill a shallow saucepan with about 4 cm (1½ in) water and set a bamboo steamer basket on top. Put the eggplant inside, cut side up. You may need to layer the eggplant to avoid overcrowding in a single layer. Cover with the lid and steam over a medium–low heat until the eggplant is completely soft, about 10–20 minutes. Top up the water in the pan as necessary.

Heat the oil in a saucepan over a medium heat. Add the ginger, garlic and sesame seeds and sizzle for 1 minute. Add the chilli and shallot and sizzle for another minute. Next, add the sesame paste, sesame oil, fermented black beans and the pork. Cook the pork, breaking it up as you go, until it is completely cooked through, about 5 minutes. Add the chilli oil, soy sauce, vinegar and the sugar, turn the heat off and taste for seasoning. It may need a bit more chilli oil or soy or vinegar – it all depends on your taste. Spoon this mixture all over the steamed eggplant and serve immediately.

Grilled broccoli shoots with anchovy butter and salsa verde

As broccoli grows, it doesn't only produce the large floreted 'crown' that we most associate with broccoli, but also sends out little shoots from its base. These are actually my favourite – you get more juicy stem and leaf and only small tips of floret at the top. If you can't find that, then swap for broccolini, which is a hybrid variety between Asian gai lan and broccoli, and mimics the broccoli shoots.

The flavours here are such a delicious mix. And I know what you're thinking: anchovy butter and salsa verde?! And the answer is yes. Try it. You won't regret it. Serve it with steamed fish or something very clean and light. You will be wanting to sop it up with bread, I promise.

Serves 4

½ quantity Salsa verde, anchovies left out (page 17)
8 anchovy fillets
30 g (1 oz) soft unsalted butter
2 bunches broccoli shoots or broccolini, bases trimmed
olive oil, for tossing
4 lemon wedges, to serve

First, mix your salsa verde and set it aside.

Crush the anchovies into a paste in a mortar and pestle and add them to the softened butter. Transfer to a large bowl, which will be used for tossing the greens.

Blanch your broccoli shoots in boiling salted water for approximately 2 minutes, or until the stems are just starting to soften. Allow to cool on a flat baking tray.

Toss the shoots with a small amount of olive oil, then salt and grill them either in a hot chargrill pan, or, better yet, on an outdoor grill until slightly charred. Toss them in the bowl with the butter and mix around until well coated.

Place the shoots on a serving platter and drizzle with some of the salsa verde. Serve with lemon wedges on the side.

Warm camembert with oven-roasted mushrooms and spring onions

This is a luxurious little dish. Camembert is an oozy French cow's milk cheese from Normandy, often sold in small wooden baskets, which are the perfect vehicle for baking them in. They are great for a cheese plate, but I think they are best when heated in the oven and served with small pieces of bread, fondue style. To go next level, shave some black truffle over the top – you won't regret it.

I think many people assume that mushrooms must be cooked in a pan, but that is not true. In fact, my preferred way of cooking mushrooms is in the oven. It's simple, it concentrates the flavour of the mushrooms, and it also gives them a great chewy, meaty texture as opposed to watery and soft, which is the result when cooked in a pan. Onions are also the perfect oven partner because their flavours really meld into one another. I love these vegetables as a side dish as well as a topping for warm cheese. If I am cooking steak, chances are, the mushrooms and onions are not too far away.

Serves 4

500 g (1 lb 2 oz) wild or cultivated mushrooms, such as porcini, chanterelle, pine or enoki, oyster or king brown (wild always preferred)
1 bunch spring onions (scallions) or bulbous spring onions
olive oil, for tossing
1×250 g (9 oz) camembert cheese in wooden basket
1 tablespoon chopped flat-leaf (Italian) parsley
sourdough bread, to serve

Preheat the oven to 220°C (430°F).

Cut the mushrooms into thick wedges, then cut the onions into chunks. Toss everything liberally with some good olive oil and spread out on the largest baking tray you have. Sprinkle with salt and roast in the oven for 30 minutes, stirring occasionally so that everything becomes golden, tender and even a bit crispy. Remove from the oven and reduce the oven temperature to 180°C (350°F).

Remove the cheese from its wrapping then return it to its wooden basket. Bake for 15 minutes until soft and gooey. Cut the top rind off the cheese by running a serrated knife around the edge, then use two spoons to lift it off. Drop the warm onions and mushrooms directly onto the cheese, sprinkle with parsley and serve with forks and pieces of sourdough so people can help themselves.

Carrot and beetroot curry

The idea for this dish came to me after receiving my weekly produce box. For a few solid weeks we had carrots and beetroot (beets) and I was stumped on ideas for using these beautiful vegetables. I always roast beetroot and throw them in a salad. Usually, I boil carrots or roast them in the oven. But instead, I decided to box-grate them, then sauté with some coconut oil and curry spices. The result was pure magic. After mentioning this revelation to a friend, his response was, 'that's very Sri Lankan'. He was right, so although my creativity took a bit of a hit, it was also confirmed by a culture that has been doing this much longer than I have!

The beauty of this dish lies in the sweetness of the vegetables. When cooked this way, their juices are reduced and their sweetness actually becomes the thing that balances the curry without the need for sugar or honey, which many curries will ask for. The result is savoury and satisfying. Rather than rice, I serve this with lettuce cups, a boiled egg, yoghurt and lots of raw, crunchy vegetables. You could serve it with a delicious dosa or poppadom on the side. It feels so nourishing and healthy that it has now become one of my most trusted weeknight meals.

Serves 2–4

12 heirloom carrots
10 small beetroot (beets)
juice of ½ lime
1 heaped tablespoon coconut oil
1 onion, sliced
1 large garlic clove, minced
2 cm (¾ in) piece fresh turmeric
1 teaspoon ground cumin
1 teaspoon black mustard seeds
¼ teaspoon anise seeds
pinch of cayenne pepper or chilli flakes
½ teaspoon nigella seeds
50 ml (1¾ fl oz) coconut cream
200 ml (7 fl oz) vegetable or chicken stock
    (see page 12, or use store-bought), or water

To serve (all optional)

lime
yoghurt (page 237)
butter lettuce leaves
radish
cabbage
cucumber
boiled eggs
coriander (cilantro)
poppadom
dosa

Peel the carrots and beetroot, then coarsely grate them on a box grater. Reserve some of the raw beetroot and squeeze the juice of half a lime over the top. Add a bit of salt and set it aside as a crunchy condiment.

In a wide sauté pan, heat the coconut oil and sauté the onion and minced garlic on a high heat for 1 minute. Add the turmeric, cumin, mustard seeds, anise seed, chilli and nigella and sauté those for another minute or two until the mustard seeds pop. Then add the carrot and beetroot and sauté for another 2 minutes. Sprinkle the vegetables with salt while they cook.

Next, add the coconut cream and stock and set a lid, slightly ajar, on top of the pan. Leave to simmer over a medium heat for 8–10 minutes until most of the liquid has evaporated and the vegetables have softened.

Serve with the reserved beetroot and lime slaw and some crunchy vegetables, half a boiled egg per person, lettuce leaves, a dollop of yoghurt and perhaps a crunchy poppadom or soft dosa.

Greens with garlic, turmeric, fenugreek and breadcrumbs

If you know me, you know that I cannot pass up a bowl of steamed greens: Chinese, Japanese, Italian, Indian, Greek, you name it – all these cultures have beautiful versions of cooked greens. Greens feel light and nourishing in a way that only leafy green vegetables can, and aside from being healthy, they are also incredibly delicious.

This recipe comes together in minutes and makes a perfect fresh and light side dish, or you can enjoy it like I do, with a fried egg on top for breakfast.

Fenugreek is an underutilised spice that was popular in the Middle East and throughout parts of the Roman Empire. You can cook with the leaves, as Persians do, but here I am calling for the seeds, available in any good spice shop or grocery store. They are often used as one of the background spices in curries and, if asked to describe them, I would say they are the flavour in a curry that you can't quite put your finger on. Don't overdo it, though, as too much can be bitter. Small quantities really round out and sweeten a dish. Also, look out for a quality turmeric powder. My preference is Allepey, which is a bit more brown and deeper in flavour than the bright yellow stuff. Feel free to leave the breadcrumbs off; they mainly add texture.

Serves 4 (or two if you're dining with me)

1½ tablespoons olive oil
7 g (¼ oz) garlic, thinly sliced
½ teaspoon Allepey turmeric powder
¼ teaspoon crushed fenugreek seeds
300 g (10½ oz) washed soft greens, such as beetroot (beet) greens or silverbeet (Swiss chard), stripped from the stems
40 g (1½ oz) Breadcrumbs, toasted (page 14; optional)

In a wide sauté pan, heat the oil over a medium heat, then add the garlic, turmeric and fenugreek seeds and sizzle for 1 minute.

Add all your greens plus 40 ml (1¼ fl oz) water and a sprinkle of salt. Place a lid, slightly ajar, on top and steam the greens for 3–4 minutes, mixing halfway through. Serve immediately with some toasted oily breadcrumbs on top.

A very green soup

It's true that a colour can inspire a dish. I suppose when you think about food as much as I do, sometimes the thought of flavour alone can become redundant. Sometimes a colour, in this case, green, is also a flavour and can be the starting point of a creation. Green feels young and fresh and new, so it makes sense that we would make something like this in the spring when everything green is sprouting. It is a bit of work to bring all the elements together and cook them perfectly, but it's totally worth it. And don't skimp on the pistou (simply 'pesto' in French) either; it ties this soup together and enlivens a simple, clean broth made from water with its verdant herbal qualities. Don't try to make this pesto in anything but a mortar and pestle; you won't achieve the same depth of flavour if you use a food processor. The act of crushing and pressing is completely different to a blade cutting through – it brings out the subtle oils and aromas from the ingredients.

Serves 6–8

150 g (5½ oz) diced shallot
150 g (5½ oz) finely diced carrot
2 tablespoons minced green garlic (see Note on page 70)
2 tablespoons olive oil, plus extra, for drizzling
200 g (7 oz) finely diced green zucchini (courgette)
300 g (10½ oz) freshly cooked borlotti beans, in their liquid, see page 115
200 g (7 oz) fresh peas
150 g (5½ oz) double-podded broad beans
150 g (5½ oz) butter beans, thinly sliced
150 g (5½ oz) sliced asparagus
500 g (1 lb 2 oz) fresh spinach leaves, well washed

Pistou

30 g (1 oz) toasted pistachio nuts
1 teaspoon minced green garlic or 1 garlic clove
60 g (2 oz) basil, leaves picked (approx. 2–3 bunches)
85 ml (2¾ fl oz) extra-virgin olive oil, plus extra for drizzling
25 g (1 oz) grated parmesan
3 cracks of black pepper

Make your pistou in a mortar and pestle. Start by pounding your pistachios to a fine crumb, then set aside. Add the garlic and pound to a paste with a pinch of salt. Add the basil, one handful at a time, reducing that to a paste before adding more. Add another pinch of salt for more abrasion. Next, add the crushed pistachios and mix them into the basil. Things should start looking a little creamier now. Start drizzling in the olive oil, little by little, mixing with the pestle as you go. When all the oil is in, mix in the cheese and black pepper, then set aside. You should have a fairly thick paste, but if it looks dry, add a little more olive oil.

To make the soup, heat a stockpot over a medium–low heat and sweat the shallot, carrot and green garlic in the olive oil until soft and translucent but not coloured. Add 1.3 litres (44 fl oz) water and bring to a simmer. Season with salt, but avoid making it too salty.

Add the zucchini and borlotti beans and simmer for 3–4 minutes until the zucchini is beginning to soften. Next, add the peas and cook for an additional 2 minutes. Add the broad beans, butter beans, asparagus and spinach and simmer for another 2 minutes. At this point, the soup is finished. Ladle into bowls and top with a good spoonful of pistou and an extra drizzle of olive oil.

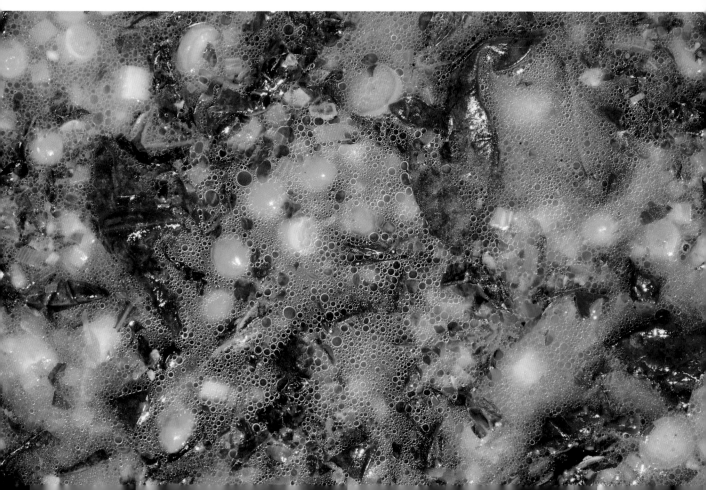

Tomato, onion and cheddar tart

The pastry for this tart is a bit different from the others in this book; it incorporates both butter and sour cream and it just makes the easiest, most delicious, delicate, flaky, buttery tart you have ever tasted. I love this pastry for savoury preparations that are baked in tins as opposed to free-form galettes, which require a sturdier dough. This recipe is inspired by my friend Martin Boetz. He made a version of this, without tomato, at a lunch we were cooking at. He told me it was his grandmother's recipe, and it just has that feel about it – it's old fashioned and I love it.

Serves 6–8

leafy salad, to serve

Pastry

250 g (9 oz/1⅔ cups) plain (all-purpose) flour, plus extra for dusting
150 g (5½ oz) cold unsalted butter, diced
½ teaspoon salt
125 g (4½ oz/½ cup) sour cream
1 egg

Filling

300 g (10½ oz) large heirloom tomatoes (approx. 1–2)
400 g (14 oz) white onion, thinly sliced
2 teaspoons chopped thyme
50 g (1¾ oz) unsalted butter
100 g (3½ oz) sour cream
100 g (3½ oz) grated cheddar cheese
3 eggs
1 tablespoon plain (all-purpose) flour
2 tablespoons cream
2 tablespoons grated parmesan

Start by making your pastry. In the bowl of a food processor, combine the flour, butter and salt and pulse until the mixture resembles fine crumbs. Add the sour cream and egg and pulse a few more times until the pastry comes together in a ball. Shape this into a disc, wrap in plastic wrap and chill for at least 1 hour in the fridge.

Preheat the oven to 180°C (350°F).

Remove the pastry from the fridge, dust with flour and roll out to a 2–3 mm (⅛ in) thickness. Try to keep as round as possible. Gently lift this into the base of a 23–25 cm (9–10 in) pie dish or tart tin. You want to leave 1–2 cm (½–¾ in) of excess pastry hanging over the edge to allow for shrinkage as it bakes. Use scissors to trim off any wider bits. Press a sheet of baking paper on top of the pastry and fill with baking weights or uncooked rice or beans to prevent the pastry puffing up as it cooks. Place the dish on a tray and bake for 20–30 minutes. When the crust is looking golden on the edges, remove the baking weights and continue baking for a further 15–20 minutes. If the crust looks like it's puffing up, poke a few holes in it with a fork to allow steam to escape. When golden all over, remove from the oven and leave to cool completely. This step could be done in advance. Reduce the oven temperature to 160°C (320°F), ready to bake the pie.

Peel your tomatoes by cutting a small X on their base, dropping them into boiling water for 10–20 seconds, then immediately refreshing in iced water. The skin should now peel off easily, starting from the X. Cut into 5 mm (¼ in) slices. Set aside.

In a sauté pan, sauté your onions and thyme in the butter until completely soft and translucent but not coloured. Season with salt and black pepper and set aside to cool. Once cool, mix with the sour cream, cheddar, eggs and flour. Pour the mixture into the base of the tart shell, then layer the sliced tomatoes over the top. Finally, sprinkle with the cream and parmesan and place on a tray. Bake for 40–60 minutes, or until the tart is no longer wobbly and is completely set. If the crust is browning too much, wrap the edge in foil to allow the custard to continue cooking. Remove from the oven and serve warm or at room temperature with a leafy salad.

Fennel braised in chicken fat

Verjus-roasted quince with gorgonzola dolce and fresh walnuts

As I mentioned already, my mom's roast chicken is my favourite. This recipe is basically just a way to get more out of the incredible roasted fennel that you find beneath a roasted chicken. By using chicken stock, chicken fat and butter, you can get a whole tray of this incredibly delicious sweet, caramelised roasted fennel. You can apply this same method to many other vegetables, such as carrots or radishes, onions or sweet potatoes, but fennel is my absolute favourite. A good kosher butcher will often sell rendered chicken fat, or you can make your own.

This is a dish that could easily fall into the cheese-for-dessert category, but with a few curly endive leaves it could also become a meal. The method for preparing the quince comes from a chef I idolise and who I am lucky to call a friend – Skye Gyngell. Skye understands clean, simple and elegant food like few other chefs I have encountered in my career. These quinces are a perfect example of that. The skin and cores are kept on and they are simply braised in delicate verjus (unfermented grape juice) with a bit of sugar and bay leaves, which complement the aromatic fruit so perfectly. As she would say, it's purely quince with the volume turned up.

Quince cannot be eaten raw, even though their raw fragrance is absolutely intoxicating. Take advantage of them while they are around briefly in the autumn and perhaps a bit of the winter, if you are lucky. If you find them at the same time that fresh walnuts arrive, then do not let that moment pass! It's pure magic, and a piquant piece of blue cheese only adds to that magic. If you can't, however, find fresh walnuts, use toasted instead.

Serves 4

3 large fennel bulbs
½ lemon, sliced
300 ml (10 fl oz) chicken stock (page 12, or use store-bought)
10 thyme sprigs
40 g (1½ oz) chicken fat
30 g (1 oz) butter

Serves 4

2 large quinces
2 tablespoons caster (superfine) sugar
150 ml (5 fl oz) verjus
2 fresh bay leaves
100 g (3½ oz) freshly shelled walnuts
150 g (5½ oz) gorgonzola dolce

Preheat the oven to 220°C (430°F).

Cut the fennel into thick wedges and lay it, along with the sliced lemon, in a metal or glass roasting tin with sides. Pour in the chicken stock and add the thyme sprigs.

Melt the chicken fat and butter in a saucepan over a low heat just until liquid and melted. Pour that over the fennel. Season everything with salt. Transfer to the oven and roast for about 40 minutes to 1 hour until the fennel is caramelised and the stock has reduced to almost dry. Be careful to not let the fennel burn as it gets close to the end, as this can happen quickly. Keep your eye on it. Once the liquid gets quite low and the fennel has caramelised, pull it out of the oven immediately.

Preheat the oven to 160°C (320°F).

Rub your quinces really well with a damp cloth to remove any of the white fuzz, then cut each into six pieces. Place them in a shallow baking tray and sprinkle with the sugar, verjus and bay leaves. Cover with aluminium foil and bake for about 1½ hours, flipping them around every 30 minutes. For the last 20 minutes, uncover them and increase the heat to 180°C (350°F) to allow them to deepen in colour and for the liquid to become sticky and thick. Serve at room temperature or warm with the fresh walnuts and some good-quality gorgonzola dolce.

Fruits and vegetables

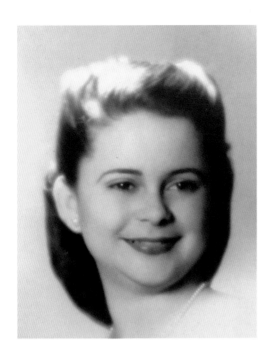

Cooking like my Cuban grandma Aida

Many people might take the expression, 'You cook like my grandmother' as a dig, but if someone said that to me (they haven't), I would jump for joy. I have always wanted to cook more like my grandmother Aida; her food felt like a warm hug. There was soul, love and confidence in every bite ... and perhaps a bit of lard too. Hers was the brand of cooking that we now dub 'ugly delicious'. It wasn't the prettiest or the most perfect, but it was always delicious. She made chicken pies, terrines, guava cakes, a type of pain perdu soaked in cinnamon syrup known as torrejas, fabada, pork roasts, seafood stews – you name it! She added a bit of this, a dash of that, and she never fully told you her secrets, so recipes replicated by anyone else were never quite right. She was an incredible cook and I miss her very much.

Aida was born in Cuba, and immigrated to the United States in the late 1950s, like so many other Cubans of her time. She was a force and she cooked with the same economy and grace that she lived her life. She trusted her palate and her intuition more than she trusted recipes. Don't get me wrong, she had lots of recipes, beautifully typed and organised, but she never needed them. I suppose, after so many years, the cooking sort of just happened. Her hands did the work, but her mind was on the myriad other responsibilities a mother has. I imagine it was like that strange sensation you get when you're driving and arrive somewhere familiar not really remembering how you got there (I realise that kind of autopilot isn't good, but it happens). She cooked everything like she had made it a thousand times, because she had, and yet every time was a little bit different. It is that intuition that I knew I needed to find in myself if I was going to accomplish anything as a cook. Professional chefs usually have very long lists of prep they must get done every day, so if you can cook through feeling versus a recipe you can move much faster. This intuition allows you to visualise the end result and constantly move towards it rather than frequently checking a recipe.

Not only did her efficiency in the kitchen impress me, but I loved how my grandmother expressed her love through food. She was always at the ready with a dessert, your favourite dinner, or simply whatever you were craving. Whether or not she knew she was going to have company didn't matter. If you surprised her, she always had little pastries in the freezer that she knew she could bake at a moment's notice. There was always a pot of beans bubbling away on the stove, and she always had a wooden spoon in her hand.

I love this kind of hospitality. It's old fashioned and rarely does anyone call anyone anymore, let alone drop in on them at home just to say hello, but maybe a restaurant can still feel this way: like my home, where friends and strangers can just drop in and I can feed them like my grandmother did for me. I know I usually have a wooden spoon in my hand.

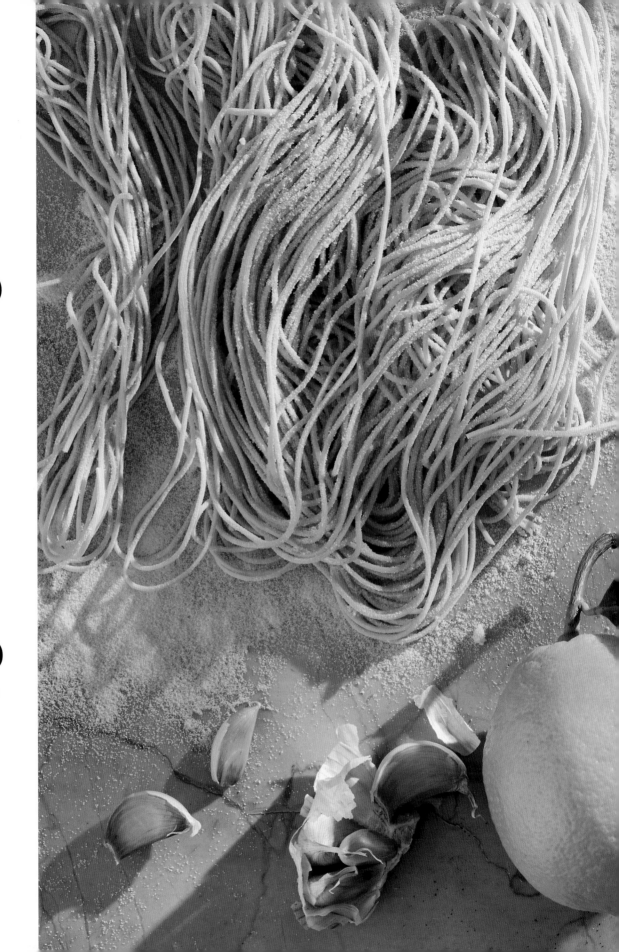

Pasta, grains and legumes

A note on pasta and its
marriage to sauce 97

Ribollita with borlotti beans
and cavolo nero 99

Barley risotto with pumpkin,
sage, roasted radicchio and
balsamic 100

Spaghetti with clams,
parsley and spinach 101

Pappardelle with
chilli-braised beef, red wine,
vinegar, egg yolk
and breadcrumbs 102

Spaghetti with cauliflower,
anchovies, currants and
almonds 104

Rigatoni with fresh tomatoes,
butter and basil 105

Pasta fredda with almonds
and chilli salsa verde 105

Fresh corn polenta with
chilli and garlic oil 108

Casarecce with pesto
Trapanese 109

Fresh pici 110

Pici with chicken, liver
and marsala ragu 111

Pappardelle with
borlotti beans, pancetta
and rosemary 114

Cooking fresh-shelling
beans 115

Green pasta with zucchini,
sage and peas 116

Socca with chickpeas,
rosemary and roasted
garlic yoghurt 118

Linguine with mussels
and nduja 119

Triangoli with asparagus
and ricotta 122

Arroz negro with abalone,
pipis and chorizo 123

Lasagna bolognese 125

Nettle and green garlic
risotto with crispy speck 128

Mussels with sausage,
capsicum and
fregola sarda 131

Pork and garlic chive
dumplings with mandarin,
chilli and soy 132

Pasta, grains and legumes

I have dedicated a chapter to this subject because it is, far and away, my favourite thing to cook for friends and family, and even myself. I love the art of mixing egg-rich pasta doughs with strength and force, followed by that delicate dance of moving thin pasta sheets through the machine while simultaneously cranking the handle. Or, perhaps, rolling thin noodles of silky soft semolina dough, one at a time. Or even stirring a pot of risotto for almost an hour and watching it transform from individual grains of rice into a luscious and creamy wave. It sounds different once it reaches a certain point, and that sound alerts me to gather friends to the table. Or maybe it's a pot of bubbling bean-thickened soup and how that instantly has the ability to comfort and make everything just a little bit better.

This is the chapter about the foods that made me want to start cooking in the first place. I wanted to know why, time and again, the simplest, humblest of ingredients ended up producing the dishes people gravitated towards. A bowl of pasta, a pot of beans or polenta bubbling away – there are great subtleties in their magic, but they seem to have universal appeal. It's comfort food. This is the kind of food grandmas make, wherever they are from. If ever I start getting too cheffy about things, I remind myself to 'cook like a grandma', because that's what everyone loves.

A note on pasta and its marriage to sauce

Pasta is something most people absolutely love, but I think we have all probably had great and bad versions of it. The difference between great and OK is all in the technique. How a pasta comes together just before it is served has a lot to do with it. Now, that doesn't mean that great ingredients don't play a part – they absolutely are the basis of the whole thing – but I find that it is the last couple of minutes of putting a pasta together that gets people confused. Thanks to excellent cookbooks, travel and after working with some great Italian chefs, I learned the art of mixing pasta in the pan with some of the cooking water. Thankfully, most home cooks I talk to now know that you don't serve naked noodles with sauce ladled on top. (Can you imagine what Italians must think when they see this?) It completely misses the point of marrying the sauce and pasta. The pasta needs to give a little of its starch so that it can receive a little of the sauce in order to come together. If done properly, it will result in the sauce clinging to the pasta when you mix the two. In fact, you can create a creamy sauce from just the starch in the pasta and the water alone. The key here is balance: you actually need a lot less sauce and a lot more pasta to achieve this. You also need to vigorously toss the pan, like chefs do, to coax the starch into thickening.

Just like great sushi or nigiri is as much about the texture of the rice as it is about the fish, great pasta is as much about the pasta as it is about the sauce. It is very difficult to cook good, non-baked pasta for a crowd. It just doesn't work. Few people have big enough pans or sufficient stove space to cook much more than four portions at a time. If you attempt large amounts, what you'll end up with is soggy, overcooked pasta and a watery sauce that doesn't really marry with the pasta, so I recommend dishes such as lasagne if feeding a crowd. For recipes like ragu, where the sauce takes hours to make and doesn't come together 'à la minute', it's best to make a large batch and freeze most of it instead of making only four or so portions at any one time. I promise the results when you make smaller batches of pasta are infinitely better than trying to feed a crowd. OK, that's my pasta rant over. On to the recipes ...

Ribollita with borlotti beans and cavolo nero

Ribollita is a hearty Tuscan soup that is typically thickened with bread. When we talk about peasant food, to me, this is the epitome of cooking with economy and grace. A little stale bread, some beans, some greens and the result is so much better than you can imagine. The trick is to cut your mirepoix very finely and sauté it for an extended period (in this case about 30 minutes) to caramelise and sweeten, and create a deep, rich base on which to build your flavours. The other important trick is a lot of really delicious new-season olive oil, like, a lot. It makes all the difference.

Serves 4

160 g (5½ oz) dried sourdough, crusts removed, bread cut into large chunks
100 ml (3½ fl oz) extra-virgin olive oil
pinch of dried chilli flakes
20 g (¾ oz) minced garlic
100 g (3½ oz) finely diced onion
100 g (3½ oz) finely diced carrot
60 g (2 oz) finely diced celery
50 g (1¾ oz) pancetta
1 teaspoon chopped rosemary leaves
4 g (⅛ oz) sage leaves
1.5 litres (51 fl oz/6 cups) rich chicken stock (page 13, or use store-bought)
220 g (8 oz) cavolo nero (Tuscan kale), stalks removed, leaves washed and cut in ribbons

Borlotti beans

250 g (9 oz) fresh borlotti beans (from approx. 500 g/1 lb 2 oz beans in the pod), see page 115
2 tablespoons extra-virgin olive oil
½ onion
½ large carrot
1 celery stalk
1 bay leaf
1 rosemary sprig
1 tablespoon salt

To garnish

freshly grated parmesan
new-season olive oil

Pod your borlotti beans and place them in a stockpot with the remaining ingredients and enough water to cover the beans by 2–3 cm (¾–1¼ in). Leave the vegetables whole so you can easily fish them out afterwards. Simmer until the beans are completely soft, but not falling apart. This should take about 45 minutes to 1 hour depending on how dry they are.

For the sourdough, either leave your bread out overnight to dry, or dry it out in a low oven (100°C/210°F). The bread doesn't have to be completely dry, just a bit drier than fresh to absorb more liquid and combine with the soup.

Set a large stockpot over a low heat. Add the olive oil, chilli flakes, garlic, onion, carrot, celery, pancetta and rosemary. Add a good pinch of salt at this stage, too. Sauté very slowly for 30 minutes, giving it a stir every few minutes. Just before the 30 minutes are up, add the sage and let that sizzle for a minute or two. Next, add the beans with half the cooking liquid and the stock. Check for seasoning, adding more salt if needed, and bring to a simmer. Next, add the bread and the cavolo nero. Allow this to simmer very gently over a low heat for 20–30 minutes to thicken, adding more cooking water to loosen if needed. Serve hot with parmesan, a good drizzle of green, new-season olive oil and black pepper.

Barley risotto with pumpkin, sage, roasted radicchio and balsamic

I find risotto difficult to make perfectly. At times, I have nailed it, and then at others, I've rushed it or mistimed, or maybe I didn't buy quality rice. When it's wrong, it's stodgy, thick, usually with overcooked rice or too much cheese and butter. When it's right, it's light but creamy, bright enough to taste the flavourings and loose enough to move like a wave heading towards the shore.

I find barley or farro to be more forgiving options for making 'risotto', and, actually, they are more nutritious. These grains, even when pearled (which just means partially polished to remove some of the tough outer grain), retain a good chew. They also carry enough starch to thicken a risotto, but not enough to make it heavy and, unlike rice risotto, which requires constant attention and immediate serving, barley risotto can sit for a minute or two while you gather your guests to the table. It is definitely heartier than rice, but that's what makes this winter version a perfect option. Pumpkin, sage, pancetta, radicchio and a good aged balsamic is a winter food equation made in heaven. Put this combination on pizza or in a pasta, or even as a warm salad and you won't be disappointed, but it's ideal in this risotto.

Serves 4

3 tablespoons extra-virgin olive oil
200 g (7 oz) radicchio
20 g (¾ oz) butter
200 g (7 oz) chopped onion
1½ teaspoons salt
160 g (5½ oz) pearled barley
100 ml (3½ fl oz) white wine
1 litre (34 fl oz/4 cups) chicken stock (page 12, or use store-bought)
1 parmesan rind
380 g (13½ oz) chopped pumpkin
8 thin slices round pancetta
24 sage leaves, half chopped, half left whole
40 g (1½ oz) grated parmesan, plus extra to serve
juice of ½ lemon
4 teaspoons good-quality aged, thick balsamic vinegar

Drizzle a bit of oil on the radicchio with a sprinkle of salt and grill the radicchio in a hot chargrill pan or on an outdoor grill. You want to get a bit of smoky char on the outside, but keep the inside raw. Set it aside to cool and, once cool, roughly chop.

Preheat the oven to 200°C (400°F).

Using a tall-sided sauté pan with a lid, place the pan over a medium heat. Add the remaining olive oil and butter and sauté the onion with ½ teaspoon salt for 5–7 minutes, or until the onion is soft and translucent.

Next, add your barley and toast in the oil for 2 minutes. Add the white wine and let that cook out, then start to slowly add your stock, about 250 ml (8½ fl oz/1 cup) at first, stirring every couple of minutes. Add the parmesan rind and place a lid, slightly ajar, on the pot. Reduce the heat to medium so the mixture simmers rapidly for 5 minutes. Remove the lid, add another 250 ml (8½ fl oz/1 cup) stock, replace the lid and simmer for ten more minutes. After this addition, add your pumpkin, another 250 ml (8½ fl oz/1 cup) stock and leave to simmer with the lid ajar for 20 minutes. At this stage, start tasting. Add the remaining salt and stock and simmer for another 5 minutes. Remember that barley will retain a bit more chew, but there should be no resistance in the centre of the grain.

While this is finishing, place the pancetta on a baking tray lined with baking paper and bake at 200°C (400°F) until crisp. When the pancetta is almost ready, throw the whole sage leaves on the tray to sizzle in the rendered fat, then remove from the oven and set aside.

Finish the risotto with the grated parmesan, chopped sage and the chopped, grilled radicchio, and taste for salt. Add the lemon juice, mix once more, and do your final taste. Adjust with more seasoning if needed.

Divide the risotto between four bowls and crumble two slices of pancetta onto each serving. Garnish with fried sage leaves and a drizzle of good balsamic. A little sprinkling of black pepper and extra parmesan, and it's ready to serve.

Spaghetti with clams, parsley and spinach

Spaghetti con vongole. Who doesn't love it? It's a simple classic, but I just can't help but add some soft greens. They also absorb more of that delicious clam liquor, which is what makes the briny sauce for the spaghetti.

Serves 4 as an entrée or 2 as a main

80 ml (2½ fl oz/⅓ cup) extra-virgin olive oil
6 garlic cloves, finely minced
25 g (1 oz) flat-leaf (Italian) parsley leaves, stalks reserved
350 g (12½ oz) vongole or other small clam that has been cleaned
200 ml (7 fl oz) white wine
300 g (10½ oz) dried spaghetti
½–1 teaspoon finely chopped fresh red chilli, or substitute with dried chilli flakes
1 bunch English or arrowleaf spinach, leaves picked and washed
1 lemon
25 g (1 oz) butter

Heat half the olive oil in a large sauté pan over a medium heat and sauté half of the garlic for 20 seconds. Add the parsley stalks and quickly drop the vongole into the pan. Pour the white wine over the clams and quickly increase the heat to high and cover with a lid. Allow the clams to steam for 1–2 minutes, then remove the lid and any of the clams that have opened, leaving the broth in the pan. If some haven't opened, return the lid and continue steaming, checking every couple of seconds, until they are all open. If any don't open, discard them. Once all the clams are out, reduce the heat to medium and taste the liquor. If it still tastes like there is any alcohol remaining, allow it to cook out a bit more. It will probably be a bit salty, but that's good. Strain this liquor through a fine-mesh sieve and set aside.

Bring a large stockpot of salted water to the boil. Add your spaghetti and cook until al dente, or just before al dente, as I prefer to do.

Rinse and wipe clean the sauté pan and return it to a medium heat. Add the remaining oil and sauté the remaining garlic with the chilli. Once soft and fragrant, add your clam liquor (you should have 150–200 ml/5–7 fl oz). If you have less, don't fret, you may just need to add some extra pasta cooking water further down to make the sauce. Let this come to a simmer. When the pasta is done, lift it out of the water using tongs and drop it straight into the pan. Add approximately 140 ml (4½ fl oz) pasta water and the spinach leaves. Toss for a couple of minutes, or until the liquid is almost cooked out and the pasta is nicely coated. Now, add your clams back in with the chopped parsley, a couple of scrapes of lemon zest, the juice of ½ the lemon (perhaps a little less if you don't like acidity), and the butter. Toss everything together and taste. Feel free to adjust the salt, lemon juice and butter – whatever you like to suit your taste. Finally, split between your bowls and serve.

Pasta, grains and legumes

Pappardelle with chilli-braised beef, red wine, vinegar, egg yolk and breadcrumbs

This is a fairly classic red wine ragu, perfect for cosy wintry days. I say fairly, because I've added some chillies to the braise and a bit of red-wine vinegar. The chilli adds a bit of spice, but I think it also brings another dimension to food that isn't all about heat: a depth that can't be achieved with anything else. I think Mexican culture really understands this and their embrace of chillies, dried and fresh, proves it. Leave out the chilli if you don't like any spice, but I recommend you try it. Just be careful to choose a chilli that isn't too high on the heat scale. The red-wine vinegar helps to cut the richness of the meat to hopefully create something that feels a bit lighter than it is. Oh, but then I add an egg yolk, so you might think those two items cancel each other out, but not really. It's all a balancing act and all those elements come together beautifully in the end.

My favourite cut of meat for ragu is oxtail, which is full of gelatinous goodness, but it may not have a huge amount of meat on it so I've mixed in some beef shins and cheeks here too, which are all great braising cuts. Another good option would be beef short ribs. Using cuts with bones in them means you get a lot of flavour without needing to make a stock beforehand.

Serves 8–10

Pasta dough

500 g (1 lb 2 oz/3⅓ cups) 00 flour, plus extra for dusting
2 eggs plus 8–9 egg yolks (combined to make 270 g/9½ oz)
2 teaspoons olive oil
pinch of salt

Ragu

500 g (1 lb 2 oz) oxtail
900 g (2 lb) beef shin
350 g (12½ oz) beef cheek
2 tablespoons olive oil
150 g (5½ oz) diced onion
2 long red chillies, split in half lengthways
3–4 garlic cloves, minced
100 g (3½ oz) sliced celery stalk
150 g (5½ oz) peeled, sliced carrot
1 rosemary sprig
200 ml (7 fl oz) red wine
3 strips lemon rind
1 tablespoon tomato paste (concentrated purée)
50 ml (1¾ fl oz) red-wine vinegar
1 litre (34 fl oz/4 cups) beef stock (or water, for a lighter sauce)

To serve

lemon juice, to taste
8–10 egg yolks
freshly grated parmesan
Breadcrumbs, toasted (page 14), to taste
chopped flat-leaf (Italian) parsley, to taste

To make the pasta dough, tip the flour onto your bench in a mound with a 'crater' in the middle. Add the remaining ingredients to the crater with 1 tablespoon water. Using a fork, slowly incorporate some of the flour from inside the crater, then move further out until almost all the flour has been incorporated, then start kneading with your hands. This is a dry dough that gives a great chew, so don't add any more water. Knead for 3–4 minutes. This dough won't come together silky smooth like other doughs you might have seen. After kneading, it may still look a bit dry and crumbly, but that's OK. Just bunch it back together as best you can and wrap it tightly in plastic wrap. Refrigerate for at least 2 hours, but ideally 24 hours, to hydrate.

Sprinkle a bit of extra flour on the outside of the dough and roll it through the widest setting on the pasta roller. Fold and repeat this 4–5 times until it looks smooth and uniform. You will have to press the dough to get it through the machine and it won't look great at first, but keep repeating the process and it will. Then, slowly work down through the width settings of the pasta roller with each pass of dough. Depending on the machine you have, the settings may vary, but for most home pasta machines you'll want to take the dough to a number somewhere in the middle. For me, that's usually 5. At this setting, the pasta is not paper thin and will still give you some chew. It's a hearty pasta and needs a strong noodle. Cut the pieces into shorter lengths while doing this, if necessary, to make it easier to manage. Dust with flour and lay the sheets on top of each other, then roll them up, like a pinwheel. Use a knife to cut the dough into pappardelle width, which is about 2–3 cm (¾–1¼ in). Separate the strands and set aside on a tray, making sure they are well dusted with flour so they don't stick together. Alternatively, you can dry them out by hanging on a clothes hanger near a window, or on the back of a chair. Dry or refrigerate if you're not going to use them straight away.

To make the ragu, start by liberally seasoning the meat with salt and pepper, then refrigerate for at least 1 hour, or overnight. Twenty minutes before you want to start cooking, take the meat out of the fridge to come back up to room temperature.

Preheat the oven to 170°C (340°F).

Heat the olive oil in a large cast-iron or Dutch oven pot over a high heat. Working in batches so you don't overcrowd the pot, add the meat and brown it on both sides. If you overcrowd the pot, the meat will steam first and then brown, and the process will take a lot longer. Remove the meat from the pan, reduce the heat to low and add your onion, chilli, garlic, celery and carrot. Sweat with a pinch of salt and the rosemary sprig for 5 minutes, stirring occasionally. Add the red wine, lemon rind, tomato paste and vinegar, and simmer for 3 minutes. Return the meat to the pot and add the stock. Bring to a simmer, place a lid on the pot, then transfer to the oven and let it do its thing for 3 hours.

After 3 hours, carefully remove the pot from the oven, remove the lid and allow the meat to cool in the liquid. Once cool, remove the meat onto a large chopping board and shred it. Pick the meat off the oxtail bone, then discard the bones. Strain the braising liquid, reserving the liquid but discarding the vegetables. This liquid will have a layer of fat on top. Try to skim a bit of this off, but reserve it. If you're serving your pasta straight away, leave the meat and liquid separate, but if you're reserving it for another day, place the meat in the liquid and refrigerate or freeze. The fat can be kept in the fridge or freezer as well.

To serve, bring a stockpot of salted water to the boil for your pasta. Set a large sauté pan over a medium–high heat. Add some of the reserved beef fat to the pan (about 2 teaspoons per portion), followed by 80 g (2¾ oz) ragu and 70–90 ml (2¼–3 fl oz) braising liquid per person. Turn the heat back up and let the liquid reduce by half. While that's happening, drop your pasta into the boiling water (calculate about 80 g/2¾ oz fresh pasta per portion) and cook for 3–4 minutes. Using tongs, pull the pasta out of the water and drop it into the pan with the meat. Cook together, tossing frequently, for about 1 minute. Add some of the pasta water to the pan to keep things juicy. Also squeeze a little fresh lemon juice into the pan, about half a lemon for 2–4 portions. Taste and see what you think. Plate each portion as you reheat it, then gently drop an egg yolk over each bowl of pasta so that it remains intact. Sprinkle with grated cheese, toasted breadcrumbs, chopped parsley and freshly cracked black pepper and serve immediately.

Pasta, grains and legumes

Spaghetti with cauliflower, anchovies, currants and almonds

This pasta is inspired by pasta Paolina, which is a pasta created by Sicilian monks in Palermo of the monastery San Francesco di Paola. Original versions of the dish used tomato sauce and spices such as cinnamon, which I have omitted here. Variations on this dish, like mine, use cauliflower, which certainly makes it feel heartier without the need for any protein beyond a few anchovies (which are more of a condiment anyway). I've taken a few more liberties by adding a bit of sweetness to this deliciously savoury pasta in the form of soaked currants, but that is not entirely out of the norm in Sicily either.

Serves 4

80 ml (2½ fl oz/⅓ cup) extra-virgin olive oil,
    plus extra to serve
170 g (6 oz) thinly sliced onion
1½ teaspoons salt
2 garlic cloves, minced
pinch of saffron threads
350 g (12½ oz) sliced cauliflower florets
15 g (½ oz) salted or oil-packed anchovy fillets
    (rinsed if salted), chopped
20 g (¾ oz) currants, soaked in hot water
2 tablespoons salt-packed capers, rinsed
250 g (9 oz) good-quality spaghetti
juice of ½ lemon

To serve

freshly grated parmesan
handful of Breadcrumbs (page 14)
20 g (¾ oz) toasted almonds, roughly chopped
grated lemon zest
25 g (1 oz) flat-leaf (Italian) parsley leaves,
    roughly chopped

Bring a large saucepan of heavily salted water to the boil for your pasta.

Grab your widest sauté pan, add half the olive oil and set it over a high heat. Add the sliced onion and ½ teaspoon of the salt, then stir to combine. Allow to brown for 8–10 minutes with minimal stirring. For the last 30 seconds of cooking, add the garlic and saffron and briefly sauté, then remove the mix from the pan and set aside in a bowl.

Add the remaining oil to the hot pan with the sliced cauliflower. Season with the remaining salt and mix to combine, but do not allow to brown. Sauté over a high heat for 5 minutes. Your stove might be stronger than mine, so adjust accordingly. You want the onion and cauliflower to be golden brown, so if the pan is getting too hot, reduce the heat to medium or even take it off the burner for a minute or two to cool down a bit.

Once the cauliflower is nice and golden, add the onions and garlic back in, then add the anchovies, drained currants, capers and 250 ml (8½ fl oz/1 cup) water. Drop the heat to low and simmer away. At this stage, your pasta water should be boiling and you can drop your spaghetti in. If the sauce ever looks like it is reducing too much and becoming dry, add a bit more water and perhaps turn the burner off until your pasta is ready.

When your pasta is al dente, remove it from the water using tongs and drop it right into the pan with the sauce and cauliflower. Take two ladles of pasta water (approx. 140 ml/4½ fl oz in total) and add it to the pan with everything else. Toss and mix, then turn your heat up to high again and simmer for a minute or two until it looks like the sauce is coating the spaghetti. At this stage, add a good few cracks of black pepper and the lemon juice, which just brightens everything up. Taste the sauce for seasoning, but it should be salty enough.

To serve, divide between bowls or plates and finish with a drizzle of good olive oil, a sprinkling of grated parmesan, some toasted breadcrumbs and the toasted almonds and lemon zest. I like a little extra black pepper and parsley on top too, but feel free to garnish however you like.

Rigatoni with fresh tomatoes, butter and basil

I will only make this pasta when tomatoes are absolutely superb. This dish is a total celebration of the tomato and I think it shows great reverence to that special time of year when tomatoes are bursting with flavour. No garlic, no lemon, no chilli – none of my usual flavour kicks – just simply tomatoes with butter, salt, a bit of parmesan and fresh basil to go with a good al dente pasta.

Serves 6–8

1 kg (2 lb 3 oz) ripest, sweet, juicy tomatoes
2 teaspoons salt
500 g (1 lb 2 oz) rigatoni
150 g (5½ oz) butter
200 g (7 oz) cherry tomatoes, halved
1 bunch basil, leaves picked
lots of grated parmesan, to serve
extra-virgin olive oil, for drizzling

Peel your tomatoes by cutting a small X on their base, dropping them into boiling water for 20 seconds, then dunking into iced water. The skins should peel off quite easily after that. Cut them along the equator and squeeze out and discard their seeds. Purée the tomato flesh in a blender with the salt, then set aside.

Bring a large saucepan of salted water to the boil and cook your pasta until just al dente, or just under al dente. Reserve about 70 ml (2¼ fl oz) of the pasta cooking water.

To another large saucepan, add the drained pasta with some of the reserved cooking water and all the tomato purée. Cook over a high heat for a minute or two until the sauce coats the pasta and, finally, add the butter and melt that in. Check for seasoning. Toss through the cherry tomatoes and serve with fresh basil leaves on top and a good sprinkling of parmesan. A drizzle of good olive oil and black pepper is all that's needed to finish it.

See image on page 106.

Pasta fredda with almonds and chilli salsa verde

I really think it is time that we brought back the pasta salad. Yes, it's been several years of terrible pesto versions lining food counters all over the world, and I could understand why you would be wary of this recipe, but trust me; it's OK to serve a cold pasta dish ... more than OK – it's delicious! Here, I suggest using my fresh chilli variation of salsa verde (see page 17) and mixing that with the cooked pasta of your choice. I like spaghetti and some toasted sliced almonds for taste and texture. It's so delicious and so perfect for a summer gathering that I think you will want to bring back the pasta salad too.

Served 6–8

500 g (1 lb 2 oz) spaghetti or other dried pasta of
    your choice
1 quantity Salsa verde (page 17)
1 tablespoon red-wine vinegar
1 tablespoon very finely minced fresh red chilli,
    seeds removed
2 teaspoons sweet paprika
80 g (2¾ oz) toasted and roughly chopped almonds

Bring a saucepan of salted water to the boil and cook your pasta until al dente. Drain and quickly rinse with cold water to stop the cooking process.

Mix the salsa verde with the additional vinegar, the chilli and paprika, then add the almonds. Toss together with the chilled pasta and serve at room temperature. Don't make this too far in advance so that the herbs stay nice and green.

See image on page 107.

Left	Rigatoni with fresh tomatoes, butter and basil (page 105)
Top	Pasta fredda with almonds and chilli salsa verde (page 105)
Right	Fresh corn polenta with chilli and garlic oil (page 108)

Fresh corn polenta with chilli and garlic oil

I think polenta is widely misunderstood. Pre-made polenta and instant polenta have made us think that it's a quick side dish option, but really, it's not.

So, what is polenta exactly? Well, it's the finished cooked porridge of dried ground corn. Not sweet corn, but starchy varieties of corn that are grown to be dried and ground. Instant polenta is a dried cornmeal, which has then been cooked, dried and processed to cook quickly. I really dislike the stuff. It comes out like a thick glue and there is not much flavour to speak of. Real polenta is made from heirloom varieties of corn, cooked slowly and lovingly over the course of an hour, gently releasing its starches so you end up with something creamy and supple. It requires some time, but little effort. Your guests will be wondering what you did to the polenta because it will steal the show! I add sautéed sweet corn to this, which I highly recommend in the summer and autumn when corn is at its best.

Serves 4–6

1.5 litres (51 fl oz/6 cups) chicken stock (page 12, or use store-bought), or water
150 g (5½ oz/1 cup) dried polenta
300–400 g (10½–14 oz) corn kernels (approx. 4 corn cobs), cobs scraped to release the 'milk'
80 g (2¾ oz) butter
2 teaspoons salt
40 g (1½ oz) grated parmesan
1 quantity Chilli garlic oil (page 57)

Bring 1 litre (34 fl oz/4 cups) of the stock to the boil in a saucepan, then slowly whisk in the polenta. It should immediately start to thicken and bubble. Reduce the heat to the lowest possible setting and cover with a lid, slightly ajar. Switch to using a wooden spoon and keep the remaining stock close at hand. (You will add it bit by bit whenever the porridge looks tight and thick.) Give it a stir every couple of minutes and ensure your polenta is just barely bubbling. If it's rapidly bubbling, you will definitely burn it. A heat diffuser on the stove is helpful here; the key is to achieve the lowest possible heat. When it's finished, it should look like a cohesive mix instead of individual grains of polenta.

Heat a sauté pan over a medium–high heat and sauté your corn with 50 g (1¾ oz) of the butter and 40 ml (1¼ fl oz) water, plus a pinch of salt, for 5 minutes. When the polenta is finished, pour in the corn. Add the salt, the remaining butter and the parmesan. Check for seasoning and adjust until you are happy. This can be served straight away or kept hot in a bain-marie until you are ready to serve. If it thickens while cooling and sitting, add a bit of water to return it to the proper consistency. Serve with a drizzle of chilli garlic oil.

See image on page 107.

Casarecce with pesto Trapanese

Pesto Trapanese is the Sicilian version of the more widely known Ligurian basil and pine nut pesto version. I do adore the Ligurian version, but I feel that in the summer, when the tomatoes are at their best, I want to put them in everything, so this pesto is the recipe I turn to. Use almonds instead of pine nuts and pecorino instead of parmesan, add a few cherry tomatoes, but keep the basil, garlic and olive oil. It's as simple as that. You've heard it before, but I'll say it again: use a mortar and pestle to make pesto; it really makes such a difference to the end result. It takes longer than you think though, so don't rush it. If your mortar is small, crush everything separately and combine in a bowl to mix. It's not ideal, but even then, the results are far superior to doing it in a blender.

Classically, I believe this dish is made with larger tomatoes, but I think cherry tomatoes give the perfect amount of sweetness without adding too much water. If you are using larger tomatoes, though, be sure to peel them first by dropping them into boiling water for a few seconds to loosen their skins.

Serves 4–6

1 garlic clove
40 g (1½ oz) basil leaves
70 g (2½ oz) toasted almonds
200 g (7 oz) ripe cherry tomatoes
150 ml (5 fl oz) good-quality olive oil
50 g (1¾ oz) ground young pecorino, plus extra to serve
450 g (1 lb) casarecce

To make your pesto, crush the garlic clove with a pinch of salt in a mortar and pestle. Add the basil leaves, bit by bit, with a small pinch of salt each time until they are all in and you have created a paste. After that, scoop the basil into a bowl and crush the almonds quite fine in the mortar, then start layering in the tomatoes and crushing them up too. Lastly, add the basil and garlic back to the mortar and begin gradually drizzling in the olive oil, stirring with the pestle. Sprinkle in the cheese and give it a final mix to combine. Set aside.

Bring a saucepan of salted water to the boil and cook the pasta until al dente. Scoop it into a large bowl with the pesto and a good ladle of the pasta water. Mix to combine and finish with an extra sprinkling of pecorino and black pepper. Serve warm or at room temperature.

Fresh pici

Pici is a rustic Tuscan hand-rolled pasta that pairs excellently with braises and richer sauces. Its beautiful chewy texture comes from the durum semolina in the dough. Durum is a type of wheat with a higher protein and gluten content than regular flour. But not all durum is created equal. I've made this same recipe with a durum that had less protein and you get a softer texture, lacking in chew. You may have to try a couple of brands until you find the one you like, but it is well worth the effort.

This is now my favourite pasta to make at home. It's incredibly easy and the best part is you only need your hands to make it. No need to bring out the pasta rollers here. The same dough can also be used to make other short pastas as well, like orecchiette. It's a great one to get your friends or children involved with too.

Serves 4

220 g (8 oz) durum semolina,
    plus extra for dusting
200 g (7 oz/1⅓ cups) 00 flour
1 tablespoon olive oil

Combine your flours with a pinch of salt in a bowl, then add the olive oil and 200 ml (7 fl oz) water. Mix to combine, then dump everything onto a bench and knead for 5–7 minutes until mostly smooth. Wrap in plastic wrap and leave to rest at room temperature for 1 hour.

Pull off 5–6 g (⅛ oz) chunks and roll them into long thin strands using your hands. I find this works best on a wooden surface that has some grit, such as a large chopping board. Dust the strands with semolina and line them up on a baking sheet until ready to use. They only need to boil for 2–3 minutes in heavily salted water, then they are ready to be thrown into a sauce.

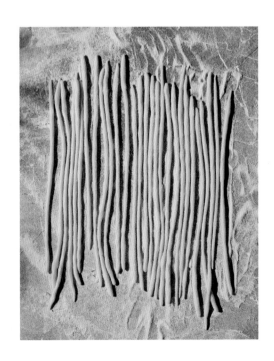

Pici with chicken, liver and marsala ragu

Before you completely overlook this recipe because you don't like liver, you should know that I have served this to several people who said they wouldn't have even known liver was in it if I hadn't told them. So why put something in a dish to not know it's there? Because it adds depth, richness and savouriness, and makes the chicken taste more like, well, chicken.

This recipe uses the more flavourful wings and legs of the chicken and braises them with seared livers, mirepoix, red wine and sweet marsala. Unlike many other meats, chicken only needs to simmer for 1 hour until it's meltingly tender and falling off the bone. Then, you just chop up all that delicious meat and skin, discarding the bones, and add that back to the braising juices. It is so unctuous and flavourful and, combined with chewy, fat pici noodles, makes an excellent dish for a cosy, cold weekend evening.

Serves 4

1.2–1.5 kg (2 lb 10 oz–3 lb 5 oz) mixed chicken
    wings and chicken Maryland pieces
    (leg quarters)
2 tablespoons olive oil
4 thyme sprigs
200 g (7 oz) cleaned chicken livers
160 g (5½ oz) diced onion
160 g (5½ oz) diced carrot
100 g (3½ oz) diced celery
15 g (½ oz) minced garlic
1 teaspoon salt
50 ml (1¾ fl oz) marsala wine
100 ml (3½ fl oz) red wine
800 ml (27 fl oz) chicken stock (page 12, or use
    store-bought)

To serve

1 quantity Fresh pici (see opposite)
30 g (1 oz) butter
1 bunch chopped flat-leaf (Italian) parsley
grated parmesan

Season your chicken pieces with salt and leave to sit for at least 15 minutes.

Heat the olive oil in a large pot or Dutch oven over a high heat and add the chicken pieces to brown. You may need to do this in two batches. Brown the chicken pieces on at least two sides, then remove and set aside. This will take approximately 20 minutes. Next, add the thyme and livers to the pot and sear those as well. Remove, then add the vegetables, garlic and salt and sauté over a low heat for at least 20 minutes. When they are starting to caramelise, add the marsala and wine and simmer for 3–4 minutes. Return all the chicken and livers to the pot, along with the stock, and bring to a simmer. Cover with a lid, slightly ajar, and simmer over a low heat for 1 hour, then turn off the heat and let everything sit for 20 minutes.

Remove the chicken pieces and thyme from the pot. Discard the thyme and pull all the meat off the bones. Discard the bones, then chop the chicken and skin finely and add it back to the pot. At this point, you should check the braise for seasoning, but if it's seasoned to your liking, it's done and you can either use it straight away or refrigerate or freeze.

To finish the dish, boil your pici for 2–3 minutes in heavily salted water until they float, then drain, reserving some cooking water, and toss with the braise in a wide sauté pan. Add the butter and some of the reserved pasta water. Taste for seasoning again, adding some black pepper and half of the chopped parsley. Toss together one more time, then divide between four bowls. Top with grated parmesan and the remaining parsley, plus a few extra cracks of black pepper.

See image on page 112.

Pasta, grains and legumes

Pappardelle with borlotti beans, pancetta and rosemary

I'm not afraid of starch on starch. I come from the land of rice and beans, so I don't see anything wrong with beans being the main component of a pasta dish. Italians know how to do this very well too. Pasta e fagioli, anyone? Potato on a pizza or in a pasta? I'm in. Add a salad on the side and it is a perfectly balanced meal. This is one of those vegetarian-ish dishes where a small amount of pancetta or anchovy is there to fortify and layer flavour as opposed to being the hero of the dish. I like to eat this way and I suggest you might too.

Serves 2

2 tablespoons extra-virgin olive oil, plus extra
    for drizzling
50 g (1¾ oz) pancetta, cut into small lardons
2 anchovy fillets, minced
2 garlic cloves, finely minced
pinch of chilli flakes
1 rosemary sprig, leaves picked and
    finely chopped
375 g (13 oz) cherry tomatoes, halved
1 teaspoon salt
120 g (4½ oz) fresh borlotti beans in
    their cooking liquid (see opposite)
125 g (4½ oz) dried pappardelle or 200 g (7 oz)
    fresh pappardelle
30 g (1 oz) picked flat-leaf (Italian) parsley
    leaves, roughly chopped
lemon juice, to serve
grated parmesan, to serve

To a wide sauté pan, add the olive oil and pancetta and bring up to a sizzle over a medium heat. When the pancetta is beginning to brown, add the anchovy, garlic and chilli flakes, and let them sizzle for about 1 minute. Next, add the rosemary, tomatoes and salt. Let that cook down for about 5–7 minutes, or until the tomatoes just begin to soften. Add the beans with all their liquid and bring to a gentle simmer. Season with some black pepper and keep warm while you cook your pasta.

Bring a large stockpot of heavily salted water to the boil and drop in your pasta. Fresh pasta should only need to cook for 2–3 minutes, dried pasta will take 5–6 minutes, or until al dente. Pull the pasta out using tongs and drop it straight into the pan with the beans. Add about 50 ml (1¾ fl oz) pasta water and toss everything together really well. Allow it to cook together in the pan for another minute over a high heat, then add the chopped parsley at the last minute with a good squeeze of lemon juice and toss once more. Serve straight away, garnished with a good glug of extra-virgin olive oil, some black pepper and grated parmesan.

Cooking fresh-shelling beans

Always start by seasoning your cooking water for shelling beans. (I believe the old rule that you should never add salt to dried beans from the beginning is also incorrect. I've added it at the end, in the middle and at the start, and found very little difference in the texture, but I did notice when adding salt at the end that the beans never actually absorbed the seasoning, therefore you needed a lot more salt to get the flavour.)

After you've cooked them, you can add them to soups, with their broth, use the beans in a pasta or toss in a salad, or just sauté them with a bit of garlic and tomato and a bit of liquid for a delicious side dish.

Fresh-shelling beans were a bit of a revelation when I first moved to California; I had never seen them before. Growing up in a Cuban household meant that I knew my way around a dried bean, but fresh? Never. Obviously, a fresh bean is just a non-dried bean, but cooking them is very different. A dried bean requires an overnight soak and a longer cook, whereas a fresh-shelling bean requires no soaking time and only needs to simmer for about 30–40 minutes. Also, if you don't live in a culture where dried beans are part of the everyday diet, they tend to sit on market shelves for way too long. Like anything, even a dried product, it does need to be used within a certain time. They don't go bad, but they do become very difficult to cook. An old, dry bean needs to cook for so long that it often falls apart before it is finished cooking, resulting in a starchy mush.

Always cool beans in their liquid. You never want to drain a bean, as the resulting lack of moisture causes the outside layers to explode and peel away, leaving the bean looking like it is shedding its skin. It will also have a mushy centre and a tough outside when you try to reheat it. Much to my surprise, I've seen chefs and cooks do this a lot, so I just want to stress again: do not strain your beans. Got it? Good, let's keep going ...

Serves 8

1 kg (2 lb 3 oz) beans in the pod, which yields approx.
    500 g (1 lb 2 oz) beans
½ small onion, peeled and left whole
2 garlic cloves, smashed
50 g (1¾ oz) carrot, peeled and left whole
1 celery stalk
8 g (¼ oz) sea salt
4 thyme sprigs
2 rosemary sprigs
1 bay leaf
80 ml (2½ fl oz/⅓ cup) extra-virgin olive oil

Combine all the ingredients in a large stockpot with 1 litre (34 fl oz/4 cups) cold water and bring to a simmer. Cook for 30–40 minutes, or until the beans are tender and creamy but not falling apart. Allow to cool in the liquid. They can be refrigerated for a couple of days or frozen and thawed for the next time you want to use them.

Green pasta with zucchini, sage and peas

Although I rarely find there is a coloured pasta that tastes intensely of the thing that is colouring it, I do believe there is beauty in it. For instance, spring is a season of renewal and greenness, so it is both beautiful and appropriate to make a seasonal green pasta dough that invigorates both your eyes and your palate, and I love a monochromatic look. This is achieved simply by puréeing fresh raw spinach and parsley with the eggs used to make the dough. We subtract a bit of the egg and water from the basic recipe to make up for the greens, which contain a lot of water. After that, you simply proceed as per my basic recipe.

The sauce for this pasta is made by cooking the peeled zucchini (courgette) until sweet, then puréeing that with the quickly blanched green skins to keep the green theme going.

Serves 4–6

200 g (7 oz) green zucchini (courgettes)
50 g (1¾ oz) thinly sliced onion
2 garlic cloves
40 g (1½ oz) butter
3 tablespoons olive oil
50 g (1¾ oz) picked sage leaves
200 g (7 oz) podded fresh peas
juice of 1 lemon
parmesan, for shaving

Pasta dough

30 g (1 oz/1½ cups) picked flat-leaf (Italian) parsley leaves
100 g (3½ oz) baby spinach
2 eggs plus 3–4 egg yolks or more to equal to 170 g (6 oz)
500 g (1 lb 2 oz/3⅓ cups) 00 flour
2 teaspoons olive oil

To make the pasta dough, start by puréeing the parsley and spinach with the eggs and yolks in a blender, then use that to make the pasta dough following the method on page 102. Rest and roll out your dough, then cut it into tagliatelle, which is about 8–10 cm (3¼–4 in) long and 7 mm (¼ in) wide.

To make the sauce, peel the zucchini and set the skins aside. Heat a wide sauté pan over a low heat and sauté the onion and garlic in half the butter and the olive oil with a pinch of salt until soft and sweet but not coloured, about 8–10 minutes. Then dice your zucchini 'meat' and add to the onion mixture with about 100 ml (3½ fl oz) water to just cook and soften the zucchini. When completely soft, turn off the heat and allow to cool.

Bring a large saucepan of salted water to the boil, drop in the zucchini skins and blanch for 20–30 seconds, then remove from the water and allow to cool completely. Keep the water boiling for the pasta. Combine the cooked skins and zucchini and onion mixture in a blender and purée. Add a bit of water as needed to achieve a smooth consistency. Set aside.

Set a wide sauté pan over a medium heat and melt the remaining butter. Add the sage leaves and sizzle. Drop the pasta and peas into the boiling salted water and cook for 2–3 minutes. Immediately add the purée to the sage and oil and mix to combine. Measure out 50 ml (1¾ fl oz) pasta water and add that to the sauce, then drain your pasta and peas and immediately add them to the sauce. Toss everything together and check for seasoning, then add the lemon juice. Divide between bowls and top with shaved parmesan and black pepper. Serve immediately.

Socca with chickpeas, rosemary and roasted garlic yoghurt

A socca is a traditional French savoury pancake with endless possibilities. Cut from the same cloth as Italian farinata (basically the same thing, except started off in a traditional, shallow, wide pan and then finished off in a wood-fired oven), a socca gets cooked from start to finish in a pan on the stove. The batter is so simple: it's just besan (chickpea flour) mixed with water, salt and olive oil. So, bonus: it's gluten-free. In Nice, it's a street-food snack and a local speciality. I love serving this for aperitivo. Dipped in roasted garlic yoghurt, it's quite simply divine, but you can go a step further and make it the base for a rocket (arugula) and tomato salad, serve it with shaved raw artichokes and pesto, or maybe as part of a salad with carrots and a coriander dressing. I think you will find many uses for this one.

Most recipes will tell you the batter needs to sit and hydrate for at least 12 hours. I have made this right after mixing and after letting it rest for a long time, and the difference is that the pancake gets crispier and takes on better colour after sitting for at least 12 hours. I don't really know why, but it is true. The whole chickpeas in the batter are optional; I just like the texture they provide.

Makes 2 pancakes

Roasted garlic yoghurt

1 garlic bulb
2 tablespoons olive oil
100 g (3½ oz) Yoghurt (page 237)
1 teaspoon salt

Socca

150 g (5½ oz) cooked chickpeas (optional)
125 g (4½ oz) besan (chickpea flour)
2 rosemary sprigs, leaves picked and chopped
70 ml (2¼ fl oz) olive oil
1 teaspoon salt

Preheat the oven to 220°C (430°F).

To make the roasted garlic yoghurt, cut off the top quarter of the garlic bulb and place it in the centre of a piece of aluminium foil. Pour over the olive oil and top with a good pinch of salt. Wrap the foil up tightly around the garlic and place it in a shallow roasting tin. Roast for 1 hour until it is completely soft. Remove from the oven and allow to cool, then squeeze out the soft garlic and mix with the yoghurt and salt. Set aside.

To make the socca, crush the whole, drained chickpeas, if using, with the back of a fork so you are left with some whole pieces and some crushed. In a mixing bowl, combine the besan, chopped rosemary, 30 ml (1 fl oz) of the oil, the salt, 170 ml (5½ fl oz/⅔ cup) water and the crushed chickpeas and set aside in the refrigerator for at least 2 hours, or up to 2 days.

Heat a small cast-iron skillet or non-stick pan on the stove over a high heat until it is smoking. Add 2 tablespoons of olive oil and immediately pour half of the batter into the pan, quickly swirling it around to cover the base of the pan. Leave on high on the stove for 1–2 minutes, or until the edges look golden brown and crispy. Give it a flip and cook for another minute or two on the other side. Add a bit more olive oil if it has all been absorbed. Place on a chopping board and cut into wedges, sprinkle with flaky salt and black pepper and serve with roasted garlic yoghurt for dipping. Repeat the cooking process to make the second pancake.

See image on page 120.

Note

You can easily scale this recipe up to make as many as you would like. To avoid sticking, cook the pancake in a non-stick or cast-iron pan.

Linguine with mussels and nduja

Nduja, pronounced 'en-doo-ya', is a type of spreadable pork salami that originated in Calabria. It's spicy and oh so delicious. It's fabulous spread on some good bread with perhaps a bit of fresh cheese, but in this instance, I add it to a pasta with mussels. It works really well with seafood and particularly shellfish that can take the spiciness without being overwhelmed. If you don't like things too spicy, I would probably skip this one, as reducing the nduja just reduces the value of the complete dish.

Serves 4–6

3 tablespoons olive oil
1 shallot, peeled and thinly sliced
1 bay leaf
2 kg (4 lb 6 oz) mussels
150 ml (5 fl oz) white wine
20 g (¾ oz) garlic, finely minced
1 heaped tablespoon nduja
1×400 g (14 oz) tin whole peeled tomatoes,
    or 6 fresh chopped, peeled tomatoes
250 ml (8½ fl oz/1 cup) chicken stock (page 12,
    or use store-bought)
500 g (1 lb 2 oz) linguine
40 g (1½ oz) butter
½ bunch flat-leaf (Italian) parsley,
    finely chopped
100 g (3½ oz) Breadcrumbs, toasted (page 14)

Heat 1 tablespoon of the oil in a wide sauté pan and sauté the shallot until softened and translucent. Add the bay leaf, then the mussels and increase the heat to high. Add the white wine and cover the pan tightly with a lid. Leave the mussels to simmer and open for about 2 minutes. Remove the mussels from the pan, discarding any that remain closed, and strain the liquid and reserve it. Once the mussels are cool, remove the meat from the shells and pull off any beards that might be attached.

In a wide sauté pan, sauté the garlic and the nduja in the remaining olive oil for 1 minute over a medium heat. Crush the tomatoes with your hands and add to the pan, but discard the liquid in the tin. Sauté for another 2 minutes. Add the stock and the reserved mussel cooking liquid. Simmer until reduced by half. At this point, taste and adjust the seasoning.

Boil the pasta in a pot of well-salted water until al dente, about 7 minutes, then remove it and add it to the sauce. Drop in the butter, mussel meat and chopped parsley and toss together well. Divide between four or six bowls and top with the breadcrumbs.

Note

The mussel beard is the little fibrous bit that a mussel uses to attach itself to a rope in the water.

Pasta, grains and legumes

Top left   Socca with chickpeas, rosemary and roasted garlic yoghurt
                  (page 118)
Bottom left   Triangoli with asparagus and ricotta (page 122)
Bottom right   Arroz negro with abalone, pipis and chorizo (page 123)

Triangoli with asparagus and ricotta

Sometimes a dish comes to you and it is so good it cannot be improved upon. These triangoli are that dish for me. They were on the opening menu of Fred's and are one of the only things that comes back around every spring, completely unchanged. Little triangle-shaped filled pasta pillows with a delicate mix of blended creamy ricotta and gently sautéed asparagus. A little bit of melted butter, parmesan cheese and toasted pistachios are the only things that dress the outside. Oh, and a squeeze of lemon, of course.

To make triangoli, or any shape of filled pasta, you need a couple of additional tools: a spray bottle filled with water, a ravioli cutter (or a knife will do) and piping (icing) bags for piping the filling. When made, line the triangoli up on semolina-dusted trays and do not let them touch one another. They must be cooked on the day you make them, or alternatively, you can freeze them, but they are never as good as when they are fresh.

Makes 40 triangoli

Dough

250 g (9 oz) 00 flour
1 egg
5 egg yolks
2 teaspoons olive oil
semolina, for dusting

Filling

60 g (2 oz) green garlic, minced (see Note on page 70)
40 g (1½ oz) butter
400 g (14 oz) asparagus
350 g (12½ oz) best-quality ricotta

To serve

6–8 spears asparagus, thinly sliced
80 g (2¾ oz) butter
grated parmesan
60 g (2 oz) toasted pistachio nuts, crushed
juice of 1 lemon

To make the dough, place the flour in a mound on your workbench. Make a little crater in the mound and drop the egg, yolks, a pinch of salt and the olive oil in the centre. Use a fork to slowly incorporate some of the flour into the centre of the mound. Eventually lose the fork and start using your hands to knead everything together. Knead for about 10 minutes until the dough becomes smooth and elastic. Add flour as needed if the dough feels sticky. Cover with a damp tea towel (dish towel) and allow to rest for 30 minutes at room temperature before proceeding to roll it out.

To make the filling, sauté the green garlic in the butter in a sauté pan over a low heat until soft and fragrant. Snap the woody ends off the asparagus, then thinly slice the rest. Increase the heat. Add the asparagus to the garlic with a splash of water. Immediately cover with a lid and allow the asparagus to steam for 1 minute. Remove the lid and sauté the asparagus for another minute or two until tender but still bright green. In the bowl of a food processor, blend the ricotta and asparagus-garlic mix until well combined but not completely smooth. Check for seasoning and add salt as needed. Scoop this mixture into a piping (icing) bag and set aside until ready to fill your pasta.

Roll your pasta thin enough to see your hand through the dough. Using a knife, cut out 7 cm (2¾ in) squares of dough and try to minimise as much waste as possible. Pipe approximately 20 g (¾ oz) filling into the centre of each square, then spray the pasta with a bit of water and fold one end over to meet the other to form a triangle. Press around the edges to seal shut and squeeze out any air from around the filling. Trim the two pressed edges with a ravioli cutter, then place on a semolina-dusted tray and continue until all pasta and filling has been used.

To complete the dish, bring a large saucepan or stockpot of well-salted water to the boil and cook the triangoli for 2 minutes. Throw the sliced asparagus into the pot for the last 30 seconds, then drain everything. Brown your butter in a large frying pan over a medium heat until it is a deep caramel colour, then toss the drained asparagus and pasta with the butter. Spoon 8–10 triangoli onto each plate. Sprinkle with parmesan and pistachios, then add a final squeeze of lemon juice.

See image on page 120

Arroz negro with abalone, pipis and chorizo

Rice tinted black with squid ink is one of the more striking things you can make. It's a Mediterranean speciality that feels celebratory and special, but really, it works any time of year. The ink adds a mild oceanic flavour and goes so well in this paella-like preparation. You could go super simple here and use prawns or squid instead of abalone, but if you have access to fresh abalone, this recipe is a great introduction to cooking and preparing it.

Abalone is quite foreign to many people, unless you are from New Zealand, Australia or the west coast of the United States. They are also found in Japan and South Africa. It's a type of shellfish, but it only has one shell instead of better-known bivalves, such as clams or mussels. In the US, you most commonly find them sliced into steaks that are then battered and fried in roadside dives along Highway 1 in California. Even though I lived in that part of the world, they were still a bit of a mystery to me.

They are easy to remove from their shells and clean, but you mustn't skip the tenderising step. If you buy frozen abalone, you may well be able to skip it as the muscle would have already relaxed, but if you're using fresh (which is best), you must spend a couple of minutes with a tea towel (dish towel) and wooden spoon tapping the muscle to tenderise it. You'll feel a change in the muscle when it has relaxed a bit, and this will make the cooking easier. The broad beans are optional, but they add a fresh green pop to an otherwise black dish.

Serves 6–8

3–4 large live abalone in the shell
45 ml (1½ fl oz) extra-virgin olive oil
80 g (2¾ oz) Spanish chorizo,
    cut into small dice
20 g (¾ oz) minced garlic
160 g (5½ oz) diced onion
130 g (4½ oz) diced carrot
100 g (3½ oz) diced celery
60 ml (2 fl oz/¼ cup) tomato passata
    (puréed tomatoes)
2 bay leaves
½ tablespoon smoked paprika
300 g (10½ oz) carnaroli or bomba rice
½ tablespoon squid ink
800 ml (27 fl oz) chicken stock (page 12, or use
    store-bought)
1 teaspoon fine sea salt
30 pipis or small clams, cleaned
1 bunch flat-leaf (Italian) parsley,
    leaves picked and chopped
60 g (2 oz/⅓ cup) podded and twice-peeled
    broad beans
lemon wedges and Aioli, to serve (page 15)

To prepare the abalone, hold it in your left hand and use a spoon to scoop and scrape underneath the muscle to dislodge it from the shell. Place the meat on a chopping board and cut away the liver and any bits that are not part of the muscle. This will be clear to you when you flip it over. Give it a good rinse. On the underside you'll see a little V-shaped beak at one end. Use a small paring knife to cut this away at an angle. Next, using kitchen scissors or a small knife, trim off the frilly edge around the outside of the abalone. Give it a good rinse and scrub and set aside while you prepare the others. To tenderise, wrap the abalone in a tea towel (dish towel) and gently tap with the back of a wooden spoon. You may need to do this for a few minutes, but you will be able to tell when it is tenderised because it will feel softer and more pliable. Sprinkle with salt and set aside until ready to cook.

Heat the oil in a wide, cast-iron frying pan over a medium heat. Add the chorizo followed by the garlic, onion, carrot and celery with a good pinch of salt. Sauté until totally soft and translucent, about 20 minutes. Next, add the passata, bay leaves and paprika and sauté for 2 minutes. Add the rice and mix to combine. Add the ink, stock and salt and mix well until everything is combined. Bring it up to a vigorous simmer over a high heat and simmer for 10 minutes. After 10 minutes, reduce the heat to low and place your abalone in the pan, along with the pipis, and simmer for another 10–15 minutes, or until the liquid is almost completely absorbed. Turn off the heat and cover the whole dish with a tea towel (dish towel) and allow it to steam for another 15 minutes. Remove the abalone from the pan, slice thinly on a chopping board, then return. Sprinkle with freshly chopped parsley and scatter the podded broad beans on top. Serve with lemon wedges and aioli.

See image on page 121.

Lasagne bolognese

Any lasagne is a true labour of love in my opinion. It takes time and I don't make this for just anyone – this one is only for family. Reading this recipe, you may be tempted to find something easier, and that's fine, but if you want to make something that is truly satisfying and you don't mind spending a few hours in the kitchen, then give it a try. Nothing is difficult, it just requires patience.

We all have memories of less-than-perfect lasagne: overfilled with dry ricotta, sautéed brown mince, or the ones that collapse on your plate in a saucy mess. It's no wonder I hated lasagne as a child, thinking back on the boxed frozen stuff that was brought out on 'special' occasions. Now I know better: a proper, homemade lasagne is a revelation, an art form. It's about delicate hand-made pasta, the right balance of sauce to béchamel, good seasoning and good construction.

You can use dried pasta sheets, but if you're going to make all the other elements, why not make the pasta as well? My main issue with the dried sheets is that they are never thin enough. You want to be able to layer your dish with lots and lots of sheets and the dried ones just don't allow for that, but by all means use them if you need to; it will still be great. The bolognese can be made in advance, but the béchamel must be made on the day you assemble it so that it's still warm and pourable.

The baking dish you choose is pretty crucial too. Try to find one that is at least 10–12 cm (4–4¾ in) deep, or you won't be able to create as many layers as needed to make this impressive. Glass, clay, earthenware, aluminium or stainless steel all work, and rectangle or square would be the easiest shape to fill.

Continued >

Serves 12–15

Bolognese (see Notes)

2 tablespoons olive oil
2 small onions, finely diced
1 large carrot, finely diced
2 celery stalks, finely diced
500 g (1 lb 2 oz) minced (ground) pork
500 g (1 lb 2 oz) minced (ground) veal
150 ml (5 fl oz) dry red wine
500 ml (17 fl oz/2 cups) veal,
    pork or chicken stock (see page 12)
200 ml (7 fl oz) full-cream (whole) milk
70 g (2½ oz) pancetta
4 garlic cloves, minced
4 thyme or rosemary sprigs, or 1 teaspoon
    dried oregano
3 tablespoons tomato paste
    (concentrated purée)
2 bay leaves
5 g (⅛ oz) dried mushrooms, such as porcini
1 parmesan rind
pinch of chilli flakes
1 tablespoon fish sauce (see Notes)

Tomato sauce

3 tablespoons olive oil
20 g (¾ oz) thinly sliced garlic
4 × 400 g (14 oz) tinned whole peeled tomatoes
2 teaspoons salt
4 basil sprigs with leaves

Béchamel

40 g (1½ oz) butter
40 g (1½ oz) plain (all-purpose) flour
800 ml (27 fl oz) cold full-cream (whole) milk
1 bay leaf
2 teaspoons salt

To assemble

2 quantities Pasta dough (page 102),
    rolled very thin and cut to the lengths
    of your baking dish
grated parmesan
300 g (10½ oz) shredded mozzarella
    (fior di latte preferred)
30 g (1 oz) butter

Start by making your bolognese. To a wide frying pan, or better yet, a Dutch oven, add your olive oil and sauté the onion, carrot and celery for no less than 1 hour on the lowest flicker of a flame. This time allows the vegetables to melt down and become super sweet. Remove from the pan and set aside. Increase the heat to high. Season the mince on the outside only with a generous amount of salt and pepper and drop it into the hot pot in large chunks – do not break it up. Let it brown and caramelise in big pieces. It takes a while, about 10–15 minutes on each side. Deglaze with the wine and simmer for 2 minutes, then add the vegetables back in along with the rest of the ingredients, except the fish sauce. Bring the mixture up to a simmer, cover with a lid (slightly ajar), then reduce the heat to low. Simmer gently for 2 hours, stirring occasionally to break up the meat. When everything is well reduced, add the fish sauce and check for seasoning, adding more salt if necessary. Set aside to cool. This makes more than you need for the lasagne (about double), so freeze any leftovers for another lasagne or to mix through pappardelle.

Next, make the tomato sauce. Heat the oil in a saucepan over a low heat and sizzle the sliced garlic with a pinch of salt until soft and translucent, about 2–3 minutes. Next, crush the tomatoes either by hand or in a food mill and add to the pan. Add the salt and bring the mixture to a low simmer. Cook for about 20 minutes. For the last 3 minutes, drop the basil in, stalks and all. Then remove it and check for seasoning. Sometimes the tomatoes can be too acidic. If your sauce is lacking sweetness, add 1 teaspoon of sugar to balance it. Set aside to cool. This makes more than you'll need for the lasagne, but I like to serve some extra sauce with it, so don't freeze it. It can be made a day or two ahead.

Make your pasta on the day you want to assemble and bake the lasagne. Exactly how much you need is hard to know as it depends on how thick you roll it and how big your baking dish is. But there is nothing worse than having too little pasta, so make the two quantities, but don't boil it all at first. Try to calculate what you'll need by working out how many sheets will cover the base of the dish, then multiply that by the 8–10 layers we want to create. It's good to cut a few extra sheets too, just in case.

Bring a large stockpot of salted water to the boil and have a large bowl of iced water near the stove. Boil the sheets, a few at a time, for 30 seconds, then immediately plunge them into the iced water. Have a few clean tea towels (dish towels) ready, or, better yet, a large, washable cotton tablecloth and lay the sheets onto the cloth next to each other but not overlapping as they will stick together. Fold the cloth over and continue layering them up until they are all cooked and ready.

Finally, make the béchamel. I do this at the end because it needs to be hot and pourable when you assemble the lasagne. Melt the butter in a saucepan over a medium heat, then add the flour and mix with a wooden spoon. Cook for about 1 minute then switch to a whisk and slowly pour in the milk, whisking constantly to avoid large lumps. (A few lumps are not an issue.) Add the bay leaf and salt. Switch back to a wooden spoon or spatula and stir continuously, scraping the bottom and side of the pan until the mixture comes to a simmer. Simmer while stirring for about 1 minute, then remove from the heat and pour into a jug. Check for seasoning, adding more salt if necessary. Remove and discard the bay leaf, then cover the top of the jug with plastic wrap to keep it hot.

When you're ready to assemble the lasagne, preheat the oven to 180°C (350°F). Use a measuring cup to measure the ingredients out for each layer to make sure it's all even. I use 120–150 ml (4–5 fl oz) tomato sauce and bolognese per layer, and 80–100 ml (2½–3½ fl oz) béchamel. The lasagne might seem quite dry as you build it, but this is intentional. I do it this way to ensure the slices stay intact and don't slide all over the place when you try to serve it. This is also the reason why I make extra sauce. Each slice of lasagne should be served with extra sauce, or just place a pot of warm sauce on the table for people to help themselves.

First, add a layer of tomato to the base of your baking dish and spread it out evenly. Top with the first layer of pasta, then drizzle the first layer of bolognese over the top, followed by the béchamel. Think of the béchamel like glue: use it sparingly on every layer to bind everything together. Next, add another layer of pasta, then tomato sauce, and a drizzle of béchamel. Sprinkle on some grated parmesan, salt and a bit of shredded mozzarella, but no more than 30–50 g (1–1¾ oz) per tomato layer. Continue, alternating between bolognese and tomato layers, until you reach the top of the baking dish. On top of your last layer, spread more tomato sauce, parmesan and mozzarella, and dot around the butter. Cover with aluminium foil and bake for 45 minutes to 1 hour on a baking tray. Remove the foil and place it under a hot grill (broiler) just to brown the cheese, then remove it from the oven and leave to sit for 20–30 minutes. Cut into portions and serve with a little extra hot tomato sauce.

Notes

This bolognese recipe makes double what you need here, so I recommend freezing leftovers for next time.

You may find the addition of fish sauce a strange one, but hear me out: it's there to add umami and seasoning. You won't notice it. But you will notice that this bolognese tastes better than others.

Pasta, grains and legumes

Nettle and green garlic risotto with crispy speck

Nettles are essentially a weed, but their flavour and nutritional profile are unlike anything else, and a risotto is one of the best ways to enjoy them. You must wear thick gloves when preparing the leaves, which have fine spikes and can sting. The sting goes away after several minutes and this shouldn't put you off using them as they are worth the minor discomfort. Once the leaves are picked, there should be no further stinging. Be sure to wash twice in cold water to remove dirt. Ask a good vegetable supplier for them, or look for them at the farmers' market. They are often available when there has been lots of rain.

The speck here is Italian, which is like a smoked, dry-cured ham. If you can't find that, substitute with thinly sliced pancetta or cold-smoked thin bacon.

I prefer to eat risotto as a small entrée or a small portion with vegetables and salad. I find that you only need a few bites to taste everything. The most important thing about risotto, though, is to serve it the moment it is ready; it cannot sit around while you gather other things. It should go from pan to plate in no more than a minute or two.

Serves 6–8 as an entrée

80 ml (2½ fl oz/⅓ cup) olive oil
180 g (6½ oz) minced onion
60 g (2 oz) minced green garlic (see Note on page 70)
1.2 litres (41 fl oz) vegetable or light chicken stock (see page 12, or use store-bought)
200 g (7 oz) carnaroli or arborio rice
150 ml (5 fl oz) white wine
2 teaspoons salt
250 g (9 oz) picked nettle leaves (thick stems removed)
18–24 thin slices speck
40 g (1½ oz) parmesan, plus extra to serve
50 g (1¾ oz) butter
juice of ½ lemon

Select a wide frying pan with tall sides; this is not a job for a sauté pan. Set it over a medium–low heat, add the olive oil and sauté the onion with a pinch of salt for at least 10 minutes before adding the green garlic. Sauté the garlic and onion for a further 10 minutes until completely soft but not coloured.

Heat the stock in a small saucepan on a back burner until just beginning to simmer. Do this before you add your rice to the pan.

Increase the heat under your pan and add the rice. Cook, stirring every couple of minutes, until the rice grains turn mostly opaque, which means they are toasted. This should take 3–5 minutes. Add the white wine and cook out for a minute or two. Then, little by little, ladle in the stock, allowing it to absorb between each addition. You should stir with a spatula or wooden spoon every few minutes, but not constantly. Add the salt to start seasoning the rice.

Preheat the oven to 180°C (350°F).

Continue ladling in the stock until it has all been used and the rice is cooked. Before you add the last of the stock, add the nettles to the pan and wilt. Stir continuously from this moment on. The whole process should take between 20–30 minutes.

While the risotto is cooking, place the speck on a lined baking tray and crisp it up in the oven, about 5 minutes. Keep warm until ready to serve.

When the rice is nearly finished but still has the tiniest bit of bite, toss it in the pan for a few minutes, stirring to pull out all the starches. This is what makes risotto creamy without the need to add cream. You may need to add a small amount of water to keep the rice loose. As a final step, turn off the heat, add the parmesan, butter and lemon juice and stir to combine. Taste for seasoning and adjust as needed.

Serve spoonfuls of the risotto in shallow bowls as soon as it is ready. Crumble a few slices of speck over the top and pour some of the fat from the speck over each bowl. Top with extra parmesan and some black pepper. Serve immediately.

Mussels with sausage, capsicum and fregola sarda

I love this kind of dish for entertaining; it's relaxed, super tasty and comes together pretty quickly. And it can be easily scaled up if you have a big enough pan. If you have a large outdoor grill, try your hand at cooking this over the fire in a paella-type dish (see Note). If you don't, don't worry! Make it on the stove in a large cast-iron pan.

Combining capsicum (bell pepper), sausage and shellfish is a really good idea. It's pretty classic in Spanish and Portuguese cuisine, and it just works. Here, I suggest adding the fregola to absorb all those delicious juices from the sausage, capsicums and mussels. Fregola is a small round semolina pasta that looks a lot like large couscous. The difference is that it is classically toasted in a wood oven, so you get this incredible toasted wheat flavour from it. All you need to serve alongside this is a lovely green salad and some Aioli (page 15), if you like, and you've got the perfect meal.

Use my sausage recipe for this dish (see page 243) or buy good-quality sausages from your local butcher.

Serves 6–8

8 sweet red capsicums (bell peppers), approx. 1 kg (2 lb 3 oz)
1 tablespoon sherry vinegar
250 g (9 oz) fregola sarda
1.5 kg (3 lb 5 oz) mussels
4 tablespoons olive oil, plus extra for drizzling
500 g (1 lb 2 oz) Sausage meat (page 243), or store-bought pork sausages (if using store-bought, remove the meat from the casings and break it into chunks)
6 garlic cloves, sliced thinly
150 ml (5 fl oz) white wine
300 ml (10 fl oz) chicken stock (page 12, or use store-bought)
juice of ½ lemon (optional)
fresh oregano or marjoram leaves, to garnish
Aioli (page 15), to serve (optional)

First, char your capsicums on an outdoor grill or on the open flame of your stove until they are black and blistered on the outside. They must also have very soft flesh, and sometimes charring on the stove doesn't achieve that. If they aren't completely soft after charring, place them in a 200°C (400°F) oven for about 10 minutes, then check on them. If the flesh is soft and floppy, they are ready. If not, give them another 5 minutes. Transfer to a bowl, cover in plastic wrap and let them cool and steam until they are cool enough to handle. Reserve any liquid that is released. Peel off the skins and remove any seeds. Cut the peppers into wide strips and sprinkle with a bit of salt and the sherry vinegar then set aside.

Bring a saucepan of salted water to the boil and cook the fregola up until a couple of minutes shy of it being completely cooked. It should be tender, but slightly al dente. Drain then set aside on a tray with a bit of olive oil to cool.

To de-beard the mussels, hold a mussel in one hand and use a small spoon or butter knife to help you grip the stringy 'beard' that hangs from the flat side of the shell. Pull it back and forth until it comes out cleanly.

Heat a paella pan over a hot outdoor grill, or a cast-iron pan over a medium–high heat. Add the olive oil, then crumble in the sausage meat and brown. Once browned all over, remove from the pan and set aside. Quickly add the garlic and sizzle that for 10 seconds, then add the mussels, white wine and chicken stock. Cover with a lid if you're cooking on the stove, but if you're doing this on the grill, leave to cook uncovered. Keep an eye on it though; you will need to add a bit more water or chicken stock to compensate for all the liquid evaporating.

Once all the mussels have opened, add the sausage back in along with the fregola and the capsicums, and any of their liquid. Stir everything to combine and let it all simmer for 2–3 minutes. Add a splash more water or chicken stock if it's looking dry. Check for seasoning and acidity, adding salt or lemon if needed. Drizzle some olive oil over the whole thing and sprinkle with the oregano.

Note

I have used a 38 cm (15 in) wide paella pan to cook this dish.

Pasta, grains and legumes

Pork and garlic chive dumplings with mandarin, chilli and soy

Dumplings are usually filled with either meat or seafood, but vegetarian versions can be made with mushrooms or greens. They are then steamed and served with quality soy sauce or dipping sauces, which vary from culture to culture. In this case, I like to serve the dumplings with a spicy condiment made quickly from mandarin peel and chilli: an unfermented, fresh version of a kosho, which is a bright Japanese condiment. Different Asian cultures favour different kinds of dumplings: fried or steamed, but for ease and clarity of flavour, I prefer steamed. These are the simple version: no fancy pleating or precise shapes, just homemade goodness. They are so fun to make, easy to prepare (no fancy equipment, just a bamboo steamer) and everyone will love them.

You can buy dumpling wrappers, but the dough for these dumplings is incredibly easy to make and well worth the effort. I prefer to make them myself as I can control what flour I use. I've also used this filling in other ways and made them into little meatballs that get dropped into a brothy soup or get cooked under the oven grill (broiler) and served with the same dipping sauce. Either way, it's a delicious little filling that has a few possible uses.

Makes approx. 40 small dumplings

tamari or soy sauce, to serve

Dough

250 g (9 oz/1⅔ cups) strong flour,
    plus extra for dusting
½ teaspoon salt
175 ml (6 fl oz) boiling water

Filling

150 g (5½ oz) Chinese cabbage (wombok),
    thinly sliced
400 g (14 oz) minced (ground) pork or chicken
20 g (¾ oz) chopped garlic chives
10 g (¼ oz) grated ginger
2 teaspoons mirin
2 tablespoons tamari
1 tablespoon red miso
1 egg
¼ teaspoon toasted sesame oil
2 teaspoons cornflour (cornstarch)

Mandarin and chilli paste

8 g (¼ oz) mandarin peel
6 red bird's eye chillies, seeds removed
1½ teaspoons flaky sea salt or ½ teaspoon
    fine salt

To make the dough, place the flour and salt in a mixing bowl. Add the water and use a spoon to mix. Once fully combined, cover with plastic wrap or a tea towel (dish towel) and rest for 1 hour. After an hour, knead the dough on a well-floured surface for 4–5 minutes until the dough looks smooth and springy. Add more flour as you go to prevent it from sticking. Cover again and allow to rest for 15 minutes, then divide the dough in two and roll into thin sheets, as thin as you can get them. Use an 8 cm (3¼ in) round cutter to cut out circles of dough. Bunch up the off-cuts and re-roll them to use up all the dough. Your dough should be floured enough that you can stack the wrappers one on top of the other without them sticking. Set aside.

Next, make the filling. Sprinkle a pinch of salt (about ½ teaspoon) on the cabbage and leave it to sit for 15–20 minutes to release its liquid. Squeeze the cabbage to release any remaining water, then combine the squeezed cabbage with the remaining ingredients and set aside until ready to fill the dumplings.

To fill the dumplings, place a wrapper in your left hand, take ½ teaspoon of the filling and place it cleanly in the centre of the wrapper. Fold one side over the other, dabbing one edge with a tiny bit of water to stick the edges together. Press the edge firmly and place on a baking tray lined with baking paper. Continue until all the wrappers and filling have been used.

Gather all your ingredients for the mandarin and chilli paste, along with a mortar and pestle. I recommend wearing gloves when handling the chillies and wearing glasses when crushing everything; a splash of spicy chilli in the eye can make things very uncomfortable. If there is any white pith still attached to the mandarin peel, take the time to gently fillet that off with a small paring knife. Finely chop the mandarin peel and chilli, then add to the mortar and pestle with the salt and crush to a fine paste. Spoon it out and set aside. This can be kept in a small jar for a few weeks in the fridge.

To cook your dumplings, set a steamer basket on top of a pan of simmering water. Place a small piece of baking paper on each layer of the basket and line up as many dumplings as you can without them touching each other. Steam for approximately 10–15 minutes, or until the filling feels cooked and firm and the dough looks slightly translucent. Serve immediately with some good-quality tamari and a small pinch of the chilli and mandarin paste.

Seafood

Oysters with coriander, lime and white pepper mignonette 139

Fish crudo with citrus ponzu 140

Snapper carpaccio with yuzu kosho, orange and fennel 142

Pot-roasted mud crab with lemon, garlic, chilli, butter and fine noodles 144

Whole roasted John Dory with brown butter, lemon, capers and nori 147

Slow-cooked ocean trout on fig leaves with kohlrabi and tomato salsa 148

Oven-roasted prawns with nasturtium and miso butter 149

Steamed cod with leek and seaweed butter 152

Squid with sweet red capsicums, basil and aioli 153

Clams with sorrel, tarragon and green garlic 154

Fragrant and sour fish curry 156

Mackerel tartare with miso, ginger and white soy 157

Tuna steaks with gribiche 158

Seared scallops with sautéed witlof and Meyer lemon salsa 161

Side note:
Women in the kitchen 162

Seafood

The world of seafood is so vast that I find it difficult to write recipes that apply universally. A mackerel in Australia is not the same as those found around England. A lobster in New England is not the same as a southern hemisphere lobster. And prawns? Well, they are different too depending on where you are. I hope you use the recipes in this section as a bit more of a guide. Go to the market and see what looks good before you decide what you are going to make. Always buy wild fish (oysters, mussels and clams excluded) over farmed, and if you must buy farmed, ensure their practices are healthy for the environment first. Most countries have guides or certifications that can help you sort through that.

Similar to cooking meat and poultry, though, some principles are universally true:

Get to know your fishmonger, but trust your instincts. The seafood business is a business like any other, and when you are working with something as perishable as seafood, the number one priority is to get the product out the door. Even if that means pushing something they know is less than perfect. Ask to see the fillet up close, to smell it and inspect it. It's not weird and, most of the time, this lets them know you are serious about freshness and they will then be a bit more honest with you. If you are lucky enough to live near a good fishmonger that you have built a relationship with, then great; you won't have to pester them too much to get the goods.

If you're trying to achieve crispy-skinned fish, allow the skin to dry out in the fridge uncovered for a couple of hours before cooking.

Most white and orange fish should be served a bit undercooked or even rare in the middle. I know this is a tough one to convince people of, but once you have experienced a piece of fish cooked this way, you'll understand. It's not dangerous provided the fish is fresh. It's succulent, delicious and how fish should be cooked.

Fresh is best. I feel strongly that, for most things, frozen seafood is just not worth it and I would prefer to eat a vegetarian meal over frozen seafood or fish. If you must buy frozen seafood, stick to prawns or squid, which fare the best in the freezer and always thaw them in the refrigerator over a longer period of time rather than trying to rush it. On the freshness point too, there are some people doing interesting things with ageing fish. My preference is still for the freshest fish possible, but I have also had some exceptional samples of dry-aged fish. Give it a try, but I would leave this one to the professionals.

Oysters with coriander, lime and white pepper mignonette

Imagine the reaction of the first person to ever discover an oyster? I mean, there is probably nothing else on the planet that packs so much flavour into such a small package. They are the essence of the ocean, distilled into this little vessel, perfect for transport. It just doesn't get much better than that. I love a baked oyster, but raw is my preference. Shucked just before eating and paired with a fresh mignonette and perhaps some lemon, they are absolute heaven. Different kinds of oysters grow all over the world, so always opt for what's local. It will give you the best sense of terroir and, almost without exception, they will be the freshest.

You've heard it before, but it's true: look for oysters that are tightly closed and feel heavy for their size. This means all their beautiful liquor is still trapped inside the shell. It takes a bit of practice to perfectly shuck an oyster, but once you've mastered it, you'll appreciate the delicate skill of enough force to pry it open but enough control not to stab the oyster. A stabbed oyster is a sad thing. Still edible, but not as sweet. Also, do not rinse them. If there is a little bit of shell caught in the oyster, use a pastry brush dipped in water to brush it out, but don't lose that beautiful salty brine.

To store oysters, keep a damp tea towel (dish towel) over them, or store them in a wet cardboard box, which provides moisture and protects them from the blowing air of a refrigerator. Oysters also like to stay at the temperature of the water in which they grew. For some parts of the world, that's cold, so they will do best in the refrigerator, but in warmer waters, you may consider leaving them out with a wet cloth over them. Check with your fishmonger or oyster provedore to be safe.

Serves 1–4

12 freshly shucked oysters
3–4 lemon wedges

Mignonette

3 tablespoons agrodolce-style
    chardonnay vinegar
1 tablespoon sherry vinegar
1 small shallot, finely diced
1 teaspoon minced coriander (cilantro) stem
½ teaspoon grated lime zest
pinch of freshly ground white pepper

Serve the oysters on a bed of crushed ice, or rock salt if you don't like them cold. Mix all the mignonette ingredients together and serve alongside the oysters with a few lemon wedges.

Fish crudo
with citrus ponzu

Ponzu is a sauce that has become so ubiquitous that you forget just how special it is. But, like anything that becomes popular, there's a reason. In this case, ponzu is the perfect accompaniment to raw fish and a myriad of other things. It's a light and fresh mixture of soy sauce, mirin and rice-wine vinegar steeped with smoked bonito shavings and kombu, then finished with bright, fresh citrus juice. If you are using quality ingredients and making this in the winter when you have an abundance of fresh citrus, you will be shocked at how special this sauce can be. It goes beautifully with most raw fish, but especially well with something fatty like kingfish or salmon. It also works on raw oysters, any kind of tataki and even cold soba noodles.

The trickiest thing about ponzu is sourcing the best quality ingredients. Visit a good Japanese food supplier or search online for what's needed.

Serves 6 as an entrée

420–540 g (15 oz–1 lb 3 oz) fish (70–90 g/
    2½–3 oz) per person
unhulled sesame seeds, to serve (optional)
snipped chives, to serve
20 ml (¾ fl oz) light sesame oil, or a high-quality
    grapeseed oil

Ponzu

30 ml (1 fl oz) rice-wine vinegar
100 ml (3½ fl oz) mirin
10 g (¼ oz) shio kombu
10 g (¼ oz) bonito flakes (katsuobushi)
120 ml (4 fl oz) white or light soy sauce
150 ml (5 fl oz) mixed citrus juice (see Note)

First, make your ponzu. Mix together the vinegar, mirin and kombu in a small saucepan and bring to a simmer. Turn off the heat and add the bonito flakes, then allow to steep for 5 minutes. Strain through a fine-mesh sieve and set aside to cool. When cool, add the soy sauce and citrus juice.

Thinly slice the raw fish and arrange on a platter. Pour the sauce over the fish or serve it on the side for dipping. Scatter the sesame seeds, if using, and chives over the fish with a small sprinkle of salt. Drizzle with the sesame oil.

Note

If you have access to fresh yuzu juice, add that, but reduce the quantity to 100 ml (3½ fl oz) as it is quite pungent. If you don't have fresh yuzus, use a mixture of mandarin, Meyer lemon or lime juices, preferably calamansi.

Snapper carpaccio with yuzu kosho, orange and fennel

Yuzu kosho is a Japanese yuzu and chilli paste that has been fermented. It is super spicy, but the citrus fragrance you get from the yuzu is incredible. It is a great pantry staple to put on fish and meat, but I like how its intense heat is balanced by something fatty, as it is here with the crème fraîche. Togarashi is another Japanese chilli mixture, but this one is a dried powder and has black sesame seeds in it. Both types of heat really complement each other and are definitely worth seeking out at Japanese food stores or online.

Serves 4

600 g (1 lb 5 oz) snapper fillet,
    skin and pin bones removed,
    trimmed of most of the bloodline
2 tablespoons Crème fraîche (page 239)
1 teaspoon yuzu kosho paste
grated zest of ¼ orange
25 g (1 oz) shallot, very finely diced
1 tablespoon lemon juice
1 tablespoon chardonnay vinegar
60 ml (2 fl oz/¼ cup) extra-virgin olive oil,
    plus a bit more for the carpaccio
1 fennel bulb, outer layers trimmed and
    fronds reserved
edible flowers, tender greens and/or baby snow
    peas (mangetout), to garnish
4 pinches togarashi, to serve

Slice the snapper fillet thinly into around 16–24 pieces. Arrange 4–6 slices on a piece of oiled baking paper. This will be one serve. Cover with another piece of baking paper and, using a rolling pin, gently but firmly tap the fish out to a thickness of 2 mm (⅛ in). You want it to be thin while still retaining some texture. Refrigerate the fish, still sandwiched between the paper, until ready to serve. Repeat with the remaining fish.

Mix the crème fraîche and yuzu kosho paste and refrigerate. You can add less yuzu paste if you do not like things too spicy.

Combine the orange zest in a bowl with the shallot, lemon juice, vinegar and a pinch of salt. Allow that to sit for 15 minutes, then add the olive oil to complete the vinaigrette. Thinly slice the fennel on a mandoline and also set aside.

When you're ready to serve, spread one-quarter of the crème fraîche mixture on the bottom of each individual plate. Peel one side of the paper from the fish and layer the slices onto the plates, along with the shaved fennel. Season the fish with salt, then pour a generous spoonful of stirred vinaigrette over the top. Finish by topping with the reserved fennel fronds, edible flowers or small, sweet snow peas and a sprinkle of togarashi.

Pot-roasted mud crab with lemon, garlic, chilli, butter and fine noodles

This is a showstopper. Anytime you bring out a platter of beautiful steaming crab, you're sure to be popular, unless you're serving someone who doesn't eat shellfish (in which case, steer clear of this dish). But if all of your guests love the sweet taste of crab, give it a go. I realise live shellfish is intimidating, and people are reluctant to try this at home, but if you aren't too squeamish and have a good large knife or cleaver, then you can handle it. Put the crabs in a bowl or bucket of iced water for 30 minutes to put them to sleep before humanely killing them with the cleaver.

This recipe could be adapted to suit whatever fresh, live crabs are available to you. In Australia, mud crabs are preferred, but spanner crabs would also be beautiful. If you're on the west coast of the US, Dungeness crab would be ideal, and, if on the east coast, blue crabs would also work well. The only thing that changes is how long they take to cook.

The pasta is optional but I strongly recommend it, otherwise some bread to mop up the juices would also do the trick.

Serves 4

1 quantity Pasta dough (page 102) (optional)
semolina, for dusting
2×1 kg (2 lb 3 oz) mud crabs
100 g (3½ oz) butter
8 garlic cloves, finely minced
2–3 long red chillies, thinly sliced
50 ml (1¾ fl oz) white wine
30 g (1 oz/1 cup) chopped
    flat-leaf (Italian) parsley
60 ml (2 fl oz/¼ cup) extra-virgin olive oil
grated zest of 1 lemon
juice of ½ lemon

If you're making pasta, roll it out to a medium number on the pasta roller to ensure your noodles are quite thick. Dust well with semolina and run it through the fine cutters of your pasta machine so you are left with delicate, thin noodles. Set aside. Bring a large saucepan of salted water to the boil while you cook the crabs.

The most difficult part of this recipe is preparing the crab, but a heavy knife or cleaver makes quick work of it. Also, full disclosure: it's a little messy, so tackle this in an area of your kitchen that is easy to clean. Remove the crabs from the iced water, then place a crab on its 'back'. Using your cleaver, give one good, strong and confident chop straight through the centre of the crab. This kills the crab instantly, but don't be surprised if the legs continue to move; it's just muscle contraction. Because mud crab shells are particularly thick, you may have to chop them a few times to split the top shell, or carapace. If you can't manage to get through it, simply pull the carapace off the rest of the body. Using the back of a knife, crack each leg joint so that, as it cooks, it absorbs the garlicky, chilli flavours, but also to make it easy to get into afterwards. Place the crab pieces in a bowl until you're ready to cook, but try to do this just before cooking.

Heat a large cast-iron Dutch oven over a medium–high heat. Add the butter, garlic and chilli and sauté for 1 minute. Next, add the crab pieces but discard any liquid they have released. Mix them around in the pot, then add the white wine. Quickly cover the pot with a heavy lid and cook for at least 15 minutes. Check on the crab every now and then to see if it's done, especially if you are using smaller crabs. When all the crab shells are bright orange, they should be cooked. Remove them from the pot and set aside.

To finish, cook your pasta for 2–3 minutes in the boiling water, then use tongs to lift it out of the water and into the Dutch oven with the butter and crab liquid. Add all the parsley, olive oil, half the lemon zest and the lemon juice. Toss this around until well coated, then check for seasoning. Pour the pasta onto the base of a large platter and top with the crab. Zest the rest of the lemon over the crab and serve straight away.

Whole roasted John Dory with brown butter, lemon, capers and nori

There really isn't anything more beautiful or satisfying than a whole roasted fish. Some fish make this preparation a little easier due to their bone structure, and John Dory is one of them. Although not a flat fish like flounder, sole, halibut or turbot, John Dory's flesh is similar in that it doesn't have thin pin bones running through it. I have also found that dory fillets off the bone are really not my favourite. It's a very lean fish, so it can get a little tough and bouncy when the fillets are cooked off the bone. Cooked on the bone, though, at high heat, it is rendered unctuous, delicate and tender. At the restaurant, we cook this fish a lot in the wood oven, but if you don't have a wood oven at home (I don't!), you can still mimic the results and it's a breeze to take off the bone.

The simple garnish of brown butter, lemon and capers is a classic, but classic for a reason: it's just a perfect accompaniment to fish. The nori adds umami, and it works really well with brown butter and lemon too.

If you want to cook this for up to four people, look for a fish that's closer to 1.4 or 1.5 kg (3 lb 1oz–3 lb 5 oz) and add about 6–10 minutes to the cooking time.

Serves 2

1×800 g (1 lb 12 oz) John Dory, cleaned and head removed
2 nori sheets
90 ml (3 fl oz) olive oil
1 whole lemon, thinly sliced
60 g (2 oz/¼ cup) butter
2 tablespoons salt-packed capers, rinsed
1 bunch flat-leaf (Italian) parsley, leaves picked and chopped
juice of 1 lemon

Preheat the oven to 250°C (480°F).

Start by seasoning your fish with salt and pepper, and set aside. You want the fish to come to room temperature before cooking it.

Next, make your nori oil. This can also be done well in advance. Toast the sheets of nori directly over the flames of a gas burner or under the grill (broiler). If toasting over flame, hold the sheets with tongs and gently brush them over the flame. Keep them moving so they don't burn. Allow to cool, then crush up and place in a blender with 50 ml (1¾ fl oz) of the oil and a pinch of salt. Blend on high until the oil looks black and smooth. Set aside.

Place the fish on a flat roasting tray and drizzle with the remaining oil. Arrange the lemon slices on top, then roast for 13–15 minutes, or longer if your fish is bigger. Remove from the oven and brush half of the nori oil over the top of the fish. Set aside to rest.

In a small pot, heat the butter over a medium heat until foaming and brown, then add the capers and parsley to sizzle for 1 minute. Pour this over the fish and squeeze over the lemon juice.

Fillet the fish by using a fork to remove the top fin bones, then do the same on the bottom. At this point you should recognise the three fillets on each side. Using the back of a spoon, gently push those fillets off the bone and place on a pre-warmed serving plate. If you've cooked it perfectly, it should look just the tiniest bit pink on the inside and you should have to push a little bit for the flesh to pry itself away from the bone. If it's definitely not coming off and you're damaging the fish, then it needs a few more minutes in the oven. The bone should still appear pink, but the flesh will be cooked. Flip it over and remove the fillets from the other side. Finish by pouring all of that beautiful sauce and remaining nori oil over the top of the fillets and serve immediately.

Slow-cooked ocean trout on fig leaves with kohlrabi and tomato salsa

Slow-cooked wild salmon or ocean trout is one of my best and easiest entertaining meals. A just-cooked piece of wild salmon is one of the greatest pleasures, and in summer, when all this produce is shining and salmon is in season, it's a real winner.

Wild salmon is really the best option if you live somewhere that has true wild salmon, but if you're in Australia, ocean trout is your next best choice. True salmon is not indigenous to Australia and can only be found farmed. In the States this is a no-no, but Australia still leads the way in sustainable, responsible aquaculture, so I suppose a little farmed fish here and there is OK, but definitely do your research; some sources are better than others.

Serves 6–8

1×1.5–2 kg (3 lb 5 oz–4 lb 6 oz) side of ocean trout or salmon, skin on
8 fig leaves
100 ml (3½ fl oz) extra-virgin olive oil, plus extra for drizzling
400 g (14 oz) cherry tomatoes
1 whole purple or green kohlrabi, about the size of a tennis ball or slightly bigger
3 tablespoons agrodolce-style chardonnay vinegar
2 tablespoons chopped herbs, such as chives, tarragon or chervil

Preheat the oven to 135°C (275°F).

Season the fish on both the skin and flesh sides and set aside for 15 minutes to come to room temperature. Line a large baking tray with baking paper and place the fig leaves, shiny side up, on top. Place the fish on top of the fig leaves, skin side down. Drizzle generously with oil and crack some pepper over it. Roast until cooked medium-rare. This should take about 15–25 minutes (because of the low temperature, the flesh will cook and flake, but still appear a deep red colour inside).

Meanwhile, halve the cherry tomatoes and sprinkle with salt, then stir to combine and leave to sit until the juices start to leak out. Peel and cut the kohlrabi into 1 cm (½ in) cubes, or whatever shape you can manage that is uniform. If your kohlrabi looks woody at one end, try to peel it down until it looks tender and crunchy. (The older the kohlrabi, the more chance of it being woody, but if you get it fresh from the farmers' market you should be OK.) Toss the kohlrabi with a bit of salt and the vinegar and allow to sit and mingle while the fish cooks.

When you're ready to serve, combine the tomatoes, kohlrabi and olive oil and check for seasoning. Pour this mixture over the fish and sprinkle with the chopped herbs. Serve warm or at room temperature.

See image on page 150.

Oven-roasted prawns with nasturtium and miso butter

Nasturtium flowers grow wild in many parts of the world, and although I think many people have seen them, they don't know that they are edible and taste of strong mustard or spicy capers. They are also incredibly beautiful and brightly coloured. Try to find some that are a bit more off the beaten path (to avoid pollution and pesticides) and be sure to give them a good rinse when you get home. You'll need a fair few flowers for this butter, so take a basket on your foraging trip. If you're not willing to forage, you can grow some easily in your garden, and some speciality grocers will have them too.

Look for large, green, fresh prawns. Frozen are fine, but fresh are far superior. These are easy to cook under your oven's grill (broiler), but can also be cooked over a hot charcoal grill by grilling only on the shell side, which keeps all the delicious butter on the prawn instead of burning in the fire.

Serves 4

100 g (3½ oz) soft butter
20 g (¾ oz) picked nasturtium petals
1 tablespoon white miso
1 kg (2 lb 3 oz) green king prawns
lemon wedges, to serve

Combine the butter, nasturtium petals and miso in a food processor and blend until smooth. Set aside.

Flip your prawns onto their backs and split them in half lengthways using a sharp chef's knife. Try to leave them attached at the tail and head by not cutting all the way through, but try to flatten them as much as possible. Spread the butter on the prawn meat and place them on a baking tray, cut side up.

Place the prawns under the grill (broiler) of your oven or over an outdoor grill, heated to high. They should be finished cooking in about 3–4 minutes depending on their size. Serve immediately with lemon wedges.

See image on page 150.

Opposite top   Oven-roasted prawns with nasturtium and miso butter (page 149)
Opposite bottom Slow-cooked ocean trout on fig leaves with kohlrabi and tomato
                   salsa (page 148)
Top right   Squid with sweet red capsicums, basil and aioli (page 153)

Steamed cod with leek and seaweed butter

Things that grow together go together, as the old saying goes, and fish and seaweed are no exception. My seaweed of choice for cooking and saucing is laver, which is found throughout Asia and is also a Welsh speciality. I like it because its texture is soft, and the flavour mild enough to be complementary but strong enough that you know it is there.

Seaweed is full of essential minerals and nutrients, but it's not something many people are used to cooking with. It's a bit salty and umami but, for me, it really hangs on to the flavour of the ocean without being overpowering. With delicately steamed fish, it works incredibly well. Many seaweeds can be found dried online. Laver, in particular, is well worth the search.

This seaweed butter is also delicious on roasted lamb and on toast with a grating of cheddar cheese over the top.

Serves 4

800 g (1 lb 12 oz) cod or other flaky white fish cut into 4 portions
1 leek
150 g (5½ oz) cold butter
10 g (¼ oz) dried laver cooked in 100 ml (3½ fl oz) water until softened, or 30 g (1 oz) prepared laverbread (see Note)
splash of white wine (optional)
2–3 teaspoons lemon juice
½ teaspoon salt

Season your fish with salt and set aside to come to room temperature.

Cut your leek down the middle lengthways and slice it into thin half-moons. Use the white and light green parts only. Heat a small sauté pan over a low heat and sauté the leek in 20 g (¾ oz) of the butter and a sprinkle of salt. Cover with a piece of baking paper so that it steams gently and doesn't colour. When the leek is meltingly tender, add the seaweed. Pour the seaweed and leek onto a chopping board and chop together finely. Return them to a small saucepan and set aside.

To cook the fish, you can use a steamer basket or a frying pan with a tight-fitting lid. Set a steamer basket over a saucepan of simmering water. Depending on the size of your basket, you may need to steam two pieces on each layer so that you don't overcrowd them; they should not be touching at all. How long they need to cook depends on the thickness of the fish. I like to pinch the fish on the sides of the fillet to check: if it still feels really firm in the centre, continue cooking, but if the fish flakes easily then it's done and you can remove it from the basket and onto serving plates. If you'd prefer to use a frying pan, simply add your fish to the pan with 100 ml (3½ fl oz) water and a splash of white wine. Cover with a lid and bring to a simmer over a medium heat. It should take 5–8 minutes to cook.

To finish the sauce, heat the saucepan of leek and laver on low and add the remaining butter, bit by bit, so it gently melts but remains emulsified. Finish with the lemon juice and salt. Check for seasoning, then spoon it over the steamed fish.

Note

If you weren't able to find prepared laverbread, you can use dried laver. To cook, simply add the laver to a saucepan with the water and cook over a medium-high heat until softened. This should take 5–8 minutes. Set aside and mix this with your cooked leeks when making the sauce. If soaking a larger amount of laver for later use, chop it after cooking and store in the fridge or freezer.

Squid with sweet red capsicums, basil and aioli

Squid are so easy to cook, but I think people get intimidated by the cleaning and prepping, so many avoid eating them at home entirely. It may not be the prettiest process, but it is quite simple. Yes, you could ask your fishmonger to do this for you, but I like to buy squid intact so I that know how fresh it is. Once they have been cleaned, they can sit around a bit longer and you wouldn't really know until you cooked them.

The other super important thing about cooking squid is the high temperature. I cannot stress this enough. You need to get your pan as hot as it can possibly be. In the restaurant we do this in the wood oven, which offers not just a hot surface but also radiant heat, which cooks them from both sides immediately. Squid release a lot of liquid when they hit the heat, so it's important that it evaporates quickly so you can achieve maximum browning without overcooking the squid. After that, it's mere seconds in the pan and out they go.

Serves 4

800 g (1 lb 12 oz) whole squid (8–10 pieces)
4 sweet red capsicums (bell peppers)
splash of sherry vinegar
1 tablespoon olive oil
1 handful basil leaves
½ lemon
1 quantity Aioli (page 15)

To clean your squid, first cut the tentacles off by cutting straight down right underneath the eyes. Then move your knife above the eyes and press down with the blade to pinch it without cutting all the way through. Push that bit away from the squid, and all the insides and the hard plastic-looking 'beak' should come out in one swipe. If not, you may have to use your fingers to pull everything out. Leave the tubes whole and do not skin them. I could never understand why people skin them since this is where much of the flavour lies. Pinch the top of the tentacles together and a small, hard round bit should pop out. Discard this. Season the tubes and tentacles with salt, then set aside.

Prep your capsicums by charring them on the open flame of a stove or on an outdoor grill. It's important that they be completely blackened so that you can pull the skin off easily. Put them in a bowl and cover with plastic wrap until cool enough to handle. They will also continue cooking and become completely soft. Remove the skin and seeds and cut the flesh into wide strips. Toss the peeled peppers with some salt and a splash of sherry vinegar, then set aside.

Heat a wide cast-iron or stainless-steel frying pan until it's smoking. Add the oil, then immediately add the squid. It shouldn't take long to cook, maybe 1 minute each side. They will become opaque white and the skin will turn pink. Immediately lift them out of the pan and reduce the heat to medium. Add the capsicums and any smoky liquid they have released. Warm them up, season with some salt, then serve on a platter with the squid. Tear the basil leaves over the top and squeeze the lemon juice over the whole thing. Serve with aioli.

See image on page 151.

Clams with sorrel, tarragon and green garlic

Sorrel pops up in farmers' markets in the spring, which is also when green garlic and tarragon can be found. I also find it in good grocery stores randomly throughout the year. If you spot it, this is a great dish to make. There really is no substitute for sorrel though, so another preparation might be better if you can't find it. Sorrel's flavour is sharp, sour and acidic, and it means you won't need to add any acid to your clams, where often I would add a squeeze of lemon or white wine.

A beautiful piece of salmon with sorrel sauce is one of the great dishes of France, but here I am combining its lovely sour flavour with the briny sweetness of a good clam. Puréeing the sorrel while cold will retain some of its colour for just a moment. As soon as sorrel hits the heat, though, it will turn a shade of olive green. There is nothing wrong with that, it's just the effect of its own acidity mixing with heat. But if you blend the sorrel while cold, the colour will stay bright for a bit longer. Serve this with some good crusty bread for mopping up the sauce.

Serves 4

1 kg (2 lb 3 oz) your favourite clams
30 g (1 oz) sorrel leaves, pulled off the stem, plus extra to garnish
30 g (1 oz) butter
40 g (1½ oz) minced green garlic (see Note on page 70), or 2 minced garlic cloves
50 ml (1¾ fl oz) cream
50 ml (1¾ fl oz) Crème fraîche (page 239)
8 g (¼ oz) picked tarragon leaves, chopped
grated zest of 1 lemon
crusty bread, to serve

Clean your clams by soaking them in several changes of cold water to ensure they don't have any sand or grit in them.

Purée your sorrel in a high-speed blender with just enough water to get the machine going, approximately 30–50 ml (1–1¾ fl oz). Blend until smooth, but not for an excessive amount of time as the heat from the blender can discolour the sorrel. Set this aside.

In a wide sauté pan with a lid, heat the butter over a medium heat, then add the garlic and sizzle gently for a minute or two. Quickly add in the clams and 80 ml (2½ fl oz/⅓ cup) water and cover with the lid. Increase the heat to high and let the clams simmer for 3–4 minutes. Check the clams to see if they have opened. If they have, remove the lid and return the heat to medium. If they haven't, continue cooking for another minute or two. If the majority are open, try to pry open the others. If any remain firmly shut, discard them.

Remove the clams from the pan and onto your platter. Add the cream and crème fraîche to the pan, mix well and taste the liquid. Perhaps it needs some salt? Adjust the seasoning, then when you are happy with it, add the sorrel purée and mix together. Immediately pour the sauce over the clams. Scatter the tarragon and lemon zest over the top of everything and finish with a few cracks of black pepper. Serve with some hot, crusty bread.

Fragrant and sour fish curry

A good fish curry seems to be a part of everyone's repertoire in Australia, but I think this is less the case in the US. Thai food is very much a part of the Australian dining scene, and people crave spiciness, sourness, sweetness and saltiness in their food: the four tastes of Thai cuisine. Australian chef David Thompson is one of the West's pre-eminent authorities on Thai food. Anything I know about authentic Thai food, I have gleaned from his tome of Thai recipes and lessons, *Thai Food*. It's an incredible book with a level of detail that is second to none. Like all my recipes, this one brings a bit of what I've learned, what I know and then a bit of intuition and my palate mixed in. It's not completely authentic, but it's not inauthentic either – just how I like it. Australian wild barramundi works very well here, but any fattier-style white fish, such as kingfish, would also be great.

The trickiest part of this dish is the curry paste. It's not even difficult, it just takes time and a bit of muscle, and you need a large mortar and pestle. Make sure each ingredient is as smooth as possible before you add the next, so that you end up with a homogeneous paste. Look for long green chillies or short and spicy green chillies, but stay away from jalapeño, which contains too much water.

Serves 4

60 g (2 oz) coconut oil
200 g (7 oz) cherry tomatoes
3 long purple eggplants (aubergines), cut into 2–3 cm (¾–1¼ in) lengths
1 litre (34 fl oz/4 cups) chicken stock (page 12, or use store-bought)
1×400 ml (13½ fl oz) tin coconut cream or milk
2 teaspoons raw (demerara) sugar
½–1 tablespoon fish sauce
800 g (1 lb 12 oz) fish fillet, such as wild barramundi or salmon, cut into 4 portions
juice of 1–2 limes
1 bunch Thai basil
1 bunch fresh coriander (cilantro) leaves (stems reserved for curry paste)
steamed jasmine rice, to serve

Curry paste

2 kaffir lime leaves, stripped from their stems
40 g (1½ oz) galangal, peeled and thinly sliced (use ginger if you can't find galangal)
3 cm (1¼ in) piece lemongrass stalk, white part only
20 g (¾ oz) peeled turmeric (or 1 teaspoon good-quality ground turmeric)
1 teaspoon cumin seeds, toasted
1 teaspoon coriander seeds, toasted
2–3 long green chillies, seeds removed
50 g (1¾ oz) shallot, peeled and diced
3 garlic cloves
15–20 g (½–¾ oz) coriander (cilantro) root or stems
1 teaspoon shrimp paste

Start by making your curry paste. In the mortar and pestle, crush the lime leaves, galangal, lemongrass and turmeric with a pinch of salt (these are the toughest to make into a paste). Once they have broken down, add the remaining ingredients, one at a time. Make sure each ingredient is fully incorporated before adding the next. Set aside.

Heat half of the coconut oil in a wide sauté pan over a high heat. Add the cherry tomatoes and eggplant and brown really well all over, then remove from the pan and set aside.

Add the remaining coconut oil and fry all the curry paste until fragrant and just beginning to brown. Next, pour in the stock, coconut cream and the sugar and simmer until it is reduced by half. Add ½ tablespoon fish sauce to begin with, then taste it. If it needs further seasoning you can either add the remaining fish sauce or some salt. Add the fish, the tomatoes and the eggplant and simmer until the fish is cooked through, about 6–8 minutes. Lastly, add the juice of 1 lime, then taste it. If it's not really sour, add the juice of the second lime until the flavour is right. It should be salty, sour, spicy and the tiniest bit sweet. Any of those flavours can be adjusted by adding a bit more sliced chilli for heat, sugar for sweetness, lime juice for sourness and fish sauce for saltiness and umami. Serve in bowls with lots of fresh Thai basil and coriander leaves, and a bowl of steamed jasmine rice on the side.

Mackerel tartare with miso, ginger and white soy

Mackerel may not be the kind of fish you most readily associate with tartare, but when incredibly fresh, there is no better way to eat it. If you can't get your hands on super fresh mackerel, try this with fresh kingfish or tuna. The strong fishyness you may associate with mackerel when cooked is not present at all in its raw form, where it is bright with saline acidity, and yet still mild.

The inspiration for this combination comes from my friend Nancy Singleton Hachisu, who has lived in Japan for several decades and has written multiple books about Japanese food. She has cooked with me a couple of times at Chez Panisse and, most recently, at Fred's, where we first made a version of this dish together. She has been an incredible teacher on all things Japanese, but the biggest lesson has been the importance of finding the best Japanese pantry ingredients. There are huge differences in quality soy sauce or tamari, miso, mirin, sesame paste, etc. If you don't have a trustworthy shop in your area, many of these items are available online. They are worth adding to your larder.

Serves 4

300 g (10½ oz) blue mackerel fillets
5 g (⅛ oz) grated ginger
1 teaspoon red miso
2 teaspoons white soy sauce
2 tablespoons grapeseed oil
½ tablespoon snipped chives
2 teaspoons Meyer lemon juice or ½ teaspoon yuzu juice
olive oil, for frying
sliced sesame baguette, or other white bread

Clean up your mackerel fillets by cutting through the centre and removing the pin bones and the bloodline. Angle your knife between the flesh and the skin, starting at the tail. While holding and pulling the skin with your left hand, push your right hand forwards to scrape the skin and separate it from the flesh. Trim off any dark red bloodline. Chop it into small dice and mix with the remaining ingredients.

Heat some olive oil in a shallow, wide sauté pan over a medium–high heat, then fry slices of sesame baguette or other white bread and serve alongside the tartare when crispy and golden.

Tuna steaks
with gribiche

This is my definition of healthy summer eating: a beautiful piece of fish, quickly grilled, and a fresh herbaceous sauce to bathe it in. This dish comes together in minutes and it is so, so tasty. Gribiche is a French sauce made using hard-boiled eggs to make something slightly emulsified, like a mayonnaise. That emulsification makes the sauce feel rich and, paired with a lean fish like tuna, that is exactly what you want. Serve with some boiled new potatoes or a simple tomato and green bean salad.

Serves 4

extra-virgin olive oil, for drizzling
800 g (1 lb 12 oz) yellowfin or other sustainably caught lean tuna, cut into 4 steaks
lemon wedges, to serve
salad greens or potatoes, to serve

Gribiche

2 eggs
2 teaspoons dijon mustard
80 ml (2½ fl oz/⅓ cup) extra-virgin olive oil
1 tablespoon white-wine vinegar
1 tablespoon snipped chives
8 cornichons, minced
1 tablespoon salt-packed capers, rinsed and finely diced
2 tablespoons finely chopped flat-leaf (Italian) parsley
1 teaspoon finely chopped tarragon

Start by making your gribiche. Place the eggs in a small saucepan of cold water and bring them up to the boil. Once the water is boiling, turn off the heat, cover the pan and set a timer for 9 minutes. After 9 minutes, remove the eggs from the water and rinse them under cold running water until they feel room temperature or cool. Peel them and separate the yolks from the whites. Place the yolks in a small bowl and use a whisk to break them up a bit, then add the mustard and gently add the olive oil, whisking constantly until emulsified. Add the remaining ingredients to the yolks and stir to combine. Check for seasoning and adjust with salt and pepper as needed. Set aside until you're ready to cook the tuna.

Drizzle a small amount of olive oil on the outside of the tuna steaks and season with salt and pepper. Leave them at room temperature for at least 30 minutes before you want to grill them so they aren't icy cold from the fridge. Set a chargrill or cast-iron pan over a high heat to get smoking hot, or set up a charcoal grill outside and get the grates as hot as possible.

When the grill is hot and the fish is at room temperature, you're ready to grill. If you're doing this in a pan, you may only be able to do one or two at a time. Place the fish down and do not touch it for 30 seconds or 1 minute, flip and do the same on the other side. The cooking time really depends on the thickness of the fish, but the idea is that you just want to get a good sear and some colour on the outside but leave the fish raw but warmed on the inside. Serve immediately with a generous spoonful of gribiche, a lemon wedge, salad or potatoes.

Seared scallops with sautéed witlof and Meyer lemon salsa

A good scallop quickly browned and caramelised in a bit of clarified butter is pretty tough to beat. There are great variances among scallops all over the world. I have been lucky enough to have wild Atlantic scallops and, I must say, these are the best for cooking. They are juicy, tender and super sweet, and you can find them along the US and Canadian coast in colder waters. Many other smaller Australian varieties are best consumed raw, in my opinion, as they can be difficult to properly caramelise if they aren't big enough. A good large size is 40–45 g (1½ oz) per scallop. I like to serve this as an entrée or a small main course.

Serves 4

600 g (1 lb 5 oz) large scallops
    (about 12–20 pieces)
2 witlof heads
25 g (1 oz) butter
40 g (1½ oz) ghee or clarified butter

Salsa

1 Meyer lemon, cut into small dice
1 small shallot, very finely diced
20 g (¾ oz) finely chopped chervil leaves
20 g (¾ oz) finely chopped flat-leaf
    (Italian) parsley
100 ml (3½ fl oz) extra-virgin olive oil

Dry your scallops on a piece of paper towel and ensure the adductor muscle has been pulled off. This is the small, more opaque-looking bit on the scallop where it attaches to the shell. Season them lightly with salt and set aside.

For the salsa, combine the Meyer lemon and shallot with a pinch of salt and allow that to macerate for at least 15 minutes, then mix in the remaining ingredients and set aside.

Set a non-stick or cast-iron pan over a medium–high heat. Cut your witlof heads in half lengthways, then cut out the cores by making an upside-down V-shaped cut on either side of it. Add the butter to the pan and let it begin to brown. Sprinkle some salt on the witlof then place them, cut side down, into the browning butter. Cook over a medium–high heat for about 5 minutes until well caramelised, then flip and cook for another minute. Remove from the pan, set aside and keep warm while you cook the scallops.

Increase the heat to high to get your pan very hot. Add the ghee and swirl it around. Dry your scallops off one last time, then add them to the pan. Do not touch the pan or move the scallops until they are properly caramelised, about 2 minutes. Flip them and allow them to cook for another 2 minutes. The other side may not caramelise as much, but that's OK. Remove the scallops from the pan and drain on paper towel.

To serve, either arrange the witlof and scallops on a share platter or divide the witlof between four plates, then serve about three to six large scallops per person, caramelised side up, and sprinkle the salsa over the top. Add a small sprinkle of flaky salt to finish. Serve immediately.

Women in the kitchen

One of the questions I get asked a lot is, 'What's it like to be a female chef in this industry?' I expected this would be something I got asked at some stage, but not over and over again. It really made me think. *What is it like*? Well, I may not be the best person to answer this, because I have mostly worked for and with women. Not by design, but because the women I worked for cooked the kind of food I was interested in: soulful, delicious, humble and not at all about themselves. I was raised in the way young women should be raised. I was empowered, I had strong female role models and I never believed there was anything I couldn't do based on my gender. So here I am, a woman in a man's world, but then again, aren't we all? Luckily, I have also worked with some pretty great men who never once made me feel like I was 'less than'. The only way to be now is aware of the world we live in, but fearless enough to continue forwards.

Poultry and meat

Poached whole chicken
with winter vegetables and
black truffle stuffing 170

Poached beef short ribs
with horseradish and
breadcrumb salsa verde 171

Sage salt and black
pepper duck breasts
with cherries 172

Mandarin and Seville
orange–braised duck legs
with carrots 174

Buttermilk-marinated
chicken with roasted
grapes and za'atar 176

Chicken al mattone with
white bean purée, lemon,
brown butter and capers 178

Braised chicken legs and
wings with almonds, olives,
raisins and preserved
lemon 180

Slow-roasted lamb
shoulder with white beans
and harissa 182

Pork neck braised with figs,
lemon and oregano 184

Pork carnitas with pineapple
and jalapeño salsa 185

Grilled flanken-style
short ribs with lemon
and olive oil 186

Grilled lamb leg spiedini
with flatbreads and
harissa-ish oil 189

Grilled côte de boeuf rested
in rosemary and thyme 190

Marinated and grilled
rack of lamb 191

Whole grilled beef tenderloin
with caramelised onions,
treviso and gorgonzola
dolce 192

Porchetta roasted
pork shoulder 194

Whole roasted pork rack
with caramelised apples
and mustard 197

Poultry and meat

A nice roast, a steak on the grill, or a whole roasted bird. Meat is something we consume far too much of these days, and it should perhaps be reserved for celebrations and not eaten every single day. However often you do choose to eat it, you need to know how to cook it. It takes a delicate touch and some confidence to get it right. Here are a few basic essential principles.

1   Allow your meat to come to room temperature before cooking. If you've ever cooked a chicken breast straight from the fridge or still partially frozen from the freezer (yikes! I've seen it) then you may understand this. Meat cooks from the outside in and knowing this means you understand that the outside should be cooking the inside, gently. If the inside is still cold, then it requires much more time and heat to cook and you end up way overcooking the outside before the inside is finished, resulting in something chewy and tough on the outside and perhaps undercooked inside. If you temper your meat properly, this won't happen. A chicken breast is actually difficult to cook well, by the way.

2   If you're unsure, use an instant-read thermometer. I pride myself on never using one, but the truth is when I'm nervous about cooking for someone, I use it because it helps confirm what your senses are telling you. And as precise as I think my touch is, a properly calibrated thermometer is an essential tool in my kitchen too.

For beef and veal

Rare: 45–50°C (113–122°F)
Medium-rare: 51–57°C (124–135°F)
Medium: 58–65°C (136–149°F)
Medium-well: 66–70°C (151–158°F)
Well: 70°C (158°F) and up

For lamb

A medium temperature of about 59–62°C (138–144°F) is ideal.

For pork

A medium temperature of 60–65°C (140–149°F) is ideal, and still gives you a perfectly safe, pink and juicy centre.

For poultry

Chicken breast: 65°C (149°F)
Chicken legs: 70°C (158°F)
Whole roast: 72–75°C (162–167°F)
Duck breast: 57–59°C (135–138°F)
A medium-rare or medium temperature is ideal for duck breast. This means it is still fully pink, but tender and juicy.
Duck legs: 70°C (158°F)

3   Keep in mind that these temperatures are for roasts and quick cooking. If you're braising or slow roasting for hours and hours until the meat falls apart, temperatures are unnecessary; you'll know that it is cooked when it is soft and tender.

4   Certain cuts of meat require long periods of salting, others don't. Any large cut of meat, such as a leg of lamb or pork shoulder or pork loin roast, and any whole birds, should have at least 8–12 hours of salting. There is no other way to ensure the interior meat will be seasoned. Also, if you're after crispy skin on anything, be it pork or duck or chicken, a 24-hour air-drying period (where the meat is left uncovered in the fridge) is necessary to dry the skin. A couple of days is even better. In the case of pork crackling, you want to be sure to score and salt the crackling for the duration of that air-drying period; the salt draws out the moisture of the thick fat cap, ensuring you'll have a blistered, crispy, tender piece of crackling. And because that fat cap is usually so thick, you don't need to worry about oversalting the meat. As for brines, I think they work well for poultry, but this is something I would only do for a turkey for Christmas or Thanksgiving, as I am not convinced the added effort is justified for your everyday roast chicken. Marinades, on the other hand, I use frequently.

5   Resting meat, after you've cooked it and before you slice it, is essential. I feel this is a message that has been well dispersed and most people know to do it, but how long should something rest for? And should you cover it or not cover it? The basic idea behind resting meat is that you are allowing the meat to drop in temperature so that all the juices that are rapidly vibrating through the meat slow down enough that they do not rush out as soon as the meat is sliced and, instead, stay in the meat, which produces a more tender, juicier texture. And remember, a piece of meat will continue rising in temperature by a couple degrees even after it has been removed from the heat source. How long do you need to rest something for? That depends on the cut. Bigger roasts could rest for 30–45 minutes. A thick steak needs 10–15 minutes,

Poultry and meat

and a whole chicken probably needs 20–30 minutes, but use your senses. If it still feels quite hot to the touch, it needs longer. The meat should feel a bit warm, but not hot. As for 'tenting' the meat? If your kitchen is cold or drafty, you should tent the meat. If it's warm, or you have a warm spot in the kitchen where you can rest the meat, it's not necessary. I find it can sometimes raise the temperature too much in the resting process and overcook the meat as well, so most of the time I leave it uncovered.

6   One last note about meat and poultry: the recipes in this chapter make up only a fraction of the total recipes in this book for the simple reason that this is how I like to cook – a simple roast or a steak to be shared, and lots of vegetables. If you ever had to choose between spending a bit more on organic vegetables or spending a bit more on organic pastured meats, you should definitely spend a bit more on organic meats. This act alone will have a significant environmental impact. It pays to find a good butcher that supplies meat like this and then support them; it is so important. I do not think meat is the enemy; on the contrary, I believe that well managed, regenerative animal farms can have a positive impact on the environment. So again, it is about supporting farms and people that do the right thing, whatever it is that they grow. And not only is this better for the environment, it's better for your health too. And if you're rolling your eyes right now, thinking this is supposed to be a light-hearted cookbook, well, it is, but this is too important a subject to glance over, so please excuse me while I get on my soapbox for a moment.

Poached whole chicken with winter vegetables and black truffle stuffing

You simply cannot imagine how delicious this is in the winter until you've tried it. This is real, home-style French comfort food, made luxurious by the addition of black truffle in the stuffing. You won't be able to make this look glamorous, but I can promise your home will be filled with intoxicating aromas of simmering chicken and sweet vegetables, and whoever eats this dish will thank you heartily. This is healing food and I look forward to making it every year when the truffles come in and it's cold outside. Choose a really good organic bird for this. No, it won't be cheap, but a good, well-raised bird tastes different. It's just better. Also, go to the extra effort of making the rich broth recipe on page 13 to poach the chicken in. It makes a huge difference to the end result.

Serves 6–8

1 × 2–3 kg (4 lb 6 oz–6 lb 10 oz) organic, heritage-breed chicken
2 litres (68 fl oz/8 cups) Rich poultry broth (page 13)
1 bunch market carrots, cleaned and peeled
1 small head celeriac, peeled and cut in wedges
1 bunch pencil leeks, well washed and cut into 2 cm (¾ in) lengths
1 bunch turnips, washed and quartered
1 swede, peeled and cut into wedges
Salsa verde (page 17) and crusty bread, to serve

Stuffing

75 g (2¾ oz) minced onion
2 garlic cloves, minced
1 tablespoon chopped thyme leaves
2 tablespoons extra-virgin olive oil
3 teaspoons salt
150 g (5½ oz) assorted, good-quality mushrooms, finely chopped (wild are preferred, but cultivated are fine)
50 ml (1¾ fl oz) white wine
50 g (1¾ oz) fresh sourdough breadcrumbs
250 g (9 oz) minced (ground) pork
1 egg
10 g (¼ oz) black truffle, microplaned or crushed with the back of a fork

Season your chicken liberally with salt about 1 hour before cooking and leave it to come to room temperature.

Start by making your stuffing. Set a sauté pan over a medium heat and sauté the onions, garlic and thyme in 1 tablespoon of the oil with ½ teaspoon salt for 4 minutes, or until the onion is soft but not coloured. Remove the onion and garlic and add another tablespoon of oil. Increase the heat to high and add the mushrooms with another ½ teaspoon salt. Cook until golden brown, then turn off the heat and add the white wine. This should cook out in the residual heat from the pan. Empty the mushrooms into a bowl with the onions, then add the breadcrumbs, mix well and set aside to cool. Once the vegetables are at room temperature, add the mince, egg, the remaining salt and black truffle. Season with 20 turns of freshly cracked black pepper and mix well. This means getting in there with your hands. If you don't mix it enough, it will fall apart. This can be made ahead and refrigerated until needed.

Fill the chicken cavity with the stuffing. It's best to form any additional stuffing into meatballs and cook them in the broth towards the end rather than overstuffing your chicken. This will depend on the size of the cavity.

Fill a large stockpot or Dutch oven with the broth and bring it to a gentle simmer. Taste the broth for seasoning; it should be seasoned, but not too highly, because the chicken carries salt too. Gently drop your bird in. The liquid should cover the bird, but a little bit sticking out the top is fine because you will flip it halfway through. Or you can add a little water to cover it. Put the lid on and simmer gently for 45 minutes to 1 hour, or until the juices between the thigh and body run clear. Once cooked, remove the chicken and leave it on a chopping board to rest.

To cook your vegetables, drop them into the broth. Try to cut them around the same size so that they cook evenly. I like them with a little crunch and texture, so I allow about 4 minutes. Divide the vegetables between serving bowls and cut up the chicken. Break up the stuffing and divide both between the bowls. Check your broth one last time for seasoning, then serve it hot on top of the chicken and vegetables. Serve with salsa verde and crusty bread.

Poached beef short ribs with horseradish and breadcrumb salsa verde

Beef short ribs braised in a red wine–laden stock and served with horseradish cream is a fairly classic way to enjoy this cut of beef. I do love a rich braise, but I also really love a light one, where the broth is thin but the meat still retains its clean flavour. The real star of the show here, though, is the salsa verde. It's another variation on my basic salsa verde (see page 17), which includes punchy horseradish, cornichons and oily breadcrumbs for a welcome crunch in an otherwise soft-textured dish. I like to serve a bit of the broth on the side for sipping, much like my mother used to do when we were children. It's fortifying, warming and delicious.

Like braising, poaching is low and slow over a few hours. The difference is we are going to submerge the beef in stock as opposed to just coming halfway up the sides. Make sure you have lots of good beef or even chicken stock to make this dish. The resulting beef will be unctuous and meltingly tender.

Serves 4–6

2 kg (4 lb 6 oz) bone-in beef short ribs
40 ml (1¼ fl oz) olive oil
1 onion
2 celery stalks
2 carrots, peeled
1 garlic bulb, halved
2 fresh bay leaves
1 tablespoon black peppercorns
2 litres (68 fl oz/8 cups) beef stock

Horseradish and breadcrumb salsa verde

1 quantity Salsa verde (page 17),
    anchovies left out
3–4 cm (1¼–1½ in) piece fresh horseradish,
    peeled and grated on a microplane
2 tablespoons finely diced cornichons
80 g (2¾ oz/1 cup) Breadcrumbs, toasted
    (page 14)

Season your ribs with salt and pepper, cover and refrigerate overnight. The following day, remove from the fridge and allow them to sit out while you preheat a large Dutch oven over a high heat. Add the oil and brown the ribs really well on all sides, working in batches to ensure the meat is in one layer. Remove from the pan and set aside. Add all the remaining ingredients, except the broth. Allow the vegetables to soften slightly, but not caramelise. Add the broth and bring it to a simmer. Add the beef back to the pan and bring back to a simmer. Skim off any foam that rises to the surface and add a bit of water if needed so that the ribs are completely submerged. Place a lid, slightly ajar, on the pan and reduce the heat to low. Simmer for 2½–3 hours, or until the meat is quite tender but not falling apart. If at any point in the cooking process the liquid evaporates too much, top up with water to keep everything submerged. Turn off the heat and allow the meat to cool for 20–30 minutes in the broth.

Mix the salsa verde ingredients together and allow them to sit for 15–20 minutes before serving.

Serve one rib per person in a bowl with a small amount of broth and lots of salsa verde. Any remaining hot broth can be served in a teacup alongside the beef to sip on.

Sage salt and black pepper duck breasts with cherries

Duck is a very special type of poultry. Many people will say they don't like it, but I think they just haven't eaten good duck, or they are scared of it. The Chinese cook duck whole and serve the skin thin, crispy and lacquered. It is an incredible process to achieve this, and it takes a lot of skill. The duck breast is always well done, but somehow still juicy. I have never had much luck cooking duck whole. The breast is usually overcooked and dry, and the legs undercooked and tough, and nothing is fully rendered. Instead, I prefer to break the meat into parts: breasts reserved for grilling or pan-frying, and legs for braising. The fat can be rendered to cook potatoes, liver and hearts are made into paté, and the bones are roasted for stock. Every little bit has a purpose. Like anything though, it is worth going the extra mile to source a quality bird so you can be sure that all that effort will turn out something delicious. I do like to buy ducks whole so that I get the most for my money, but if you're able to just buy breasts, this comes together really quickly and it's very impressive. I like to cook duck breasts more to the medium end, as I fear duck that is too rare is chewy and hard to eat.

I suggest pairing this with cherries, but anything sweet, such as citrus, figs or plums, is a great complement to duck. To deepen the colour of the skin on the duck, you can splash it with a mixture of white wine mixed with sweet wine, such as muscat Beaumes de Venise, or something similar, before cooking.

Serves 2

2 × 220 g (8 oz) duck breasts (see Note)
8 g (¼ oz) sage leaves
10 g (¼ oz) salt
1 garlic clove
12 pitted fresh cherries
30 ml (1 fl oz) red wine
1 teaspoon honey
15 g (½ oz) butter

Prepare your duck breasts by scoring the fat of the skin with a sharp knife in a fine diamond pattern. Be careful not to cut into the flesh. This step is important, as it allows the fat to melt out when cooking, so you end up with something crispy and fully rendered, not flabby. Flip the duck breast onto the skin side and check for any sinew. If there is sinew, which is a white band on one side of the breast, use a small paring knife to gently pry your way underneath and cut that bit off. Set aside.

Next, make your sage salt by crushing the sage leaves and salt in a mortar and pestle until it almost looks like a paste. You won't use all the salt on two duck breasts, but you can put the rest in a jar and save for another time. Season the breasts liberally, then crush the garlic clove in the mortar and also rub that onto each breast. Crack some black pepper all over and leave to sit for at least 20–30 minutes.

Heat a chargrill or flat cast-iron pan over the lowest possible heat. You want to cook the duck over as low a heat as possible to render as much fat off the breast as you can. Place the duck, skin side down, in the pan for 12–15 minutes. If you see the meat starting to brown on the sides, remove the pan from the heat for a few minutes to cool down. Each stove is different, so just keep the heat as low as possible so that you are only cooking the skin. Flip the breasts over and cook for another 3–5 minutes. It's a good idea to move the duck breasts around at this stage to make sure all sides get some heat. The breast is not completely flat, so you maybe need to cook it on its sides for 30 seconds or so, to ensure even cooking.

Remove the breasts from the pan and allow to rest on a chopping board. Pour off most of the fat from the pan, but leave a little behind and add the pitted cherries. Return the pan to a low heat and allow the cherries to soften slightly for 2 minutes. Next, add the red wine and let that cook out and reduce by half. Add the honey and the butter and mix well. Add a pinch of salt and taste for seasoning.

To serve, slice the duck breast against the grain and pour the sauce over the top.

Note

You can marinate the skin of the duck in a sweet marinade before cooking, if you like. Combine 10 ml (¼ fl oz) sweet wine with 20 ml (¾ fl oz) white wine and mix well. Place the duck breasts, skin side down, in the marinade and leave for 20 minutes to 1 hour before cooking. This helps to brown the skin.

Poultry and meat

Mandarin and Seville orange–braised duck legs with carrots

As I mentioned in the previous recipe, sweet things tend to go really well with duck. In this case, sweet citrus and spices complement the darker duck leg meat. Duck leg meat really requires a low, slow and moist cooking environment. Being an animal that really uses its legs for swimming and walking, duck meat is rich in flavour but can also be quite tough if not dealt with properly. This is a dish to cook in the autumn and winter months, when citrus is at its peak. Serve with some crushed, buttered turnips or swede, and you have something that soaks up all the delicious juices beautifully.

Serves 4

4 × 300 g (10½ oz) duck legs
1 tablespoon duck fat, clarified butter or olive oil
300 g (10½ oz) medium carrots, peeled and
    halved lengthways
200 ml (7 fl oz) duck or chicken stock (see
    page 12, or use store-bought)
120 ml (4 fl oz) Seville orange juice
120 ml (4 fl oz) mandarin juice
8 thyme sprigs
3 bay leaves
2 cloves
2 star anise
1 whole mandarin, sliced
1 whole Seville orange, sliced
1 cinnamon stick
1 tablespoon dark brown sugar
20 g (¾ oz) butter (if necessary)
splash of sherry vinegar (if necessary)

Season your duck legs well with salt and pepper, then leave them to rest at room temperature for 1 hour. Preheat the oven to 180°C (350°F).

Select an ovenproof pan that has sides 3–4 cm (1¼–1½ in) high and melt the duck fat over a medium–high heat. Brown the duck legs, skin side down, for 6–8 minutes until golden, then flip and cook on the meat side for another 2 minutes. Remove the legs from the pan and add all the remaining ingredients, except the butter and sherry vinegar. Bring to a simmer, then add the legs, skin side up, back in. The liquid should only come halfway up the sides of the legs; they should not be submerged. Cover with a lid or aluminium foil and cook in the oven for 1 hour. After an hour, remove the lid and take out the cinnamon stick. Flip the duck legs over so they are skin side down in the liquid and return to the oven for another 25 minutes. After this time, the skin and meat should be starting to pull away from the joint or muscle and the drumstick should be loose when pushed against the thigh. If this is not the case, cook for another 15 minutes. Once everything is looking tender and beginning to separate from the bone, flip the duck legs back over, skin side up, and increase the heat to 200°C (400°F) for another 15–20 minutes. You want the skin to look nice and golden and the carrots to be brown as well. Remove from the oven and allow to cool slightly.

Adjusting the braising liquid is not essential, but it really takes this dish from delicious to amazing. I like a sauce that has a little bit of thickness to it, so to do that we need to reduce the liquid. Simply pour the liquid from the pan into a small pot (straining it as you go to remove the cloves and star anise) and simmer until it is reduced by almost half. At this stage, I taste it to make sure it is seasoned enough and, if not, I add a bit of salt. If it is too sour or doesn't feel balanced, I'll add the butter. If it needs more sourness, I'll add a splash of sherry vinegar. If all is good, I pour the liquid back over the carrots and top with the legs, then reheat in the oven (if it has cooled) or serve straight away.

Buttermilk-marinated chicken with roasted grapes and za'atar

This is a great dish to make in the autumn when wine grapes are around. If you don't have access to wine grapes, use sweet red table grapes instead. Brining, or to be more technically correct, marinating in a mixture of milk and buttermilk, tenderises meat due to the interaction of the calcium and certain acids found in milk, but another happy coincidence is that the sugar in the milk, also known as lactose, helps produce a beautiful golden colour.

Ask your butcher to butterfly the chicken for you – it will make life easier.

Serves 4

1×2 kg (4 lb 6 oz) chicken, butterflied
600 ml (20½ fl oz) buttermilk
1.5 litres (51 fl oz/6 cups) full-cream (whole) milk
extra-virgin olive oil, for drizzling
1 tablespoon za'atar
150 g (5½ oz) red wine grapes
50 ml (1¾ fl oz) verjus, or red or white wine
50 ml (1¾ fl oz) chicken stock (page 12, or use store-bought)
25 g (1 oz) butter
1 teaspoon sherry or red-wine vinegar
5 brined grape leaves (optional)

Season your bird with salt and refrigerate for 30 minutes, then place your chicken in a bowl that will hold it snugly. If the bowl is too large, the liquid won't cover the chicken. Alternatively, you can use a sealable plastic bag. Pour the buttermilk and milk over the bird and leave it to marinate in the refrigerator for 24 hours.

Preheat the oven to 200°C (400°F).

The next day, remove the bird from the liquid and set it directly in a roasting tin, skin side up, and allow it to come to room temperature. Set a chargrill pan over a medium–high heat or get an outdoor grill quite hot. Drizzle the chicken skin with a little oil and place the whole flattened bird on the grill to get it nicely coloured. Sear for about 5–7 minutes. Once you have good grill marks, flip the bird over and place it directly on a roasting rack, skin side up. Roast the chicken in the oven for 20–30 minutes, or until the internal temperature reaches 70°C (158°F) on a cooking thermometer. Approximately 10 minutes before your chicken is finished, drizzle it with some extra olive oil and sprinkle the za'atar over the top. When the bird is cooked, remove it from the oven and set it on a chopping board to rest for 20 minutes.

Next, check the roasting tray. If the fat and dripping look quite burned, rinse it off before adding your grapes to the tin, but if the dripping is just deeply caramelised, place your grapes on top of that spot on the tray. Pour the verjus onto the grapes and sprinkle them with salt and olive oil. Return the tray to the oven and roast at 220°C (430°F) for 10–15 minutes, or until the grapes swell and look like they will burst. Remove from the oven and set the grapes aside. To make a little sauce, place the roasting tin over a medium–low heat on the stove and add the chicken stock and any juices the chicken has released while resting. Add the butter and let it simmer, reduce and thicken. Add the vinegar to the sauce once reduced. It may need a bit more salt or butter depending on the sourness of the grapes, so have a taste. Set aside for pouring over the chicken.

I like to fry some brined grape leaves in olive oil until they are crispy, but this is not essential, just beautiful and tasty. Carve your chicken and serve with the roasted grapes and all the juice poured over it, and the grape leaves, if you've done them.

Chicken al mattone with white bean purée, lemon, brown butter and capers

Chicken al mattone is such a good way to cook a piece of chicken. Al mattone is Italian and literally translates as 'under a brick', meaning the chicken is cooked under a weight that keeps most of the skin in contact with the hot pan, resulting in a golden, crispy crust. This really works best with a whole leg that has been deboned. The juices and fat contained in the leg make this a perfect cut for this preparation. You can ask your butcher to prepare it for you, or if you feel comfortable with a boning knife, simply scrape the meat off the bone with the tip of the knife and just be careful not to pierce the skin.

I love the combination of velvety purée, salty capers, sour lemons and sweet brown butter, but feel free to combine the chicken with any number of vegetables and salads. As usual, try to find the best chicken possible; something organic is preferable.

Serves 2

2 boneless, skin-on chicken legs
3 tablespoons clarified butter
40 g (1½ oz) butter
1½ tablespoons salt-packed capers, rinsed
1 small lemon or ½ a large one, peeled, segmented and diced
20 g (¾ oz) chopped flat-leaf (Italian) parsley

White bean purée

1 garlic bulb
2 tablespoons olive oil
400 g (14 oz) freshly cooked cannellini or borlotti beans (cooking liquid reserved)

Note

If using dried beans, soak them overnight. The following day, cook in well-seasoned, simmering water with a pinch of bicarbonate of soda (baking soda) added, until they are tender. The bicarb helps to soften the skins.

To achieve crispy skin, you need to dry out the skin of the chicken. Refrigerate uncovered for one or two nights. If you don't have time for this, dry out the skin as best you can with paper towel. On the day you want to cook the chicken, remove it from the fridge, season with salt and leave it to come to room temperature.

Preheat the oven to 180°C (350°F).

To make the white bean purée, start by cutting the top quarter off the garlic bulb. Place it on a piece of aluminium foil and pour the oil on top with a pinch of salt. Wrap the garlic in the foil and bake for 30–40 minutes until it is soft and golden. Remove from the oven, unwrap and allow to cool, being careful to reserve all the oil it was cooked in. Put the beans in a blender and blitz to a purée with some of their cooking liquid. Squeeze the soft garlic out of its skin and into the blender, along with the reserved garlic oil. Blend until smooth, then check for seasoning. Add a bit more liquid or water as needed to achieve a smooth but not runny consistency. Scrape it into a small saucepan, ready to warm up before serving.

Heat a wide cast-iron pan over a high heat. When it is very hot, add the clarified butter and place one piece of chicken, skin side down, in the pan, then reduce the heat to medium. You will need to cook the chicken one piece at a time to ensure crispiness. Place a small piece of baking paper or aluminium foil on top of the chicken and use another heavy pan to weigh it down. It will take 6–8 minutes to brown the skin. Start checking it after 5 minutes. When brown and crispy, remove the chicken from the pan and repeat the process with the other piece. To finish cooking, place both pieces of chicken back in the pan, flesh side down, and cook for another 3–4 minutes until just cooked through. Remove the chicken from the pan and allow to rest. Discard the remaining oil, then add 30 ml (1 fl oz) water to the pan and deglaze, scraping all the bits from the bottom. Use this as a pan sauce. Set aside.

Clean the pan and set over a medium heat. Brown the butter until golden, fragrant and foamy. Immediately throw in the capers and sizzle in the butter. Add the lemon pieces and parsley.

To serve, place a bit of the warmed purée on the base of each plate and top with the chicken. Spoon some of the pan sauce on top and, finally, spoon over the butter caper sauce. Serve immediately.

178

Braised chicken legs and wings with almonds, olives, raisins and preserved lemon

A chicken wing is one of my favourite things in the world. If I cook a whole chicken, I always save the two chicken wings for myself. Maybe because I grew up on American-style barbecue, or hot sauce–slathered chicken wings, but I really think they are one of the most underrated cuts out there. They stay juicy no matter what you do to them, the ratio of meat to skin (the best part!) is excellent and, typically, they are cheap as chips. Sure, there isn't a lot of meat on them and they really can only be eaten with your hands, but to balance out those factors, I suggest braising them with chicken leg pieces so that you get a bit of extra meatiness.

This combination of raisins, olives and almonds may suggest a more Middle Eastern–style flavour profile, but altogether, those components really just make this dish a bit sweet, salty and savoury. Serve it on top of some polenta or with some steamed couscous and you have a delicious, comforting meal.

Serves 4

4 whole chicken legs or chicken Marylands (leg quarters)
8–12 chicken wings (wing tip separated and reserved for stock, wing split at the joint)
2 tablespoons olive oil, plus extra if needed
1 preserved lemon, rinsed
1 bunch spring onions (scallions), green parts cut off and reserved, white parts quartered
10 garlic cloves
2 tablespoons plain (all-purpose) flour
100 ml (3½ fl oz) white wine
800 ml (27 fl oz) chicken stock (page 12, or use store-bought)
1 tablespoon honey
1 tablespoon sherry vinegar
2 bay leaves
15 whole pitted green olives
30 g (1 oz) sultanas or raisins
30 g (1 oz) toasted almonds

Season your chicken legs and wings with salt and pepper and leave to sit at room temperature for 15–20 minutes.

Heat the oil in a wide ovenproof sauté pan over a medium–high heat and brown the chicken pieces all over. Do not move them around or flip them too much while browning. If all the wing pieces don't fit at the same time, you can do this in two batches, just add a bit more olive oil if needed.

Preheat the oven to 200°C (400°F).

To prepare the preserved lemon, cut the flesh out of the lemon and discard. Finely slice the pith and skin and set aside.

Remove the chicken from the pan and immediately add the quartered onion and garlic cloves. Allow those to soften and begin to colour for about 10 minutes over a medium heat. Add the flour and stir to moisten it with the oil and cook it out. Next, add the white wine and simmer for 2 minutes. Add the stock and bring up to a simmer. Once simmering, add the honey, vinegar, bay leaves, preserved lemon, olives and sultanas and stir to combine. Return the chicken to the pan, skin side down. Bring the whole lot to a simmer, then place a lid on the pan, slightly ajar, or a piece of baking paper (cartouche). Alternatively, transfer everything to a baking dish and cover with aluminium foil. Place in the oven, then drop the temperature to 180°C (350°F). Simmer for 45 minutes to 1 hour, or until the chicken is tender. Flip the chicken over onto the skin side, remove the lid or cartouche and cook for another 20 minutes, so that the liquid can reduce a bit further.

Remove the pan from the oven and set it aside, semi covered, for about 20 minutes. Roughly crush the almonds in a mortar and pestle so they remain fairly chunky, then sprinkle on top of the chicken. Serve immediately or cool and reheat when ready.

Slow-roasted lamb shoulder with white beans and harissa

A whole slow-roasted lamb shoulder is a beautiful way to prepare lamb for a few people. Cooked over a few hours in a low oven, the meat becomes meltingly tender and can easily be pulled apart with two forks. The romesco is a purée of charred red peppers, crushed nuts, breadcrumbs and roasted and raw garlic. It's a delicious, smoky, sweet and savoury accompaniment to lamb, but it also works very well with grilled fish, squid or even chicken.

Soak your beans overnight and cook them gently so that they remain intact and don't burst open while cooking. If they do burst open, do not despair; they will still be delicious. But under no circumstances should you drain the beans until you are ready to serve them. Instead, allow them to cool in their cooking liquid. Don't worry; they won't overcook.

Serves 6

1×2.25–2.5 kg (5–5½ lb) lamb shoulder,
    on the bone
2 tablespoons olive oil, plus extra to serve
juice of 1 lemon
½ bunch thyme, leaves picked

Beans

300 g (10½ oz) dried white beans,
    such as cannellini or flageolet
1 onion, peeled and halved
2 carrots, peeled and halved
2 tablespoons olive oil
2 tablespoons salt
2 bay leaves
½ bunch thyme

Romesco

900 g–1 kg (2 lb–2 lb 3 oz) red bullhorn peppers
    (or any sweet red pepper/capsicum variety)
1 garlic bulb plus 1 garlic clove
3 tablespoons olive oil
60 g (2 oz) hazelnuts, toasted
60 g (2 oz) almonds, toasted
1 teaspoon mild smoked paprika
1 tablespoon sherry vinegar
2 teaspoons red-wine vinegar
60 g (2 oz) Breadcrumbs, toasted (page 14)

The beans can be made a day or two ahead. Soak them in cold water overnight and cover the beans with more water than you think they need. They will double in size during the soaking process, and if some stick out of the water, they will not soak evenly and will therefore cook unevenly. The following day, drain them and place them in a large saucepan with 1.5 litres (51 fl oz/ 6 cups) cold water and the remaining ingredients (tie the herbs together so they are easy to remove later on). Bring the water up to a simmer and skim off any brown foam that floats to the top. Simmer until they are completely creamy and tender. This could take anywhere between 1 and 2 hours depending on the size of the beans. Add a bit more water during the cooking process if it seems like it is evaporating too quickly. Allow to cool in the liquid, then reheat, still in the liquid, to serve.

Preheat the oven to 180°C (350°F).

To make your romesco, char the peppers completely over a stovetop flame or outside on a grill. It's important that they are blackened so that the skins come off easily. Place them in a bowl and cover with a lid so they steam and cool. Once cooled, peel them, removing any seeds or stem that is still attached. Add to a blender and blitz to a paste. You don't want a super-fine paste, but something with a bit of texture to it. To roast your garlic, cut the top quarter off, place it on a piece of aluminium foil and pour over 1 tablespoon oil and a sprinkle of salt. Wrap it up tightly in the foil then bake in the oven for 45 minutes until it is soft and beginning to turn golden. Set aside to cool. Crush your toasted nuts in a mortar and pestle until finely crushed but not yet a paste. In a bowl, combine the crushed nuts with the pepper purée, squeeze the soft garlic out of its skin and add it along with any of its roasting oil, the smoked paprika, remaining olive oil and vinegars, and grate in the raw clove of garlic. Add the breadcrumbs just before serving so that they don't go soggy.

The night before you want to cook your lamb, season it liberally with salt and pepper and refrigerate, uncovered, overnight. The next day, remove it from the fridge and allow it to come to room temperature. Preheat the oven to 160°C (320°F). Pour the olive oil and lemon juice over the lamb and rub it with the thyme leaves. Place it on a tray and roast for 6–7 hours until very tender. The meat should fall off the bone. If the shoulder needs extra caramelisation, increase the heat to 220°C (430°F) for the last 20 minutes of cooking to brown the outside. Rest the meat for 20 minutes on a serving platter so that its juices will mingle with the beans.

Spoon the hot beans around the lamb and drizzle with some good olive oil and a final seasoning of salt and pepper. Serve with the romesco.

Pork neck braised with figs, lemon and oregano

This is a very traditional way of braising any type of meat that likes a low and slow type of cook. Brown the meat, sweat the mirepoix, add some wine and some stock and cook slowly for several hours. What is not very traditional is the figs and fig leaves in the braise. Fig leaves add a sweet, almost vanilla type flavour to this braise and the figs impart sweetness. It's aromatic, a perfect accompaniment to pork and oh so delicious. It's a perfect early autumn dish when the temperature starts to drop but summer produce is still hanging on.

Pork neck can be cooked low and slow or quick and hot in a pan or over a grill, it's very versatile. It is a cut that has beautiful intermuscular fat and great flavour, one of my favourites for pork.

Serves 6

1×2–2.5 kg (4 lb 6 oz–5½ lb) pork neck fillet (collar)
2 onions, peeled and diced
2 carrots, peeled and diced
2 celery stalks, diced
3 crushed garlic cloves
300 ml (10 fl oz) white wine
200 ml (7 fl oz) verjus
500 ml (17 fl oz/2 cups) chicken or pork stock
2 rosemary sprigs
6 figs, torn in half
3 fig leaves
2 fresh bay leaves
peel of 2 lemons (peels in large pieces using a vegetable peeler, not a microplane)
1 bunch oregano
polenta, to serve (see page 108)

Season your pork with salt and black pepper the day before you want to cook it and leave it in the fridge overnight.

Preheat the oven to 170°C (340°F).

Using an enamel-coated Dutch oven over a medium–high heat, brown the pork neck on all sides. When browned remove it from the pan and set aside. Next, turn the heat down to medium and add the onions, carrots, celery and garlic cloves to the pan and sauté until starting to soften. When translucent, after about 10 minutes, deglaze with the white wine and verjus. Be careful not to burn the edges of the pan. Add a bit of water to bring down the heat in the pan if it looks like things are caramelising before they are soft.

Return the pork neck to the pot. Next, add in enough stock to come up halfway to the sides of the pork in the pan, approximately 500 ml (17 fl oz/2 cups) stock. Season the stock with a bit of salt (remembering that it will reduce). Add the rosemary, figs, fig leaves, bay leaves, lemon peel and the oregano. Cover with a lid and braise in the oven for an hour and a half. At this stage, remove the covering, flip the roast and allow to continue roasting for another hour and a half, or until tender but not falling apart.

Remove the fig leaves and rosemary from the braise and discard. Slice the meat after allowing it to cool for about 20–30 minutes and return to the liquid. Serve with its braising liquid on top of some soft fresh corn polenta.

Pork carnitas with pineapple and jalapeño salsa

I feel an affinity with this Mexican dish because there is something very similar in Cuban cuisine called masitas de puerco. Meltingly tender chunks of pork are braised slowly in water, aromatics and fat before being browned and made crispy in their own fat once the water has cooked off. Yes, it's a bit rich, but you don't eat much of it and the pineapple salsa cuts through much of the fat and complements it with a lovely sweetness. Carnitas should be served in full Mexican style with some soft corn tortillas, pickled red onions, avocado and some shredded cabbage … and probably another red-hot sauce if you're eating with me. It's a fabulous and fun way to serve a meal for friends. Load all the condiments and pork in the middle of the table for everyone to help themselves, and you need little else. Maybe just some cold beers or margaritas and perhaps some rice and beans.

Serves 8–10

2 kg (4 lb 6 oz) boneless, skinless pork shoulder, cut into large chunks
2 white onions
1 garlic bulb, split in half along the equator
3 bay leaves
2 dried chillies
500 g (1 lb 2 oz) lard (see Note)
warm corn tortillas, sliced avocado, shredded cabbage, lime wedges and pickled onion, to serve

Pineapple salsa

250 g (9 oz) peeled and cored pineapple
40 g (1½ oz) jalapeños (seeds included), diced
50 g (1¾ oz) coriander (cilantro)
2 tablespoons lime juice
2 teaspoons salt

Season your pork with salt and refrigerate, covered, overnight.

The next day, remove the pork from the fridge and allow it to come to room temperature.

Preheat the oven to 180°C (350°F).

Place the pork in a large Dutch oven, add 750 ml (25½ fl oz/3 cups) cold water and add the onion, garlic, bay leaves, chillies and lard. Bring to a simmer on the stove, then carefully transfer to the oven and cook, uncovered, for 2 hours, stirring occasionally.

To make the salsa, blend all the ingredients in a blender. If your jalapeños are particularly spicy, remove the seeds or just use less.

After 2 hours, return the pot to the stove and remove as many of the aromatics as you can pick out. Place over a medium heat and simmer until all the liquid has evaporated and the meat is beginning to brown in its own fat. Cover with a lid, slightly ajar, at this stage so the popping fat doesn't escape. Stir carefully to brown evenly on all sides. Once the meat is caramelised, remove from the fat and drain on paper towel. Serve immediately.

Serve the pork with tortillas, pineapple salsa, sliced avocados, shredded cabbage, lime wedges and pickled onions.

Note

Try to buy rendered lard from your butcher. If they don't have any, ask for 1 kg (2 lb 3 oz) minced (ground) pork fat. To render it, simply place it in a saucepan with a few splashes of water, cover with a lid and heat over the lowest possible heat until rendered. Stir it every so often to make sure it's melting evenly. If browning stars to occur before much of the fat has melted, add another splash of water. Strain and reserve. It can be kept in the freezer for months.

Grilled flanken-style short ribs with lemon and olive oil

Flanken-style or 'asado-style' short ribs are short ribs that have been cut through the grain and through the bone. They are sliced thinly (about 1.5 cm/½ in) and each slice will have at least 3–4 pieces of bone in it. Unlike English-cut short ribs, which is the cut most of us are familiar with and that requires hours of braising, flanken-style ribs grill up beautifully and quickly. I'm sure if you've eaten Korean food before you will have tried this cut Kalbi-style, marinated in ginger, soy and sugar and grilled to a sweet caramelised char. This cut has more texture and chew than something like fillet, but, on the flip side, it also has so much more flavour.

This is a delicious dish, and by foregoing highly seasoned marinating ingredients and just grilling the meat, you're left with the beefiest tasting cut out there. Served simply with olive oil and lemon it is a real purist's way of eating it. Without question, you need quality beef to start with, so go to a butcher you trust and ask for the best beef you can buy. It must have excellent marbling and fat throughout.

Serves 4

1.2 kg (2 lb 10 oz) flanken-style short ribs
extra-virgin olive oil, for brushing and drizzling
lemon juice, for drizzling

Heat your grill to a very high heat.

Brush the ribs with a small amount of olive oil and season well with salt. Leave to sit for at least 15 minutes before grilling. Also, be sure that your ribs are at room temperature before grilling.

Grill the ribs to a nice char on both sides, ensuring that the middle is still a little bit pink. This should only take 2–3 minutes on each side if your grill is extremely hot. Do not bring the lid of the grill down while these cook. Allow them to rest on a warm serving platter for a few minutes before serving, then simply drizzle with good olive oil and lemon juice.

Grilled lamb leg spiedini with flatbreads and harissa-ish oil

I've cooked many a lamb leg in my day. Lamb leg 'à la ficelle' is a bit of a fixture in my professional cooking life. This is where you hang a partially boned leg of lamb by a string in front of an open fire in a hearth. The heat slowly turns the lamb leg so you get beautiful even, smoke-kissed cooking. I do not think most people have open fireplaces in their hearths these days, but if you do, that is my absolute favourite way of cooking a leg of lamb. My second favourite way is this: small chunks, diced up, marinated and grilled over charcoal. Ask your butcher for a piece with a good fat cap on it. The rump is a good place to start.

I like to serve it with what I call harissa-ish oil. It's a mixture of cumin, coriander and chilli blended with olive oil. A classic harissa is made by soaking and puréeing dried chillies with ground coriander, garlic and tomato, so yes, this is not classic, but it's delicious nonetheless, and far easier to make.

Serve with some of my Yoghurt and spelt flatbreads (page 232) and perhaps some yoghurt and lemon for a little bit of acidity.

Serves 4

1 kg (2 lb 3 oz) boneless fatty lamb leg
2 garlic cloves, crushed
2 tablespoons olive oil
4 g (⅛ oz) thyme leaves
4 g (⅛ oz) fresh oregano leaves
Yoghurt and spelt flatbreads (page 232), lemon
    wedges and Yoghurt (page 237), to serve

Harissa-ish oil

2 tablespoons coriander seeds
2 tablespoons cumin seeds
1 small garlic clove
2 tablespoons Aleppo chilli flakes
180 ml (6 fl oz) olive oil

To make the harissa-ish oil, toast your spices in a dry frying pan until they are warm and aromatic. Combine all the ingredients in a blender and blitz on high speed until the spices are crushed and well combined. Set aside. This could be done well in advance and kept in the fridge.

Dice your lamb into 2 cm (¾ in) pieces and combine with all the ingredients in a bowl. Cover and leave to marinate overnight, or for at least a few hours.

Set up a charcoal grill and get the coals white hot. Thread your lamb pieces onto either metal or bamboo skewers (remember to soak them first if using bamboo), then season with salt. Cook over the fire for 2–3 minutes on each side (you will only flip them once). If your grill is flaring up too much, simply move them for a minute or move the coals around a bit underneath them. Serve immediately with warm yoghurt flatbreads, some harissa oil, lemon wedges and a dollop of yoghurt.

Grilled côte de boeuf rested in rosemary and thyme

Really, this method could be applied to any number of cuts of grilled beef or even lamb. The idea is simple: grill the meat then rest it in a beautiful herbaceous, garlicky mixture. Think of it like reverse marinating. I think it's a lovely way to enhance the flavours of grilled meats without changing them too much.

I will always advocate for grass-fed meat, but find the best quality meat you can buy with a great fat content. Grass-fed meat will never be as fatty as grain-fed meat, but as we know, fat is flavour and there are great farmers out there helping to achieve the best ratio of fat to meat, even in grass-fed meats.

When it comes to grilling, you will never achieve the same flavour of charcoal or wood on a gas grill. It just won't happen. And unless you have a very powerful gas grill that gets super hot, you won't get a good sear either. I have cooked at friends' houses who said, 'Yeah, yeah, I've got a great grill' only to find myself finishing the meat in a frying pan on the stove because the grill just never got hot enough to caramelise the meat. A simple Japanese grill combined with a cheap charcoal chimney to light the charcoal has produced some of the best steaks I have ever had. It doesn't need to be fancy, just super hot to produce that deeply seared and crispy outside crust. And be patient when cooking over charcoal; the coals must be white before you attempt to cook on them, or you will only impart the taste of charcoal versus enhancing the flavour of your meat by allowing it to be kissed by the smoke.

Serves 2

1 × 600–800 g (1 lb 5 oz–1 lb 12 oz) slice
    côte de boeuf (approx. 3 cm/1¼ in thick)
1 tablespoon extra-virgin olive oil,
    plus extra for drizzling
3 rosemary sprigs
4 thyme sprigs
2 large garlic cloves, crushed
squeeze of lemon juice

Bring your meat to room temperature. While that's happening, light your grill and let it get super hot. Drizzle the meat with the tiniest bit of olive oil, then sprinkle it generously with sea salt and freshly cracked black pepper.

Next, set up your resting dish. Add the herbs, stripped from their stems, the oil and the garlic. Mix well and bring it with you to the grill.

As the meat cooks, its fat will render and drip. To avoid these drips catching, ensure the grill is positioned about 15–20 cm (6–8 in) above the coals. This will ensure you get maximum heat and any flare-ups won't char the meat. Place the steak on the hottest part of the grill and try not to touch it for 4 whole minutes. Flip it over and grill the other side for 4 minutes, untouched. Flip once more for another minute on the first side. You want to avoid enormous flare-ups that engulf the meat. This is why you only coat it in a little oil, as dripping fat equals flames. Those cooking times will give you a medium-rare steak, which is my preference for beef. If you want something closer to medium add another 1–2 minutes per side (see page 166 for internal meat temperatures). Ideally, you would have an instant-read thermometer on hand so you can accurately gauge the temperature, since all steaks are a bit different.

Rest the meat directly on top of the herbs and cover with aluminium foil for 10 minutes. Slice the steak thinly against the grain and pour the resting juices over the meat. Sprinkle with a bit more salt and drizzle with olive oil and a small squeeze of lemon.

Marinated and grilled rack of lamb

I remember one of my first big challenges on the grill at Chez Panisse was the lamb. Three different cuts, grilled separately, then served alongside each other on the plate. We broke down whole animals for this kind of preparation and there was usually very little lamb to spare at the end of the service, which meant there was very little room for error. It was pretty tough to get them all just right, but that is what was required and so it went. A little magic, a little skill and quality produce, and I often heard people say in utter disbelief, 'I've never had lamb that good'. Wood smoke, charcoal and lamb definitely go hand in hand, but start with a good-quality young lamb and you can't go wrong. In case 'good quality' seems like too vague a statement, what you want is young, tender lamb with a good amount of fat and a sweet flavour. Their flavour can change with the seasons, but spring is widely regarded as the best time for sweet, tender lamb.

I don't like to French the racks because I adore that meat in between the bones. 'Frenching' is a butchering technique where the bones are cut and scraped dry for a neat and tidy presentation. Neat and tidy has never been my biggest goal in the kitchen, but flavour, on the other hand, has. You should never feel bad about picking up a bone with your hands. In fact, if I see someone doing it, I think, 'Here is someone who knows good food'. It's also a compliment to the chef, so I encourage this kind of behaviour.

Serves 2–3

1 × 800 g (1 lb 12 oz) rack of lamb (not Frenched)

Marinade

2 rosemary sprigs, leaves picked and finely chopped
12 thyme sprigs, leaves picked and finely chopped
2 garlic cloves, crushed in the mortar and pestle
1 tablespoon extra-virgin olive oil

To make your marinade, combine all the ingredients in a small bowl. Season your lamb with salt and pepper, then spread the marinade on it and leave to sit at room temperature for 1 hour. Light your grill, but the goal is to keep it at a medium–low heat. You don't want to cook this cut of meat at extremely high heat, as that would char and dry the outside a bit too much before you achieved a perfect medium temperature inside.

Unlike steaks, where you don't want to move the steak too much during grilling, it's a good idea to move a rack of lamb around often to keep the fat rendering but without charring or causing a flare-up. Turn it over every couple of minutes until you've reached an internal temperature of approximately 60–62°C (140–144°F). If you like your lamb medium-well, leave it on the grill until it reaches 70°C (158°F). Pull it off the grill and rest it in a warm place for 15 minutes. Lamb fat re-solidifies at room temperature, so your lamb won't be as enjoyable with a long resting time, unlike beef. Try to serve it while it's still pretty warm. Slice in between the bones and into individual cutlets, then serve immediately.

Whole grilled beef tenderloin with caramelised onions, treviso and gorgonzola dolce

From the outside, this dish seems like it should be for special occasions only, but the truth is it's so simple to prepare you really can make it any time you want. My mom made this kind of thing a lot whenever the beef tenderloin was on sale at the store and, as kids, we begged for it. The high price of this cut of meat can feel prohibitive, but sometimes you can get lucky. It's a cut that has a bad rap for its lack of fat (because as we all know fat is where much of the flavour lies), but that is where this delicious creamy gorgonzola sauce comes in. There are those who I'm sure are not fans of beef and blue cheese, but I urge you to try it anyway. It's much milder than you might think, and the cheese adds a good kick of umami savouriness to an otherwise mild cut of beef.

Cooking this cut over charcoal or wood is also very important. You just won't get the flavour from a chargrill pan on the stove. Be sure to get the grill super hot before you start grilling, and make sure the coals are white before you place the meat on the grill. Don't be afraid of seasoning either; the meat really needs lots of black pepper and salt. You can also cook fillet steaks instead of a whole tenderloin if you are cooking for a smaller group.

Serves 6–8

2 kg (4 lb 6 oz) whole beef tenderloin, trimmed and tied
olive oil, for rubbing

Gorgonzola sauce

600 ml (20½ fl oz) cream
180 g (6½ oz) gorgonzola dolce
1 teaspoon lemon juice

Onions

2 onions, peeled and sliced thinly
2 tablespoons olive oil, plus extra to serve
1 tablespoon Worcestershire sauce
1 tablespoon red-wine or sherry vinegar
50 ml (1¾ fl oz) red wine

To serve

1 head treviso
red-wine vinegar

To make your sauce, simmer the cream slowly in a small saucepan until it is reduced by half. To avoid the cream bubbling over, keep a stainless-steel spoon in the pan as it simmers, but be careful when touching the spoon as it can be very hot. Once reduced, add the blue cheese and salt and pepper, then set aside. The sauce can be rewarmed gently and just needs the lemon juice added at the end. Don't chill and rewarm this sauce as it can split.

To make your onions, heat a sauté pan over a low heat. Sweat the onions in the oil with a pinch of salt until they are tender and have released most of their water, about 5 minutes. Increase the heat and begin to brown them. Unlike recipes where you cook them slowly and allow them to caramelise gently, here, we want to brown them quickly so that they maintain some texture and integrity. Once they are nice and brown, turn the heat back down to low and add the Worcestershire sauce, vinegar and red wine. Allow to cook out and reduce for about 2 minutes, then set aside.

To cook your beef, rub it gently with a small amount of olive oil, then season it liberally with salt and roughly cracked black pepper. Be sure that it has come to room temperature before you cook it. Get your grill nice and hot. Place the meat on the hottest part of the charcoal grill to try to achieve maximum char on all sides. The browning process should take 8–10 minutes depending on the size of the beef and the heat coming from your grill. At this stage, check the temperature. You're looking for 50°C (122°F) for rare and 51–58°C (124–136°F) for medium-rare. If the meat is not quite there yet, keep cooking it on the cooler sections of the grill and rotate it until the desired temperature is achieved. As soon as the meat is ready, remove it from the grill and wrap it tightly in aluminium foil. Leave it to rest in a warm spot, such as an oven with the pilot on, or an oven set to 50°C (122°F). It should rest for at least 20 minutes.

To finish, warm the onions and gorgonzola sauce and slice the beef. Dress the treviso with a good few splashes of red-wine vinegar, some olive oil and salt and pepper, and either plate each dish with a few of each component, or serve it all in the middle of the table so people can choose how much sauce they want.

Porchetta roasted pork shoulder

Most agree the origins of porchetta are in Umbria, also known as Italy's green heart. There, lush, rolling hills provide a perfect home for pastured pigs. In its most authentic form, porchetta is a full boned-out pig marinated with garlic, wild fennel and maybe rosemary, then rolled up and tied in a big log, often with the head still attached. It's a tremendously beautiful and impressive thing, often reserved for celebrations. Chefs will make simplified versions using a fully boneless loin with belly. To make things even easier at home, I suggest adding all those flavours to a pork shoulder and slow roasting that in your oven instead, so you don't have to worry about boning out a pig or finding butchers' string and tying it up perfectly. Seasoning a cut like this 12–24 hours in advance is crucial. It's the only way to get salt into a piece of meat so large, and it's also the best way to guarantee a crackling skin. Serve this with my fresh corn polenta (page 108) and perhaps some salsa verde (see page 17) and you have a spectacular meal worthy of any celebration.

The porchetta should be baked in a roasting tin with sides at least 2 cm (¾ in) high, as the pork will release a lot of fat and liquid when cooking.

Serves 10–12

1×5 kg (11 lb) whole pork shoulder, skin on, shank and blade removed
10 dried bay leaves
4 rosemary sprigs
4 thyme sprigs
2 tablespoons wild fennel flowers, or 1 tablespoon fennel seeds if flowers unavailable
20 g (¾ oz) garlic, crushed into a paste in the mortar and pestle

Score the skin of the pork in a diamond pattern, then season the skin side liberally with salt. Flip it over and season the flesh side liberally with salt and lots of freshly cracked black pepper. Crush the bay leaves in your hands and combine with the picked rosemary, thyme and fennel. Spread the garlic liberally all over the flesh side, but not the skin side, then cover the flesh side with all the herbs and fennel and press them in so they stick. Flip it back over so that the skin side is up and refrigerate, uncovered, for 12–24 hours.

Remove it from the fridge and allow it to come to room temperature for 2 hours. Preheat the oven to 200°C (400°F), then roast for 1 hour. Reduce the heat to 150°C (300°F) and cook for another 5–6 hours. To get crackling skin once the meat is tender and fully cooked, place the pork under the grill (broiler) of your oven, but don't walk away from it. It goes from blistered and bubbly to burnt pretty quickly.

Note

When it comes to slow roasting, a lot of people will ask, how do you know it's done? In this form of cooking, you are not looking for an end temperature. You are fully cooking the meat then allowing it to continue cooking to break down the muscles and connective tissue further, so the result is meat that is melting and falling off the bone, a lot like a braise or American barbecue. You'll know it's done when you can easily pull the meat from the bone without needing to cut it.

Whole roasted pork rack with caramelised apples and mustard

This is such a good dish to cook for a crowd. The delight on people's faces when a big roasted rack of pork with blistered, crackling skin hits the table is incredible. I also love how the roasted sweet apples and the mustard and crème fraîche become a perfect sweet and savoury sauce. The pork on its own is good, but with the sauce is divine.

Look for pork that has a good fat content and good provenance. If you can find a piece that is not wrapped in plastic from a butcher, even better. It will mean the skin will have already been air-dried, which is the key to crispy crackling. If your pork does come wrapped in plastic, it must first be refrigerated, uncovered, for 1–2 days to air-dry. I serve this roast medium, which means it is a little bit pink. If you buy high-quality pork, this is perfectly fine – and not just fine, but the ideal temperature to produce a juicy and tender slice.

Serves 4–6

1.25 kg (2 lb 12 oz) pork rack, bone in, skin on
8 g (¼ oz) sage leaves
10 g (¼ oz) salt
5–6 sweet apples, cored and quartered
1 teaspoon dijon mustard
1 teaspoon wholegrain mustard
2 tablespoons Crème fraîche (page 239)

To prepare the pork rack for roasting, score the skin in thin narrow lines from top to bottom. You want to cut through the fat, but not into the flesh. This will allow the fat to melt out and the skin to blister. If your kitchen knife isn't super sharp, a small serrated knife makes this job easy.

Next, make your sage salt by crushing the leaves and salt together in a mortar and pestle until you get something that is almost paste-like in consistency. Rub the sage salt around the flesh of the pork, but not the skin. Crack black pepper on the meat as well, then sprinkle plain sea salt on the skin and refrigerate, uncovered, overnight.

The next day, remove your pork from the fridge and allow it to come to room temperature.

Preheat the oven to 220°C (430°F).

Place the pork, skin side up, on a tray lined with baking paper. Roast for about 20 minutes, then add the apples to the tray and turn to coat them in a bit of the rendered pork fat. Roast for another 30 minutes, or until the internal temperature at the thickest part of the meat reads between 58–65°C (136–149°F). At this stage, place your roast under the grill (broiler) for a minute or two, but do not walk away from it. This last little blast of heat will make any last bit of skin blister and puff into crackling, but it can burn very easily. Remove it from the oven and place on a chopping board. Let it rest for at least 15 minutes while you finish the sauce.

Remove the apples from the roasting tray and pour off the juices and fat into a small saucepan. Set over a medium heat and add the mustards and crème fraîche. Bring to a simmer, then check for seasoning and set aside.

Cut the pork rack in between the bones into chops. Serve one warm chop per person with a few wedges of apple. Finally, spoon a generous tablespoon of warm sauce on top of each chop and serve straight away. A little sprinkle of salt on top of the sliced meat is also a good idea.

Dessert

Cape gooseberry
clafoutis 201

Pineapple and ginger
upside-down cake 203

Strawberry and rhubarb
crumble 204

Chocolate miso tart 204

Lime curd tart with toasted
meringue 206

Strawberry and brown sugar
galette 208

Mom's flan with poached
cherries 211

A simple apple galette 213

Chocolate torte with
baked plums 215

Ice creams 216

Blueberry frozen yoghurt 216

Custard apple and kaffir lime
ice cream 217

Almond and cherry custard
ice cream 217

Citrus and chocolate
mousse trifle 221

Buckwheat, brown butter,
almond and apple cake 223

Dessert

Dessert is a bit of an indulgence, but when consumed in moderation, it is the perfect end to a special meal. There could be nothing more satisfying than a fresh fruit galette, homemade ice cream, or a delicious chocolate cake, so I don't try anything overly elaborate. Finishing a meal on a high doesn't require you to be a pastry chef, which I am, admittedly, not. I know the things that I like and the things that I feel confident making and I stick to those. I feel as though I approach most cooking with senses of taste and smell and touch, and most pastry cannot really be approached this way, which is why I have a harder time with it. You see, cakes and tarts really need to start with great recipes, more than many other things, and at a certain point you just need to trust that you followed all the steps correctly. In much of baking and pastry, there is a certain alchemy that happens when something is in the oven, at which point it is out of your control. It challenges the part of my mind that wants to eyeball everything and use my instincts. Instead, I am forced to focus, follow instructions and concentrate and ensure that I am prepared. It's a great lesson to come back to and it also makes for great day-off cooking.

With any kind of baking, preparation is important. Before you start baking, ensure you have all the ingredients on hand and check the expiration date on ingredients such as baking powder, baking soda or yeast. You wouldn't believe how many times I have skipped that step and jumped right in only to spend all day baking a cake that never rose because my baking powder was two years out of date.

Cape gooseberry clafoutis

Cape gooseberries, also known as physalis, are a curious little fruit. Not related to gooseberries at all, instead, they are related to tomatillos and are a part of the nightshade family. Their name derives from early plantings of the fruit in the Cape of Good Hope in South Africa, although the plant originated in Peru and South America. They now grow in temperate and tropical regions all over the world, and if you have never tried one but manage to find them, you're in for a real treat. They are little tropical fruit bombs that taste a bit of passionfruit and kiwi, but strangely also retain a bit of a savoury note. Their short season is different wherever they are, but usually they are found in the late winter and into spring.

Clafoutis is essentially pancake batter that has been poured over fruit and is baked in a hot oven until caramelised and set. It is a great way to showcase the excellent flavour of the gooseberry, but if you can't find them, use other fruits, such as ever-classic cherries, or perhaps apricots, peaches or pears, depending on the time of year. It's the best kind of dessert to pop in the oven as you are cleaning up from dinner and drop in the centre of the table 15–20 minutes later with a few scoops of vanilla ice cream and some spoons to dig in.

Serves 4–6

250 ml (8½ fl oz/1 cup) full-cream (whole) milk
85 g (3 oz) plain (all-purpose) flour
70 g (2½ oz) caster (superfine) sugar, plus 1 tablespoon extra
60 ml (2 fl oz/¼ cup) cream
3 eggs
1 tablespoon muscat Beaumes de Venise or other sweet wine (replace with kirsch if using cherries)
1 teaspoon vanilla extract
25 g (1 oz) soft butter, plus extra for greasing
40 cape gooseberries
1 handful toasted sliced almonds

To serve

icing (confectioners') sugar
vanilla or crème fraîche ice cream

Preheat the oven to 200°C (400°F).

To the bowl of a freestanding electric mixer fitted with the whisk attachment, add the milk, flour, sugar, cream, eggs, a pinch of salt, sweet wine and vanilla and whip on medium speed for 5 minutes until aerated. Butter a 30 cm (12 in) cast-iron frying pan or ceramic or glass baking dish with butter, then tip in the fruit. Pour the batter over the fruit, sprinkle with the extra sugar and dot with the soft butter. Place in the oven. About 10 minutes into the baking time, scatter the top of the clafoutis with almonds. Continue baking until no longer soft in the middle, about 5–10 minutes longer. Place under the grill (broiler) for a minute or two if the top needs more browning. Sprinkle with icing sugar and serve with ice cream.

Pineapple and ginger upside-down cake

I have a lot of love for upside-down cakes. They're a perfect way to bring fruit and cake together without making separate components. The way the fruit softens and caramelises and then mixes with the cake batter, which absorbs its sweet juices, is just perfection. And it looks so gorgeous. The best part is, this cake could be adapted to any fruit really: plums, nectarines, peaches, apricots, strawberries, blueberries, or, in this case, my favourite of all the upside-down cakes, pineapple. The ginger adds a spicy note that works well with the pineapple, but it doesn't overpower. The cake element for an upside-down cake is very tricky, and this one took me a while to get right. Not enough air, or support, and the cake batter mixes with the fruit juices too quickly and becomes soggy. But, thanks to the combination of baking powder, bicarbonate of soda (baking soda) and whipped egg whites, this batter lifts beautifully from the beginning, leaving a perfect, fluffy, buttery crumb.

You must start with ripe fruit. Yes, the sugar and the cooking of the fruit will improve things, but if you want this to be a fabulous cake as opposed to an alright cake, make sure the fruit is fabulous to start.

Serves 8–10

225 g (8 oz) soft butter, plus extra for greasing
200 g (7 oz) caster (superfine) sugar
4 eggs, separated
20 g (¾ oz) grated fresh ginger
1 teaspoon vanilla extract
220 g (8 oz) plain (all-purpose) flour
½ teaspoon salt
2¼ teaspoon baking powder
½ teaspoon bicarbonate of soda (baking soda)
100 ml (3½ fl oz) full-cream (whole) milk
ice cream, to serve

Topping

25 g (1 oz) butter
80 g (2¾ oz/⅓ cup) brown sugar
½ pineapple, peeled, cored, sliced and
    cut into pieces

Grease and line a round 22–25 cm (8¾–10 in) round cake tin with baking paper.

Start by making the topping. Melt the butter and brown sugar in a small saucepan until the sugar crystals have melted and the mix is bubbling. Simmer for 1 minute, then pour this molten mix into the prepared tin. Arrange the pineapple pieces on top of this caramel in any pattern you like. Try to cover as much surface area as possible so you can have a lot of fruit in each slice.

Preheat the oven to 180°C (350°F).

Cream together the butter and sugar in a freestanding electric mixer until light and fluffy, then add the egg yolks, ginger and vanilla and mix until well incorporated. Separately, whip the egg whites in a clean bowl, either by hand or with an electric whisk, until soft peaks form. Set aside.

Combine the dry ingredients in a bowl and whisk them together. Add half the dry ingredients to the butter and gently mix, then, with the machine still running, add all the milk and mix. Carefully add the remaining dry ingredients and finish mixing with a spatula. Fold in the whipped egg whites. Pour this on top of the pineapple in the tin and spread it out evenly. Gently tap the tin on your work surface to ensure the cake batter has dropped into place. Bake for 1 hour to 1 hour 15 minutes, or until a skewer inserted in the middle of the cake comes out clean. Allow to cool slightly before flipping the cake out. To flip it over, place a flat plate or cake tray on top of the tin, then, holding the plate in place with your hand, flip the cake over quickly and carefully. Once flipped, simply pull the tin off and peel back the baking paper. Serve warm or when completely cooled.

Strawberry and rhubarb crumble

A good crumble should be part of every cook's repertoire. You can use it on top of almost all fruit – apricots, plums, apples, you name it – but my all-time favourite has to be strawberries and rhubarb. It's sour, sweet, crisp, buttery and very comforting. Serve with vanilla ice cream, vanilla custard or a dollop of crème fraîche. This crumble can be made ahead and frozen. I often make double the recipe just so I can have back-up in the freezer waiting for me when I need a last-minute dessert. Bake it in a ceramic or glass baking dish that you can take straight from the oven to the table.

Serves 8–10

250 g (9 oz/1⅔ cups) hulled strawberries
1 bunch rhubarb, leaves and woody stalk trimmed off, cut into 2–3 cm (¾–1¼ in) pieces
2 tablespoons caster (superfine) sugar
1 tablespoon plain (all-purpose) flour
ice cream, custard or Crème fraîche (page 239), to serve

Crumble topping

60 g (2 oz) plain (all-purpose) flour
35 g (1¼ oz) spelt flour
30 g (1 oz) rolled oats
75 g (2¾ oz) brown sugar
50 g (1¾ oz) caster (superfine) sugar
40 g (1½ oz) slivered almonds
40 g (1½ oz) crushed walnuts
½ teaspoon salt
100 g (3½ oz) butter, diced

Preheat the oven to 170°C (340°F).

Cut the hulled strawberries in half and mix in a bowl with the rhubarb pieces, sugar and flour. Pour the mixture into a 23 cm (9 in) round or square baking dish.

To make the crumble, combine all ingredients except the butter in a bowl and, using your hands, crush the butter into the mixture until it looks crumbly, but well combined. There should not be any floury bits or large clumps of butter. Sprinkle this mixture on top of the fruit and place the dish on a baking tray. Bake for 25–35 minutes until golden and bubbly. Serve hot with ice cream, custard or crème fraîche.

Chocolate miso tart

Dark chocolate tarts made with ganache are often a bit too heavy and rich for me. This version, blended with eggs, cream and milk, gets baked, so it's more like a chocolate custard filling. To me, this makes it feel lighter while still being heavy on the chocolate flavour. The other interesting ingredient here is miso. The miso is that surprising little bit of saltiness that you wouldn't expect in a tart like this. It's best served with some cream that has been lightly whipped and lightly sweetened.

Serves 8–10

1 quantity Pâté sucrée (page 228)
120 ml (4 fl oz) full-cream (whole) milk
350 ml (12 fl oz) cream
3 tablespoons caster (superfine) sugar
35 g (1¼ oz) red miso
2 large eggs
300 g (10½ oz) 70 per cent dark chocolate, roughly chopped
lightly whipped cream, to serve

Follow the recipe to make the pastry, then blind bake it. Set aside to cool. You can make the tart shell a day in advance.

To make the chocolate filling, heat the milk, cream and sugar in a saucepan until scalding but not boiling.

Separately, mix together the miso and egg in a mixing bowl and whisk vigorously. Slowly add the hot cream mixture to the eggs, whisking constantly to avoid curdling the eggs.

Preheat the oven to 150°C (300°F).

Place the chocolate in another mixing bowl and pour the hot cream mixture on top. Stir until the chocolate has melted, then pour into a blender and blitz on high speed for 30 seconds. Strain through a fine-mesh sieve and pour into your prepared tart shell. Bake for 15–20 minutes then remove from the oven and allow to cool before serving. Serve with lightly sweetened whipped cream.

Left   Strawberry and rhubarb crumble
Right   Chocolate miso tart

Lime curd tart with toasted meringue

Somewhere between a key lime pie (a speciality from my Floridian roots) and lemon meringue pie is this delicious tart. As much as I love lemon, I do think the flavour of lime is more interesting. It has floral notes, it's more tropical and you cannot make a margarita without it. Growing up, we had a lime tree in the backyard, and I remember every night before dinner, Mom would say, 'Go and grab a lime'. I can remember running outside with bare feet, stepping on small little pebbles on the way and finally hitting the patch of grass where the tree grew. The good ones were always too high up the tree for me to reach, so I could only grab the low-hanging fruit. I learned to figure out early which limes were ripe and which were green due to youth. This is probably where my incessant need for a splash of lemon on everything came from – ironically, with a splash of lime. This tart is an excellent use of juicy, fragrant ripe limes.

Serves 8–10

1 quantity Pâté sucrée (page 228)

Lime curd

5 large egg yolks
120 g (4½ oz) caster (superfine) sugar
120 ml (4 fl oz) fresh lime juice
      (approx. 5–6 limes), plus the
      microplaned zest of the limes
120 g (4½ oz) butter, cubed

Meringue

6 large egg whites
340 g (12 oz) caster (superfine) sugar
¼ teaspoon salt
¼ teaspoon cream of tartar (optional;
      but it helps to stabilise the meringue)

Follow the recipe to make the pastry, then blind bake it. Set aside to cool.

First, make the curd. Set a heatproof bowl on top of a saucepan of simmering water. Make sure the bottom of the bowl does not touch the water. In that bowl, off the heat, whisk together the egg yolks, sugar and lime zest until light and fluffy, about 3 minutes. Add the lime juice and a pinch of salt and mix to combine. Place the bowl over the saucepan of water and whisk constantly until the mixture has reached 79°C (174°F) on a cooking thermometer and is nice and thick. Immediately pass the curd through a fine-mesh sieve into a bowl. Add the butter and whisk until the butter has fully melted. Place a piece of plastic wrap directly on top of the curd and refrigerate to chill slightly. Once cool to the touch, mix the curd until smooth again and pour it into the pre-baked pastry case. Refrigerate to set and cool, about 2–3 hours.

To make the meringue, combine the egg whites, sugar, salt and cream of tartar in the heatproof bowl of a freestanding electric mixer. Place the bowl over a saucepan of simmering water, much like you did with the curd, and use a spatula to mix and stir until a thermometer inserted directly in the whites reads 70°C (158°F). This should take about 10 minutes. Once you hit that temperature, transfer the bowl to the machine fitted with the whisk attachment. Whip on high speed until the whites are voluminous and glossy. This takes about 5 minutes. Transfer the meringue into a piping (icing) bag.

Pipe the meringue on top of the set tart in whatever pattern you like. Use a blow torn or the grill (broiler) to toast the meringue before cutting slices and serving.

Strawberry and brown sugar galette

For the base of this strawberry galette, I suggest a bit of brown sugar cookie-like batter to bake the strawberries on. It adds a really lovely chewy and gooey characteristic to this delicious warm-weather galette.

Serves 8–10

1 quantity Flaky dough (page 227)
300 ml (10 fl oz) sweetened whipped cream mixed with 150 ml (5 fl oz) Crème fraîche (page 239) or vanilla ice cream
500 g (1 lb 2 oz/3⅓ cups) strawberries
2 tablespoons raw (demerara) sugar

Cookie dough

60 g (2 fl oz/¼ cup) melted butter
110 g (4 oz) brown sugar
1 egg
1 teaspoon vanilla extract
100 g (3½ oz/⅔ cup) plain (all-purpose) flour
¼ teaspoon bicarbonate of soda (baking soda)
¼ teaspoon salt

Egg wash

1 beaten egg plus 1 tablespoon water

First, roll out your flaky dough as thinly as possible and keep it cold in the fridge on a piece of baking paper.

Preheat the oven to 220°C (430°F) with a baking stone on the middle rack.

To make the cookie dough, combine the butter and sugar in a bowl and beat in the egg by hand using a wooden spoon. We're not creaming the butter and sugar like you would for a cake; just mixing it to create a base for the fruit. Add the vanilla and the remaining dry ingredients and mix just enough to combine. Spread the cookie dough out over the base of the pastry, but leave a 3–4 cm (1¼–1½ in) edge.

Prepare your egg wash by combining the egg and water in a small bowl. Set aside. Combine the whipped cream and crème fraîche and set aside.

Slice your strawberries thinly and place them on top of the filling in concentric circles, starting from the outside until you reach the centre. Fold the edges over the fruit to create a crust. Brush the crust with the egg wash and sprinkle with half the raw sugar. Sprinkle the other tablespoon of sugar on the strawberries. Lift the galette up with the baking paper and carefully place it directly on the preheated baking stone in the oven. Bake for 45 minutes to 1 hour, giving it a few turns every now and then so that it caramelises evenly. Pull it out onto a flat, overturned tray by carefully pulling the baking paper towards you and sliding the galette onto the tray. Now slide it onto a cooling rack and pull the baking paper out from underneath so it cools and remains crunchy.

Serve warm or at room temperature with a dollop of the prepared cream mixture.

Mom's flan with poached cherries

If you're asking a Cuban who invented flan, they will say they did, but the truth is, the origins of flan are in Europe. It is a baked custard and burnt sugar dessert that you will find throughout South America and the Caribbean thanks to Spanish colonisation. To Cubans, though, this dessert is particularly important and they take it seriously. To the extent that every family has their version. Whole eggs versus egg yolks, or a combination of the two? Milk and cream, or just milk or sweetened condensed milk plus evaporated milk? My mom's recipe included sweetened condensed and evaporated milk because, aside from some eggs, this would have been the most economical and readily available option. You see, when my family came to the United States as immigrants, they came with almost nothing. It was a struggle to survive and put food on the table, but they always had sugar; it was in their blood.

My mom's family grew and processed sugar cane into sugar. It was the family business. Real sugar went in the coffee and there was almost certainly a dessert every night, even in the toughest of times. They all had a sweet tooth, Mom included. She loved a good dessert and this flan is her gift to me. I've made the tiniest of amendments because I'm a chef and I can't help it, but this recipe comes from her and it will always be a flavour of home that I cherish: simple ingredients, prepared with a bit of love and patience. You do have to chill this overnight, after all.

Serve with poached cherries or completely ungarnished; it's perfect on its own.

Serves 8–10

150 g (5½ oz) caster (superfine) sugar
1 × 375 ml (12½ fl oz/1½ cups) tin evaporated milk
1 × 355 ml (12 fl oz) tin sweetened
    condensed milk
120 ml (4 fl oz) full-cream (whole) milk
2 eggs, plus 5 egg yolks
2 teaspoons vanilla extract

Poached cherries

100 g (3½ oz) caster (superfine) sugar
2 strips lemon peel
1 vanilla bean, split
400 g (14 oz) sour or sweet fresh cherries;
    see Note (if using sweet cherries, add the
    juice of 1 lemon to the poaching liquid)

Note

You can leave the cherries unpitted, just be sure to warn your guests.

Preheat the oven to 150°C (300°F) and boil a full kettle of water.

Melt the sugar in a non-stick frying pan over a medium heat until it turns a dark amber colour. Use a wooden spoon to mix it once it starts caramelising to ensure that it all melts evenly. Immediately pour the caramel into the base of a non-stick loaf (bar) tin. Whisk together the remaining ingredients and a pinch of salt in a bowl, then pour the custard through a fine-mesh sieve directly onto the caramel. Cover the tin with aluminium foil and place it inside a larger baking dish. Place the dish in the oven, then pour in enough boiling water to come halfway up the side of the loaf tin. Bake for 1 hour and 20 minutes. At this point, check the texture: it should still be quite wobbly, but not liquid. If it is still liquid in the centre, continue cooking for another 15–20 minutes. Remove from the oven and allow to cool in the water bath. Once cooled, refrigerate, still covered, overnight.

To make the poached cherries, combine the sugar, lemon peel, vanilla bean, 200 ml (7 fl oz) water and a pinch of salt in a saucepan and bring to a simmer on the stove. Pit your cherries using a cherry pitter, or push them out using a metal straw. Add the cherries to the pot and simmer until they are soft but not bursting, about 5 minutes. Set aside until ready to serve.

To unmould, cut around the sides of the custard and invert onto a flat plate. Cut slices and serve with or without the poached cherries.

A simple apple galette

Not only is this my favourite rendition of apple in tart form, but what makes it even more perfect is that the entire apple gets used. Cores and skins are cooked into a syrup that glazes the finished tart and gives you the most beautiful sheen, which also tastes like apple. If you use a different fruit for this recipe, simply glaze with melted fruit jam for the same effect.

Try and find unwaxed, new-season apples for this recipe. My absolute favourite variety is one called crimson snow, and not just because of its romantic name. It's fragrant, sweet and sour, and its skins are the most beautiful colour I have ever seen in an apple: an almost purple-pink crimson, as the name suggests. Use your favourite variety, or the best, freshest apple you can find here.

You can also swap out the apples for plums, peaches, apricots, nectarines, figs or whatever sliceable fruit you like. Replace the calvados with a liqueur flavoured with whatever fruit you're using, such as kirsch for cherries.

Serves 8–10

1 quantity Flaky dough (page 227)
1 kg (2 lb 3 oz) apples of your choice
½ tablespoon plain (all-purpose) flour
20 g (¾ oz) butter
1 tablespoon lemon juice
15 g (½ oz) caster (superfine) sugar,
    plus 1 tablespoon extra
1 tablespoon calvados (optional)
1 egg, beaten with a splash of cream,
    full-cream (whole) milk or water
ice cream, Crème fraîche (page 239) or lightly
    whipped cream, to serve

Apple peel glaze

50 g (1¾ oz) caster (superfine) sugar

Follow the recipe to make the dough, then roll it out into a circular shape about 2 mm (⅛ in) thick and place it on a piece of baking paper. Refrigerate.

Preheat the oven to 200°C (400°F) and place a baking stone on the middle shelf.

Next, prepare your apples by peeling, quartering and coring them. Place the peels and cores in a small saucepan with the sugar for the apple glaze. Add 300 ml (10 fl oz) water, cover with a lid and simmer over a medium heat for 15 minutes.

Take your apple quarters and cut each quarter into 6–8 thin slices. Keep the slices together so you can arrange them nicely on the dough.

Sprinkle the prepared dough with the flour then spread it out evenly over the base using your hand. Arrange the apple slices on top in whatever pattern looks nicest to you. Concentric circles always look good, starting from the outside in, making sure you tightly fill the space with fruit. (It will shrink and move as it cooks, so make sure you use plenty.) Leave a 2 cm (¾ in) edge.

Melt the butter and mix in the lemon juice, sugar and calvados, if using. Spoon this mixture over the top of the apples only. Fold the edge of the dough up around the fruit. Brush the egg mixture over the folded edge of dough and sprinkle with the extra sugar. Try to land as much sugar as possible directly on the crust and as little as possible on the baking paper.

By this point, your apple peel glaze should be ready. Strain it into a clean saucepan and put it back on the stove to simmer and reduce until thickened and 'glazy'. You only need about a tablespoon or so.

Continued >

Transfer the galette to the oven, sliding it onto the baking stone using the baking paper. Immediately reduce the oven temperature to 180°C (350°F) and bake for 30 minutes. After 30 minutes, increase the temperature to 200°C (400°F) and continue baking for 20–30 minutes until the crust is beautifully golden and the apples are browned on the edges. At this stage, flip a baking tray upside down and carefully pull the galette onto the baking tray using the baking paper. Transfer to a wire rack to cool and, finally, pull the baking paper out from underneath. If you leave the paper underneath, the base of the galette will steam and go soft.

When cooled but still slightly warm, brush your apple glaze on top of the apples. Enjoy with ice cream, crème fraîche, lightly whipped cream or just on its own.

Chocolate torte
with baked plums

This flourless chocolate cake is a fairly simple combination of melted chocolate, butter, sugar, eggs and vanilla. Egg yolks and whites get whipped separately and folded into the melted chocolate, creating a light and airy dessert. This is a staple recipe that you can bring out time and time again. I love to pair it with sweet and sour plums, but feel free to use the fruit of your choice or perhaps fresh nuts and caramel instead.

Serves 8–10

225 g (8 oz) 70 per cent or higher
    dark chocolate
220 g (8 oz) butter, plus extra for greasing
1 teaspoon vanilla extract
8 eggs, separated
200 g (7 oz) caster (superfine) sugar
300 ml (10 fl oz) cream, lightly whipped, to serve

Plums

1 kg (2 lb 3 oz) juicy, ripe plums, halved and
    stones removed
30 g (1 oz) butter, melted
2 tablespoons caster (superfine) sugar

Grease and line a 28 cm (11 in) round cake tin.

Combine the chocolate and butter in a heatproof bowl set over a saucepan of simmering water and melt, then set aside and allow to cool slightly. Once cooled, mix in the vanilla.

In a separate bowl, whisk the egg yolks and half the sugar until lightened and beginning to form ribbons.

In another bowl, whisk the egg whites with a pinch of salt until they become foamy, then gradually add the remaining sugar, little by little, while continuing to whisk. This is done easily in a freestanding electric mixer fitted with the whisk attachment.

Preheat the oven to 170°C (340°F).

Fold the whipped egg yolks into the melted chocolate, then fold in the whites in three stages. Stop folding when there are no more visible white streaks. Pour the mixture into your tin and bake for 40–50 minutes, or until the middle is no longer wobbly when tested with a skewer. Remove from the oven and allow to cool. Increase the oven temperature to 190°C (375°F).

To prepare the plums, place them in a baking dish lined with baking paper. Pour the melted butter over the top, then sprinkle with the sugar. Bake for 15–20 minutes, then remove from the oven and allow to cool slightly.

Serve slices of torte with a bit of lightly whipped cream and warm roasted plums.

Ice creams

The world of ice creams is vast. If you can imagine a combination, someone has probably made it. I call most frozen desserts an ice cream, but, to be specific, there are a few categories that tell you a bit about what's in them, and those are: gelatos, custard ice creams, ice milks, frozen yoghurts, sherbets and sorbets. A quick summary is this: custard ice creams are made with egg yolks and, no surprise, are made into a custard before freezing. Gelato is Italian in origin and is similar to a custard ice cream, except that it tends to use milk instead of cream, therefore it has less fat and is often served at a warmer temperature, so it feels softer. Ice milks are basically ice creams made with milk instead of cream, and no eggs. Frozen yoghurts contain no eggs and are made entirely with yoghurt or yoghurt mixed with cream or milk. Sherbets are often fruit based, more like a sorbet without any eggs, but will often contain some milk. A sorbet has no dairy or eggs. And then, of course, there are a few anomalies in between.

Ice cream is probably the only thing that I make at home that requires a specific piece of equipment. I'm sure some more creative people might have cracked it, but I have not yet figured out a way to make good ice cream without an ice-cream maker. Yes, it's probably a lot easier to buy ice cream, but I think it is one of the best desserts that uses ripe fruit in the summer and I happen to crave ice cream in the winter too, so I make it all year round. Show me someone who would fail to be impressed by homemade ice cream and I'll stop making it at home. Until then, I'll carry on.

The one thing I always do with frozen desserts is add a little splash of the appropriate alcohol to the base before freezing. Sometimes you want a boozy ice cream, but most of the time you won't taste it and it becomes more of a background flavour. You see, alcohol lowers the freezing point below zero, making it softer and more scoopable straight from the freezer, because who wants to wait for tempering ice cream? Not me. On that note, I am told this is not appropriate for children, so leave out the alcohol if you're making it for kids.

Here are a couple of my favourite homemade variations.

Blueberry frozen yoghurt

This frozen yoghurt is striking in its purple-blue colour, which alone will get everyone excited to taste it. A few people I made this for proclaimed it to be 'the best ice cream they ever had'. I'll take that compliment!

Makes 800 ml (27 fl oz)/Serves 6–8

250 g (9 oz) fresh blueberries
190 g (6½ oz) caster (superfine) sugar
230 ml (8 fl oz) cream
230 g (8 oz) Yoghurt (page 237), or store-bought
1 tablespoon lemon juice
1 tablespoon kirsch
sliced mango, whipped cream and angel food cake,
    to serve

Combine the blueberries, sugar, two pinches of salt and 2 tablespoons water in a small saucepan and bring to a simmer. Simmer until the sugar has dissolved and the blueberries have burst. Pass through a fine-mesh sieve to remove any skins. Add the remaining ingredients, whisk until smooth, and freeze according to the ice-cream maker's instructions.

I love to serve this frozen yoghurt with fresh mango slices, whipped cream and angel food cake.

Custard apple and kaffir lime ice cream

A custard apple is a fairly unusual fruit, but it is so exciting when you find them and can use ripe ones. They are native to South and Central America, but now grow in Australia and in North America too. They are actually a hybrid of cherimoya fruit and sugar apples, although either of those could be used in the same way if you happen to find them. They should be soft to the touch, but not collapsing under your thumb. I serve this ice cream on its own because it is so unusual and because it is a great joy to taste something so exotic.

Makes 800 ml (27 fl oz)/Serves 6–8

4 ripe custard apples
500 ml (17 fl oz/2 cups) cream
150 g (5½ oz) caster (superfine) sugar
4 kaffir lime leaves, crushed in a mortar and pestle

Peel your custard apples using a small paring knife, then place the apple pulp, seeds and all, in a stainless-steel or other heatproof bowl and cover super tightly with plastic wrap. Make a rope of plastic wrap and tie it around the edge of the bowl to ensure no steam will escape.

Place the bowl over a saucepan of simmering water, like a bain-marie. Ensure the bowl fits snugly into the saucepan and doesn't overhang the sides of the pan too much. Steam for 20 minutes, then push the pulp through a fine-mesh sieve. Discard the remaining pulp and seeds. Mix in the cream, sugar and crushed kaffir leaves and whisk to dissolve the sugar. Add a few pinches of salt at this stage. Chill for several hours before straining once more through a fine-mesh sieve, then freeze according to your ice-cream maker's instructions.

Almond and cherry custard ice cream

This is a good base recipe for any ice cream flavour you can dream up. Omit the almonds and cherries and replace with chunks of ripe peach, or fresh crushed strawberries, or toasted hazelnuts and Frangelico, or even drizzle some melted chocolate in at the last minute to create a chocolate chip ice cream. Do whatever takes your fancy.

Makes 1 litre (34 fl oz/4 cups)/Serves 8

420 ml (14 fl oz) full-cream (whole) milk
500 ml (17 fl oz/2 cups) cream
220 g (8 oz) caster (superfine) sugar
4 large egg yolks
1 teaspoon vanilla extract
1 teaspoon almond extract
2 tablespoons amaretto or kirsch
65 g (2¼ oz) toasted slivered almonds
400 g (14 oz) fresh pitted or frozen sour cherries

Combine the milk, half the cream, the sugar and a pinch of salt in a saucepan over a medium–low heat. Warm until scalded and small bubbles appear on the edge of the pan.

To a bowl, add the remaining cream. Set a fine-mesh sieve on top of the bowl, then set aside.

Place the egg yolks in a mixing bowl and whisk until smooth. When your milk mixture has scalded, begin ladling it into the eggs while still hot, whisking with the opposite hand. Pour the whole mixture back into the pan and cook over a low heat, stirring continuously with a rubber spatula and making sure to scrape the bottom and side of the pan. When the mixture is visibly thickened and coats the back of a spoon (just before it begins to simmer and curdle the eggs), pour it through the sieve into the bowl with the cream to stop the cooking process. Mix to combine, then add the vanilla, almond extract and alcohol. Refrigerate until cold, then freeze according to your ice-cream maker's instructions. Add the nuts and cherries to the ice cream about 5 minutes before it has finished churning in the machine.

See image on page 218.

Opposite Almond and cherry custard ice cream (page 217)

Citrus and chocolate mousse trifle

In the southern hemisphere, there aren't really any holidays in the winter months that warrant this level of decadence, but do you really need a special occasion to make a trifle? No! I created this recipe for a dear friend's birthday and, even though I was only serving three people, I divided up the rest for each to take home and it was happily shared.

Trifles can feel like a lot of steps, and a lot of mixing bowls, but they are easy to manage as the whole thing can be made and assembled a day ahead. In fact, that is encouraged. That time in the fridge allows the cake to absorb the custard and become a lovely sponge.

As a side note, dulcey is a type of caramelised white chocolate made by Valrhona, which tastes like dulce de leche and biscuits. If you don't have access to that, use a good 60–70 per cent dark chocolate that you like. Or, if you simply prefer dark chocolate, go for that from the start. Also, swap the poached kumquats for orange marmalade if you can't find them.

One last note: all of the components are delicious on their own, so feel free to use each of these recipes for other applications or desserts.

Serves 12–14

Sponge cake

30 g (1 oz) butter, plus extra for greasing
60 ml (2 fl oz/¼ cup) full-cream (whole) milk
1 teaspoon vanilla extract
100 g (3½ oz/⅔ cup) plain (all-purpose) flour, plus extra for dusting
1 teaspoon baking powder
¼ teaspoon salt
35 g (1¼ oz) cocoa powder
3 eggs plus 3 egg yolks
170 g (6 oz/¾ cup) caster (superfine) sugar

Poached kumquat

150 g (5½ oz) whole kumquats
150 g (5½ oz) sugar

Continued >

Start by baking your cakes. Preheat the oven to 175°C (345°F) and set a rack in the middle of the oven. Grease and flour two 21 cm (8¼ in) round cake tins and place a round of baking paper in the bases. Heat the milk and butter in a small saucepan over a low heat until the butter has just melted, then add the vanilla, set aside and keep warm.

Combine the flour, baking powder, salt and cocoa powder in a mixing bowl and whisk a few times to combine and get rid of any lumps.

In the bowl of a freestanding electric mixer fitted with the whisk attachment, whip your eggs and yolks with the sugar on high speed until ribbons form. The eggs should have significantly lightened in colour, tripled in size and, when you pull the whisk out of the mixture, it should briefly leave a ribbon on the surface before falling into the mixture.

Fold one-third of the egg mixture into the dry ingredients, then alternate adding the warm butter and milk mixture and the egg mixture to the dry ingredients until everything is light, fluffy and combined. Folding gently is key here; you want as much air in the mixture as possible. Divide the batter evenly between the prepared tins and bake for 30 minutes until the cakes are set, springy and bouncy, and a skewer inserted in the middle comes out clean. Remove from the oven and allow to cool in the tins on a wire rack.

Next, poach your kumquats. This can be done days in advance and refrigerated. Slice the kumquats, skin and all, as thinly and evenly as possible, and remove any seeds. Combine the sugar with 150 ml (5 fl oz) water in a small saucepan and bring to the boil. Add the kumquat and poach gently over a medium heat for 7–10 minutes until the fruit is slightly more tender and softened. Set aside to cool in the liquid.

Continued >

Custard

30 g (1 oz) cornflour (cornstarch)
4 egg yolks
100 g (3½ oz) sugar
500 ml (17 fl oz/2 cups) full-cream (whole) milk
1 vanilla bean, split and seeds scraped
2 tablespoons Cointreau
150 ml (5 fl oz) cream

Chocolate mousse

160 g (5½ oz) Valrhona dulcey chocolate
    (or use 60–70 per cent dark chocolate
    with 40 g/1½ oz caster/superfine sugar),
    roughly chopped
grated zest of ½ orange
2 eggs, separated
180 ml (6 fl oz) cream

To assemble

80 ml (2½ fl oz/⅓ cup) Cointreau
400 ml (13½ fl oz) cream
2 tablespoons caster (superfine) sugar
60 g (2 oz) cacao nibs
zest of ½ orange

For your custard, combine the cornflour, egg yolks and sugar in a mixing bowl and whisk until lightened and the sugar has dissolved. At the same time, heat your milk, vanilla bean and a pinch of salt in a saucepan over a medium–low heat. Stir every so often with a spatula to make sure the bottom isn't catching. Once small bubbles appear around the edge of the pan, the milk is hot enough. Begin ladling a small amount of the hot milk mixture into the eggs while whisking at the same time. Once you have ladled about half the milk into the eggs, pour everything back into the saucepan. Place over a low heat and stir with a spatula until the mixture is thickened and bubbling. Once it is bubbling, allow it to bubble for another full minute. The cornflour doesn't activate until it has reached a certain temperature, and don't worry about the eggs curdling either; the starch deactivates the proteins in the eggs that coagulate at high temperatures. Remove the vanilla bean, as it should have done its job by now, and pour the mixture through a fine-mesh sieve into another bowl. At this stage, add the Cointreau and whisk to combine. Cover the bowl with a piece of baking paper so a skin doesn't form as the custard cools. Set aside. Once cooled, lightly whip the cream in another bowl and fold this into the custard. Transfer the mixture to piping (icing) bags, or just cover with plastic wrap and refrigerate until ready to use.

To prepare the mousse, heat the chocolate with the orange zest in a heatproof bowl set over a saucepan of simmering water. Once melted, set aside.

In one bowl, whip your egg yolks by hand until light and fluffy. In another bowl, whip the whites to soft peaks. If using dark chocolate, add the extra sugar to your egg whites during the whipping process. The sugar will dissolve and create more stability in the mix if added towards the middle instead of at the beginning.

To put everything together, fold the yolks into the chocolate, followed by the whites. Once you have folded in the whites, whip the cold cream to soft peaks in the same bowl used for the egg whites. Finally, fold this into the chocolate mix gently and set aside. For ease, I suggest putting the mousse into a piping bag for assembling the trifle later, but it's not absolutely necessary.

To assemble, spoon one-third of the custard into the bottom of a trifle bowl. Next, add a layer of cake (aim to use a trifle dish the same diameter as your cakes, but if the size isn't quite right, just break up the cake and add it in one tight layer). Spoon half the Cointreau onto the cake, then add another one-third of the custard. Sprinkle half the poached kumquat on top of this. Next, pipe on a layer of mousse, starting from the outside working your way in. Repeat the layers with the remaining cake, Cointreau, custard, kumquats and mousse. At this stage, cover the bowl with plastic wrap and refrigerate until you're ready to serve. An hour before you want to serve your trifle, remove it from the fridge to allow the mousse to soften slightly.

For the final steps, whip the cream with the sugar until soft peaks form. Pour that over the trifle and sprinkle the top with cacao nibs and orange zest. Serve immediately.

Buckwheat, brown butter, almond and apple cake

Before summer is over, the apples start to arrive. It always strikes me as premature; I'm not ready to give up the long sunny days just yet! But, sure enough, their arrival means the crisp air is just around the corner. And then, almost entirely in sync, I start to crave a good apple cake. Something to have with a cup of coffee in the morning, with afternoon tea, or served warm with some vanilla crème anglaise as a luxurious finish to an autumnal dinner party. It's just delicious. Fragrant with warm spices, dark from the brown sugar and buckwheat, and just a little bit gooey. Gluten-free but not intentionally so; I just love how buckwheat and apples complement each other. I think this will become a seasonal favourite of yours, too. Use an apple of your choice. Personally, I think sweeter as opposed to sour varieties work better here, but it works either way.

Serves 8–10

150 g (5½ oz) butter, plus extra for greasing
200 g (7 oz) dark brown or muscovado sugar
165 ml (5½ fl oz) full-cream (whole) milk
2 teaspoons vanilla extract
1 teaspoon apple-cider vinegar
1 egg
200 g (7 oz) light buckwheat flour
100 g (3½ oz/1 cup) almond meal (ground almonds)
1 teaspoon ground cinnamon
¼ teaspoon ground cloves
¼ teaspoon ground allspice
⅛ teaspoon ground nutmeg
¼ teaspoon fine sea salt
1½ teaspoons bicarbonate of soda (baking soda)
400 g (14 oz) apples, peeled, cored and diced into 2 cm (¾ in) pieces, plus 2 apples, peeled, cored and thinly sliced

Preheat the oven to 175°C (345°F) with a rack in the middle of the oven. Grease a 27 cm (10¾ in) round cake tin, then cut a piece of baking paper to fit the base of the tin and line it. Set aside.

Melt the butter in a small, tall-sided saucepan over a medium heat until it turns brown. Be careful when doing this, as the butter will bubble and rise over the edges towards the end. It's ready when golden in colour and the bubbles on top have turned into more of a foam. It should also smell nutty and delicious. Set aside to cool.

Mix the sugar, milk, vanilla, vinegar and egg in a large bowl. Whisk in the cooled brown butter (scrape all the brown bits into the bowl) and mix until combined.

In another bowl, mix together the dry ingredients, then, all at once, pour onto the wet ingredients and mix just enough to combine – a few small lumps are OK. Add your diced apples and mix with a spatula to combine. The mixture will be thick, so pour and spread it into the tin, then arrange the sliced apples on the surface in a circular pattern. Bake for 50 minutes to 1 hour 15 minutes until a skewer inserted in the middle of the cake comes out clean.

III.
Projects

1   Pastry 226

2   Bread 230

3   Dairy 236

4   Meat 240

5   Pickles 246

Pastry

Making good pastry requires some attention. It is so elegant in its simplicity, yet it gives a lot of people trouble. I think because it's so simple it deceives people into thinking it is easy, so they rush through it and perhaps ignore certain points about temperature or handling. Simple does not necessarily mean quick or straightforward. Pastry might only have a few ingredients, but there are many variables. I've tried to explain in detail two of my most useful pastry recipes. One is for more rustic flaky galettes or pies, and the other is for lining tart moulds; it's crisp and short. Read the recipes in full before you begin and pay attention to the details because they make all the difference.

Flaky dough

Makes 345 g (12 oz),
enough for 8–10 slices

65–80 ml (2¼–2½ fl oz)
    cold water
100 g (3½ oz) cold butter
170 g (6 oz) plain (all-purpose)
    flour, plus extra
    for dusting
1 teaspoon caster
    (superfine) sugar
½ teaspoon salt
1 egg, beaten with a splash
    of cream, full-cream
    (whole) milk or water

The key to making good dough is to keep everything super, super cold. I usually measure out my water first and put it in the freezer. I will also cut my butter and just toss with the dry ingredients and put that bowl in the freezer too for about 5 minutes. You'll also find what brand of butter works for you. A butter with a higher fat-to-liquid ratio is best, because it stays super hard even in warmer temperatures.

Once everything is very cold, begin to crumble the butter into the flour using your fingertips. Work the butter into the flour until you have bean-sized lumps. Begin to rub the dough between the palms of your hands as if trying to wipe your hands off. This is what creates those thin sheets of butter that form flaky layers. Add half the cold water and mix with your hands. Try not to stretch or knead the dough; you just want it to come together. At this stage, I like to dump it onto a bench so I can press the dough together. If it comes together easily without any dry, floury spots, then it has enough water. If there are some powdery, dry clumps, add a bit more water until everything comes together. Wrap the dough in plastic wrap and press it into a disc. Rub the outside of the plastic wrap to create a smooth edge (this will help get a more even circle when rolling it out). Refrigerate to cool and rest for at least 30 minutes.

If you have a marble benchtop, that is ideal for rolling out pastry as it stays cold. A wooden bench has the advantage of not being sticky. Whatever you have, try to find a space in your kitchen with enough flat surface to give you room to move. When the dough is still cold, but has warmed enough to be slightly pliable, dust it with flour. Roll the dough out from the centre in all directions, trying to keep the round shape as much as possible. I purposely wrote this recipe to give you enough extra dough so that you can roll it out wider than you need to then cut a neat round of dough, so don't worry about the edges being cracked or uneven. Continue rolling and rotating the dough to ensure it doesn't stick, until it reaches a diameter of 33 cm (13 in) and a thickness of 2 mm (⅛ in). Use a little extra flour when rolling to prevent it sticking, but don't throw handfuls of flour at it. Trim the edges so you are left with a neat circle (but not too perfect). Gently roll the dough up on a rolling pin and place it on a piece of baking paper. Transfer the baking paper and dough to a round pizza pan. If you don't have a pizza pan, you'll just lift the baking paper straight onto a baking stone when ready to bake. This is when you will add your toppings.

As far as rolling up the edges, you can make flat folds or elaborate, decorative edges, but my preferred fold is a pretty crimp, which I always think makes the humble galette look much more professional, but if that's not your vibe, make it rustic.

To make said crimp, start at any point along the edge and fold a small section over itself to create a crust about 2 cm (¾ in) wide (I like a thick crust). Continue folding the dough over on itself to create a pretty fold. If you don't want to bake the galette straight away, you can refrigerate it for up to 24 hours at this point, and a bit of chill time is preferred to help firm up the dough. Once you've added the topping, bake within the next few hours to prevent the crust from getting soggy.

You want to bake this in a hot oven, and by hot I mean 200–220°C (400–430°F). This is what gives you that gorgeous deep golden and caramelised crust. Before going into the oven, brush the edge with the egg wash. Transfer the galette to the oven, either on the pizza pan on top of the baking stone, or place the galette, still on its baking paper, directly on the stone. Drop the oven temperature to 180°C (350°F) and bake for 30 minutes. If you are using a pizza pan, carefully hold the pan with an oven mitt or tea towel (dish towel) and, holding the baking paper on the opposite side, slide the galette off the tray and place it directly on the baking stone. Increase the oven temperature to 200°C (400°F) and continue baking for 20–30 minutes until the crust and filling are golden. Once baked, flip a baking tray upside down and pull your galette, using the baking paper, off the stone and onto the tray. Transfer to a wire rack to cool and, finally, pull the baking paper out from underneath the galette. If you leave the baking paper underneath, the crust will steam and the pastry won't be crisp.

Note

You can also make the dough and freeze it, but you'll need to defrost it overnight in the fridge before you use it.

Equipment

Baking stone, rolling pin

Pâté sucrée (sweet pastry)

Pâté sucrée is the pastry used for fluted tarts, usually filled with custard, chocolate ganache or citrus curd. Unlike the galette dough, you need to blind-bake this pastry, weighed down with baking weights, without the filling, to partially cook it before filling and baking again.

For years, this recipe has been my nemesis. I have really, really struggled with it and made every mistake known to man. Not just with the pastry itself, but the shaping of it in the tart mould too. I used to watch pastry chefs do it and, frustratingly, everyone did it slightly differently. They would say: you must do this and you must do that, but each time, I did not achieve a thin, tender, sweet crust that unmoulded perfectly. Nightmare. However, I persisted and, instead, came up with my own way after a lot of trial and error, mostly error.

Some recipes tell you to incorporate the butter into the flour using a food processor, or cube and crumble it in, like you would with galette dough. My issue with this method is that it has weak spots: the butter melts, leading to cracking and leaking filling. My answer to this? Cream the butter and sugar together like you would for a cookie dough.

Some recipes suggest using icing (confectioners') sugar instead of caster (superfine) sugar. This works in recipes that tell you to cut the butter into the dough, but because I favour the creaming method, I steer clear of it here.

My next issue is rolling and shaping the pastry. Too much flour when rolling, and you'll have a dry crust. Too little and the pastry is so short it will crumble when you try to lift it. Simply lifting the pastry up and placing it in the tart mould never seems to work for me. Instead, I find rolling it out between two sheets of baking paper is essential to a successful transfer. Use extra-wide baking paper for this; the regular stuff just isn't big enough. The other method suggested for shaping a tart is pressing the dough in, and this has never worked for me either. It ends up too thick and doesn't have the delicate edges we associate with sucrée. Another mistake I've made is not chilling the dough twice, leading to shrinkage. And another is trimming the excess dough before baking. You must chill the pastry both before and after shaping it, and always leave 1–2 cm (½–¾ in) of excess to allow for shrinkage while baking. I know it's painful, but resist the urge to neaten it up until it's almost finished baking, and do it with a small serrated knife for a clean edge.

Unfortunately, I do ask that you make this with a freestanding electric mixer. You can push yourself to exhaustion perfectly creaming the butter and sugar by hand, but if you're someone who loves baking, then I bet you already have a good mixer.

Makes approx. 500 g
(1 lb 2 oz), enough for
8–10 slices

230 g (8 oz) unsalted butter
170 g (6 oz/¾ cup) caster
    (superfine) sugar
1 egg plus 1 egg yolk, at room
    temperature
1 tablespoon vanilla extract
2 teaspoons salt
35 ml (1¼ fl oz) cream
500 g (1 lb 2 oz/3⅓ cups)
    plain (all-purpose) flour

Bring your butter to just below room temperature, so it's cool to the touch but pliable. Drop it into the bowl of a freestanding electric mixer fitted with the paddle attachment. (If you have one of those fancy paddles with rubber sides that scrapes the edges, use that one.) Add the sugar and cream together on a medium–high speed for 5 minutes. Stop the machine and scrape down the sides a couple of times during the 5 minutes. Next, add the eggs and vanilla and beat until combined. Add the salt, cream and flour and beat on low speed to incorporate so the flour doesn't fly everywhere. When it just comes together, dump it onto your bench. Divide it into two equal balls, flatten into discs and wrap tightly in plastic wrap. Refrigerate for at least 2 hours, or freeze if not using that day. Allow to defrost in the fridge overnight.

If you're making individual tartlets, divide the pastry into 6–8 pieces, depending on the size of your moulds. From here, the instructions are the same whether you're making one tart or multiple small ones.

Roll the dough out between two pieces of baking paper until it is 2 mm (⅛ in) thick. Remove the top sheet of baking paper, then flip the dough onto a tart mould with a removable base. Pull off the other sheet of baking paper and gently push the pastry into the creases of the tin. If any pastry snaps off, simply press it back into the gaps until the tin is completely covered and you have a bit of excess hanging off the side. If you have too much excess, simply trim with scissors, but leave enough to allow for shrinkage during baking. Place the tin on a baking tray and put it in the fridge or freezer to chill for 1 hour. This second chilling stage will prevent the pastry from shrinking too much.

Preheat the oven to 175°C (345°F) and set an oven rack in the lower third of the oven with a baking stone on top.

Remove your pastry from the fridge and place a piece of baking paper on top. Fill the tart with baking weights or dried beans or rice. Bake for 30 minutes until the edges are just beginning to brown. Remove the weights and baking paper and return the tart to the oven for another 10–20 minutes, until the base and side are also golden. If the edges are brown but the base is still slightly undercooked, cover the edges with aluminium foil and continue to bake until the base is cooked. Remember the crust will continue baking once it's out of the oven, so remove it when it's one shade lighter than you want it to be.

Allow it to cool completely before unmoulding the crust onto your display plate. Fill with pastry cream and fresh fruit, or with lemon or lime curd, and serve it straight away. My chocolate miso filling (see page 204) is also great here, though note that it requires some extra baking.

Equipment

Electric mixer with paddle attachment, fluted tart tin, rolling pin

Pastry

Bread

Making fresh breads has to be one of the most rewarding home-cooking projects. I have baked many sourdough loaves at home, and I love the entire process, but I don't always have a consistent enough schedule to make that happen. The following breads use dried yeast and are therefore a little less time consuming. They are simple, yet are absolute crowd pleasers, and are easy to make.

Potato rolls

Potato rolls are, for me, the ultimate dinner roll, and they're a pretty easy entry into the world of breadmaking. This isn't one of those overnight, complex-flavoured sourdoughs; it's a simple, soft, moist and slightly sweet roll that can be made in a few hours. They're a Thanksgiving staple at my house, and I'm sure they will become an Aussie barbecue staple. They're a real crowd pleaser and great for a sandwich the next day. Choose a potato with yellow, starchy flesh, such as Dutch cream or Yukon gold.

I have given instructions for making this recipe with a freestanding electric mixer with a dough hook, but if you don't have a machine, do it by hand. It takes a little bit longer, but you will be able to feel the dough and better understand what 'knead until it comes together' or 'mix until fully incorporated and not sticky' means. These are all principles that will help you in making other types of bread.

Put the whole, cleaned potatoes into a pot of cold salted water and bring to the boil. Cook until tender (a knife inserted in the centre of a potato should come out easily). Remove the potatoes but reserve 115 ml (4 fl oz) of the cooking water for the dough. Try to keep it warm and add 1 teaspoon of caster sugar to it. When the potatoes are cool enough to handle, peel then mash them with a fork, potato ricer or a mouli, and measure out 250 g (9 oz). Leave the mash to cool to nearly room temperature.

Separately, dissolve the yeast in the reserved potato water and set aside for 5 minutes. If the yeast becomes foamy, you'll know it's still active. If you're confident that your yeast is fresh, you needn't wait the 5 minutes, but if you've pulled it from the back of the cupboard after God knows how long, wait and make sure it goes foamy.

In the bowl of a freestanding electric mixer fitted with the paddle attachment, mix the mashed potato, butter, eggs, sugar, honey and salt. Mix on low speed for about 1 minute. If you're not using a mixer, beat with a wooden spoon for 2 minutes.

Warm your milk slightly and add the yeast mixture. Stir to combine. Next, add this mixture to the potato mixture and mix on low speed until blended (or use a spoon).

Gradually add the flour to the potato mixture, one cup or handful at a time, until a soft dough forms. You may not use all the flour; moisture in the air and the type of flour you use all affect how much you need.

If you're using a machine, switch to the dough hook attachment and knead for about 5 minutes at low speed. If working by hand, knead the dough for 7–8 minutes.

Once the dough is soft and elastic, place it in a lightly oiled bowl. Put the bowl in a slightly warm place, covered with a damp tea towel (dish towel) and leave until it's doubled in size. Keep checking it every 20 minutes; it may take an hour or two.

Once the dough has doubled, punch it down and weigh into 50 g (1¾ oz) balls. To shape them, place the dough balls on a lightly floured work surface. Cup your lightly floured hand around a ball and begin to make circular movements (use your dominant hand and either go counter-clockwise with your right hand or clockwise with your left. When you get really good, you can do this with both hands simultaneously). Press down on the heel of your hand to lightly catch that bit of dough underneath it, creating some tension that will pull the dough mass into a smooth round ball. Place the rolls 1.5–2 cm (½–¾ in) apart on baking trays lined with baking paper.

Brush the tops of the balls generously with melted butter, cover with a damp cloth and leave to rise again in a warm spot until doubled in size. This may take 30 minutes to 1 hour. Preheat the oven to 200°C (400°F). Once doubled in size, sprinkle with coarse, flaky salt and you're ready to bake.

Bake for about 15–20 minutes, or until puffed and beautifully golden. Remove from the oven, brush with a little more butter and serve straight away. They're amazing hot out of the oven, but will also stay soft and be delicious at room temperature.

Makes approx. 28–30 dinner rolls

350–400 g (12½–14 oz) starchy, yellow-fleshed potatoes
115 ml (4 fl oz) lukewarm reserved potato water with 1 teaspoon caster (superfine) sugar added
7 g (¼ oz) active dried yeast
150 g (5½ oz) butter, softened, plus another 50 g (1¾ oz) for melting and brushing
2 eggs
60 g (2 oz) caster (superfine) sugar
2 tablespoons honey
1½ tablespoons fine sea salt
240 ml (8 fl oz) full-cream (whole) milk
1 kg (2 lb 3 oz) plain (all-purpose) flour, plus extra for dusting
flaky salt, for sprinkling

Equipment

Bench scraper, electric mixer with a dough hook

Yoghurt and spelt flatbreads

It's hard to know what each component of a bread recipe does to create the unique chemistry that allows you to make thin breads or puffy breads or chewy breads or soft breads. Although the basic ingredients are flour, yeast, salt and water, the quantities are what creates unique and different characteristics. For example, this dough uses a very small amount of yeast, a lot like good pizza dough, and that's because we want to stretch it thin and allow for a long, overnight fermentation process. Have you ever tried to stretch dough and it kept shrinking back? I think we all have at some point. This is because the dough probably had a short fermentation and too much yeast was used.

The other interesting thing about this dough is the yoghurt and olive oil. The fat and acidity both play a role in giving us a tender, supple dough. The fat in the dough shortens the gluten strands so the dough is not super chewy (a characteristic of a good flatbread) and the acidity in the yoghurt tenderises and relaxes the gluten, making it a bit easier to stretch so you can get it thin enough.

As for the flours, I use a mixture of plain (all-purpose) and spelt here. I just love the taste of wholegrain flours; they add nuttiness and another dimension in an otherwise plain white dough. They are a little bit more difficult to get right when used as the only flour in the recipe, but mixing both flours gives you the best of both worlds.

Makes 8 flatbreads

175 ml (6 fl oz) warm water
3 g (⅛ oz) active dried yeast
30 ml (1 fl oz) olive oil, plus extra for brushing
120 g (4½ oz) Yoghurt (page 237), or store-bought
250 g (9 oz/1⅔ cup) plain (all-purpose) flour
140 g (5 oz) spelt flour
2 teaspoons fine sea salt

Combine the water and yeast and allow it to dissolve and become foamy. Add the olive oil and yoghurt and mix to combine. Add the flours and salt to the bowl of a freestanding electric mixer fitted with the dough hook attachment, then pour in the wet ingredients and knead on low speed until everything comes together. Once the dough is combined, knead for 5 minutes until it looks smooth and elastic. If doing this by hand, knead for 8 minutes. Place in a lightly oiled bowl and cover with plastic wrap or a damp tea towel (dish towel) and refrigerate overnight or for at least 8 hours.

The next day, remove the dough from the fridge and divide into eight even, small balls. Roll the balls as explained in the potato roll recipe (see page 231) and set on a lightly floured benchtop or tray in a warm place. Cover the balls with a damp tea towel and leave to prove for 1 hour. Using your hands and not a rolling pin, stretch, press and pull the dough balls into a flat, round shape a lot like a pizza base.

To cook the flatbreads, either grill them over a medium grill or use a chargrill pan on the stove over a medium–high heat. Lightly brush them with oil and cook for approximately 2 minutes per side until golden. Serve immediately.

Equipment

Electric mixer with dough hook, outdoor grill or grill pan

Focaccia

Focaccia is a well-known bread from Italy. It is the abundance of good olive oil that makes this simple yeasted dough unique and utterly delicious. The oil not only flavours the dough but makes it quite tender and soft. There are many versions of focaccia throughout Italy, and it really depends on what region you're in. It could be quite thin, it could be crispy, and it could be topped with a multitude of things, from fresh herbs and tomatoes to potatoes and other vegetables. This is a basic recipe, so feel free to add whatever topping you fancy. The only special piece of equipment you need is a shallow sheet tray. I prefer the commercial American-style aluminium trays that measure 46×33 cm (18×13 in), but anything with similar dimensions should work. Just try to find a tray with sides about 2.5 cm (1 in) high. I give instructions for kneading in a machine, but, as always, you can do this by hand, just double kneading times.

Makes 1 × 46×33 cm
(18×13 in) focaccia

15 g (½ oz) active dried yeast
1½ tablespoons caster
   (superfine) sugar
450 ml (15 fl oz) slightly warm
   water
100 ml (3½ fl oz) olive oil
25 g (1 oz) salt
750 g (1 lb 11 oz/5 cups) plain
   (all-purpose) flour, plus
   extra for dusting
100 ml (3½ fl oz) extra-virgin
   olive oil
2 tablespoons yellow coarse
   semolina or polenta
1 teaspoon flaky coarse salt

Optional toppings

30 g (1 oz) picked rosemary
   leaves
250 g (9 oz) cherry tomatoes
250 g (9 oz) purple grapes
70 g (2½ oz) thinly sliced red
   onion
30 pre-roasted garlic cloves
1 large potato, thinly sliced on
   a mandoline
30 g (1 oz) picked sage
   leaves

Mix the yeast, sugar, water and oil and set aside for about 10 minutes until the yeast begins to get foamy, then mix in the salt. To a freestanding electric mixer fitted with the dough hook attachment, add the flour, then pour in all the wet ingredients. Mix on medium speed until the dough comes together and looks even and smooth, about 8–10 minutes.

Remove the dough from the mixer and roughly shape into a round. Place in a lightly floured bowl and cover tightly with a damp tea towel (dish towel). Allow to rise for 1–1½ hours, or until the dough has doubled in size. This may take much longer depending on the temperature of the room. If you're doing this in winter, you can place it in an oven with the pilot light on to accelerate the process a bit.

Pour half the extra-virgin olive oil onto the base of the sheet tray and sprinkle the semolina on top. Once the dough has proved, remove it from the bowl and place directly on the tray. Pour some of the remaining olive oil onto the dough, then use your fingers to push the dough out to the edges (shape your hands like you were playing the piano). The idea is to create small indentations that give the dough its unique look and texture, and a place for the oil to pool and 'fry' the pockets. Once the dough starts pulling back, stop and let it rest for 10 minutes, then come back, add the remaining olive oil and press it out evenly a bit further. Stop, allow it to rest for another 10 minutes and repeat until the dough looks even and has reached the edges of the tray. If you wanted to add any toppings, press them into the dough on the final round of stretching and pressing. Press them in firmly without breaking the dough; once they bake, the indentations will puff back up and push the toppings out, causing them to burn. Season the top with flaky sea salt, then cover loosely with baking paper or a tea towel (dish towel) and prove for a further 30 minutes in a warm spot.

Preheat the oven to 220°C (430°F) and, if you have a baking stone, set it in the oven.

Peel the baking paper off the top and bake the focaccia for 20–30 minutes on the stone, or until well puffed and deep golden brown on top. Remove from the oven and allow to cool slightly before cutting and serving.

Equipment

Electric mixer with dough
hook, shallow sheet tray

Fougasse

This is probably the recipe I was most worried about including in this book. It is not the beloved Fred's fougasse, but an equally delicious recipe. The bread we bake at Fred's daily is one of those recipes that can't really be replicated at home. You see, we bake it in a wood-burning oven, which I believe is the real secret to its beautiful flavour. The small amount of burning and toasting flour on the floor of the oven is really what's responsible for this dough's excellent flavour. And although I would like to imagine people constructing their own wood-burning ovens so they could bake fresh bread daily, it's just not realistic.

The idea came to me after several failed attempts at sourdough. A baker friend of mine, Simon Cancio of the famed Sydney bakery Brickfields, suggested I make a high-hydration, more rustic dough made for baking in wood ovens. Hydration, by the way, just means the ratio of water to flour in a recipe. He suggested ciabatta-type doughs, but after a bit of research, I landed on fougasse. Fougasse is a French bread from Provence. It is essentially a large slab of bread with a series of cuts that, when baked, fan out to look like a leaf. It is strikingly beautiful, and all those cuts mean you get the textures of soft and chewy with lots of crispy, crusty edges as well. During my research, I discovered the name originates from the Latin word for focus, which meant hearth or oven. It was too poetic to ignore.

I developed the recipe to be very similar to a baguette, lean style of dough, which gives excellent chew. Baguettes are usually started by making what's called a poolish. Poolish is a French term for a pre-fermented bit of dough that then gets mixed with the full recipe of dough. It contributes aroma, flavour and texture to the finished bread. It takes longer to make bread using a starter like this, but you simply cannot get the same flavour without it.

You can also add ingredients to flavour the dough, such as chopped fresh rosemary leaves, pitted black olives or chopped sun-dried tomatoes as I have done here.

Makes 1 fougasse

Poolish

100 g (3½ oz/⅔ cup) plain (all-purpose) flour, plus extra for dusting
2 g (⅛ oz) active dried yeast

Dough

500 g (1 lb 2 oz/3⅓ cups) strong flour
4 g (⅛ oz) active dried yeast
10 g (¼ oz) salt
120 g (4½ oz) kalamata olives, pitted and roughly chopped
1 tablespoon picked and chopped rosemary leaves

For brushing

2 tablespoons full-cream (whole) milk
flaky sea salt
2 tablespoons olive oil

Mix your poolish ingredients with 100 ml (3½ fl oz) water in a small bowl with a spatula, then let it sit, covered with a tea towel (dish towel), for 2–3 hours, or until small bubbles start to appear on the surface.

Combine all the dough ingredients, except the olives and rosemary, with 300 ml (10 fl oz) water in the bowl of a freestanding electric mixer fitted with the dough hook attachment and add the poolish. Mix on low speed for 4 minutes, then mix on medium speed for 4 minutes. Add the olives and rosemary (or other desired flavourings) and mix for another minute. Turn the dough out onto a well-dusted benchtop and knead 10–20 times until the dough no longer sticks to your hands. Use a bit of flour as needed to prevent sticking. Shape into a ball and place in a clean bowl. Cover with a damp tea towel and leave to ferment for 1 hour.

Dump the dough onto a dusted benchtop and shape it into a rough rectangle. Pull the left side up and place it in the centre of the dough, then repeat on the right side, then pull the top piece up and towards the centre. Stretch the bottom piece up and pull it all the way over the whole thing so you are left with a tight little package. If the dough looks slack and still feels loose instead of taut, repeat this stretching and shaping process a couple of times until it holds. Leave it covered with a damp tea towel on the bench. If your room is particularly cold, place an overturned bowl over the dough to keep its temperature warm. Allow this to prove for 1 hour.

Place the dough on a baking tray lined with baking paper and stretch and pull it into a rectangular, or, if you can manage it, a leaf shape. Then, using a bench scraper, make two long cuts all the way through the length of the dough, but leaving the edges intact. Then make three 30° angled cuts on each side. Pull on the dough to separate the cuts and reveal something that looks like a leaf.

Place this tray into a cold oven on the middle rack and place a small saucepan of boiling water on the tray below. This will create a perfect warm, moist proving chamber for your dough to rise one last time. Allow 45 minutes to 1 hour this time, then remove the tray from the oven.

Preheat the oven to 240°C (465°F).

Brush the dough with milk, sprinkle with sea salt and place the tray in the oven with another small saucepan of boiling water underneath it. Bake for 10 minutes, then remove the saucepan of water and continue baking for another 20 minutes, rotating the tray once halfway through. This may take slightly more or less time depending on your oven, but you want the bread to be nice and dark golden brown. Pull it out of the oven and immediately brush it with the olive oil. Allow it to cool slightly before serving.

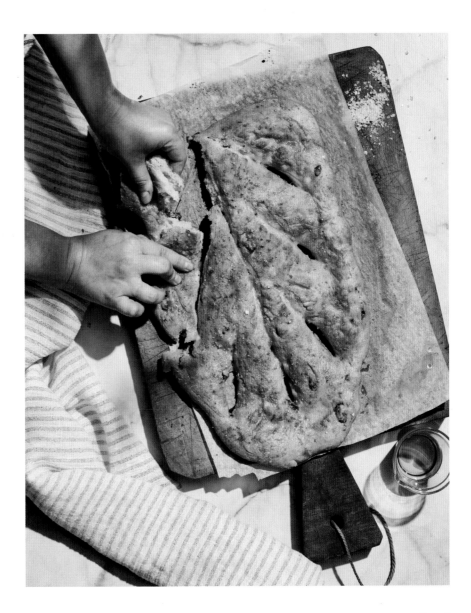

Equipment

Baking stone, electric mixer with dough hook, bench scraper

Dairy

All three of these projects are quite simple, but the trick to having things go smoothly is being prepared with all the bits of equipment that you need before you commence. As someone who often starts something before realising I'm missing an integral element, I can tell you, you will have a better time in the kitchen if you have thought things through before starting. As projects, some recipes may require a few added tools and a bit of time.

Yoghurt

Yoghurt is so easy to buy, so why bother making your own? Well, if you're like me, sometimes you just want to understand how things are made and either use that information to make your own for special occasions, or make it a part of your weekly routine. There are times when I make yoghurt regularly and times when I just have some nice milk that I know I won't be able to finish and I'll turn it into yoghurt, which lasts much longer. The truth is, though, however much you do or don't eat yoghurt, there are a number of uses for good yoghurt and it's a great thing to have in the fridge. It also couldn't be simpler to make. The hardest part is figuring out the right incubation chamber to hold your milk as it is fermenting. All you're really doing is heating milk, cooling it down, adding a bit of live active yoghurt, then maintaining it at a specific temperature for a minimum of 5 hours, or much longer if you prefer a very sour flavour (I like to ferment mine for 12–14 hours). Either way, holding the yoghurt at this temperature is pretty crucial. You are creating a good environment where healthy or good bacteria can thrive and reproduce. This prevents bad or unhealthy bacteria from growing and spoiling your milk. Once you find the right yoghurt starter and an incubation chamber that works for you, you should be able to get consistent results. Don't be discouraged if your first batch doesn't work out, however. Sometimes they just don't set, or you need to play with your set-up a little.

A few options for incubation chambers:

Set your mixed yoghurt in a covered bowl or jar inside a larger bowl of hot water. Place the whole thing in a super low oven or an oven that has a pilot light.

Place your mixed yoghurt inside a thermos or jars and place that in a cooler filled with other jars of hot water or a couple of hot water bottles.

Place your yoghurt in jars and wrap them with a heated blanket.

Place your yoghurt in jars and place the jars in a crock pot or slow cooker on the lowest setting. Add enough hot water to come three-quarters of the way up the jars and place a lid on the pot. Incubate overnight.

Makes 1 kg (2 lb 3 oz)

1 litre (34 fl oz/4 cups) full-cream (whole) milk
80 g (2¾ oz) live active plain yoghurt

Equipment

Instant-read thermometer, glass jars with lids, incubation materials

Slowly heat your milk in a saucepan over a low heat until it reaches 82°C (180°F). Whisk it every few minutes to make sure it doesn't catch and burn on the bottom. When it reaches 82°C (180°F), turn the heat off and remove from the stove. You can place your pot directly in an ice bath and whisk until the temperature reaches somewhere between 43–46°C (109–115°F). Alternatively, you can let this cool on its own on your benchtop, just be aware this takes surprisingly long.

While your milk is cooling, prepare your incubation chamber by prewarming it. Place your yoghurt in a small bowl and, when the temperature of the milk has dropped, ladle a small amount into the bowl and whisk it, then add this back to the rest of the milk and whisk to combine. At this stage, either pour into jars or cover your bowl with plastic wrap. Incubate at a temperature between 43–46°C (109–115°F) for a minimum of 5 hours. You can also do this overnight or even longer, it will just get a bit sourer.

Next, place the yoghurt in the fridge for about 8 hours to ensure it is completely set. At this point, it is ready to eat. You can also carefully and gently strain the yoghurt through a fine-mesh sieve for a further 8 hours in the fridge, to get a thicker, Greek-style consistency.

Ricotta

The ricotta I describe here is, sadly, not true ricotta. True ricotta is a by-product of cheesemaking. Ricotta in Italian translates to recooked, indicating that after cheesemakers have made their cheese, they would then take the remaining whey and cook that a second time to pull any remaining proteins out of the whey and make a fresh, delicate curd cheese for themselves. You get very little ricotta from a huge amount of milk if made this way, so it's not really practical to do at home. Instead, milk can be heated to make a fresh cheese or ricotta from the initial milk. This produces a much more abundant amount, which you can use for a variety of different things or simply spread on toast.

There are a few things you can use to acidulate the milk so that it curdles when heated. One is lemon juice, the other is buttermilk, and my preference is citric acid dissolved in water. I like that the citric acid doesn't interfere at all with the clean flavour of the milk and that I can keep it indefinitely in the cupboard so it's on hand whenever I want to make cheese. Alternatively, you can just use lemon juice, but expect it to have a lemony flavour, which is not always desired.

The trick to making good ricotta at home is a very slow heat up to 90°C (194°F). I learned this from a local cheesemaker here in Sydney named Kirsten Allen, who makes some of the most delicate and luxurious ricotta I have ever had. These days, she teaches lessons on cheesemaking and I have tried to glean as many tips from her as I can. She says you can literally take all day to reach 90°C (194°F), but I have had some excellent results doing this over the course of an hour or two. If you heat the milk too quickly or too high, you end up with grainy, tough and dry-textured curds. Heat it over a double boiler and you shouldn't have any issues with that. The other important thing here is that you really need a ricotta basket, which can be sourced online from cheesemaking supply shops. They are designed to capture delicate, soft curds, which is what you are looking for.

Makes approx. 200 g (7 oz)

1 litre (34 fl oz/4 cups)
    full-cream (whole) milk
½ teaspoon fine sea salt
1 teaspoon citric acid
    dissolved in
    1 tablespoon water
lemon juice (optional)

Combine the milk and salt in a heatproof bowl and set it over a saucepan of gently simmering water. Very slowly heat until the milk mixture reads 80°C (176°F) on a cooking thermometer. Stir every few minutes to ensure the milk is heating evenly. Once it reaches 80°C (176°F), stir in the citric acid and water and you should see the curds begin to form immediately. If the milk doesn't split immediately into curds and whey (which is more yellow looking), add another teaspoon citric acid dissolved in water, or teaspoons of lemon juice, one at a time, until it splits (see Notes). Stop stirring immediately at this point. Keep the mixture on the heat until it reaches 90°C (194°F), then hold it for 5 minutes at this temperature. Turn off the heat and allow the mix to settle for 10 more minutes.

Gently scoop out the curds using a mesh skimmer and drop them into the cheese mould, which can be placed inside another bowl to capture any remaining whey. Allow this to drain in the refrigerator for 8 or so hours, or until fully chilled.

Use on toast, to fill pasta or as part of a salad.

Notes

A few times when making ricotta, my milk just hasn't split into curds and whey, even once I have added more acid. I've asked some cheesemakers about this, and they say it is due to nutritional variations in cows' diets. This variation can cause weakening of the protein bonds in the milk, which do not bind using lemon juice, citric acid and heat. There's not much you can do about it. If this happens to you, try a different brand of milk and use the uncurdled milk in a blended soup.

If you want a creamier-style ricotta, add a couple of tablespoons of cream to the finished ricotta and mix to combine.

Equipment

Instant-read thermometer, mesh skimmer, ricotta or fresh cheese basket

Crème fraîche

Lastly for the dairy projects is crème fraîche. This is, by far, the easiest thing to make; no heating or straining required. You simply mix fresh cream with some live-cultured buttermilk and allow it to sit out on the benchtop for 24–48 hours. That's it! I can find a million uses for crème fraîche. I'll often mix a bit into vinaigrettes to soften them or toss some into cream-based sauces or sweet whipped cream because I like the delicate acidity. It is a great thing to always have in the fridge and a little can go a long way. If you wanted to even take this crème fraîche a step further, you could whip it in a freestanding electric mixer and make your own cultured butter.

Makes 600 g (1 lb 5 oz)

600 ml (20½ fl oz) cream
80 ml (2½ fl oz/⅓ cup) live-cultured buttermilk (see Note)

Mix the cream and buttermilk together and place in a jar or plastic container, leaving the lid off. Place a sheet of paper towel or muslin (cheesecloth) over the top and tie it onto the jar to hold it in place and prevent anything from dropping in. Leave to sit at room temperature for 24–48 hours depending on the temperature in the room. Once coagulated, it will appear thickened. Pull off the paper, replace the lid on the jar and refrigerate for several hours to fully cool. This should last a few weeks in the refrigerator.

Note

It is essential to find live cultured buttermilk to make crème fraîche. Be sure to read the label of the buttermilk you are buying. Substitute with live active kefir if you can't find a cultured buttermilk.

Meat

This is potentially one of the more intimidating sections of the book, I'm not going to lie. I won't be offended if you don't jump straight into making liver parfait or terrines, but you should definitely make your own sausage mix. Maybe you can work your way up to terrines and parfait; they are so satisfying to make once you feel confident enough. They also make use of those lesser-loved cuts of meat, which are often wasted. A true art form, but with a good recipe, they go from unknown and scary to achievable and delicious.

Bacon and chicken liver parfait

Makes 1 terrine

Reduction

60 g (2 oz) shallot, peeled
   and sliced
½ tablespoon olive oil
1 bay leaf
60 g (2 oz) dry-cured smoked
   bacon, diced
150 ml (5 fl oz) Madeira
pinch of ground allspice

Parfait

500 g (1 lb 2 oz) chicken
   livers, at room
   temperature
3 eggs, at room temperature
7 g (¼ oz) nitrate salt for
   cooked goods
3 g (⅛ oz) salt
2 g (⅛ oz) caster
   (superfine) sugar
pinch of freshly ground
   white pepper
pinch of ground allspice
360 g (12½ oz) clarified, warm
   unsalted butter or ghee

To finish

50 ml (1¾ fl oz) clarified
   butter or ghee

Equipment

Very fine sieve, high-speed
blender, terrine mould

A parfait is a smooth paste made by emulsifying melted clarified butter with puréed livers and baking them in a terrine mould. It is different to pâté in that it is always completely smooth, whereas a pâté can be chunky. As a self-confessed liver sceptic, I love this dish. The liver is subtle and the bacon helps to round out the flavour of the liver as well. Again, like my chicken ragu and liver pasta, if you think you don't like liver, you should try this; it may change your mind.

You do need to source some nitrate curing salt specifically for 'cooked goods' for this recipe. This helps to preserve it and can be found online. The parfait will be good for about a week in your refrigerator as the quantity makes one full terrine, but feel free to halve it if you have a smaller vessel. After all, you don't want to eat too much of this as it is quite rich. It makes an excellent canapé or appetiser at a holiday function or gathering and also is a fantastic schmear in a homemade banh mi sandwich. Serve with something acidic and sweet, like good-quality aged balsamic vinegar or a fruit chutney and grilled sourdough bread.

Make the reduction well before making the parfait so it has time to chill. Sweat the shallot over a low heat in the oil with the bay leaf to bring out all the sweetness. Cover with baking paper or a lid, slightly ajar, and allow to sweat gently until lightly brown in colour. Add the bacon and increase the heat to medium. Let everything become golden but not dark brown or burnt. You may need to add a splash of water to prevent it catching.

Add the Madeira and reduce by two-thirds. Season with a pinch of pepper, allspice and salt. Remove the bay leaf and discard, then blend the mixture to a paste in a high-speed blender.

Pass through a fine-mesh sieve by pressing on the paste with a ladle. You will end up with approximately 75–100 ml (2½–3½ fl oz) liquid. Allow to cool, then set aside. This can be made a day or two in advance and stored in the fridge.

Before making the parfait, make sure all your ingredients, including the reduction, are slightly warm or at room temperature. The idea is to keep everything at the same temperature when mixing so as not to break the emulsion of the butter, eggs and livers.

Clean the livers very well of any sinew and weigh them. You need to end up with 400 g (14 oz) once cleaned. Blend the livers with all the remaining ingredients except the butter until smooth, then slowly add the warm butter with the machine running on low speed. Finally, add the warmed reduction and blend. Pass through a fine-mesh sieve into a bowl. Pour this mixture into a 30×11 cm (12×4½ in) terrine mould and cover tightly with aluminium foil.

Preheat the oven to 150°C (300°F).

Place the terrine in a deep roasting tin and pour enough water into the roasting tin to come halfway up the side of the terrine. Bake until the internal temperature of the parfait reaches 58°C (136°F) on a cooking thermometer. Remove it from the oven and water bath and leave to cool completely, then refrigerate overnight.

The following day, remove the parfait from the refrigerator and use a spoon to scrape the grey top layer away. Try to smooth the top out as much as possible. Pour the clarified butter over the top to completely cover and seal it, then refrigerate again to firm up. To serve, scoop out spoonfuls and serve with a drizzle of aged balsamic vinegar and grilled sourdough or crostini, or a sharp and sweet fruit chutney.

Pork, duck and pistachio terrine

This terrine really makes me feel like I know what I'm doing in the kitchen, which doesn't happen as often as you might think! The art of charcuterie is not something I claim to be an expert on, but I have learned that even though most foods that fall into this category are made with humble ingredients, there is tremendous skill involved in making them well, so you really must be patient and follow all the instructions to the letter. Don't cut any corners, start with great fresh ingredients and you'll have a beautiful and professional-looking terrine. I would serve this with grilled bread and fruit chutney, or with frisée lettuce and a mustardy dressing.

Makes 1 terrine

3 tablespoons duck fat
120 g (4½ oz) finely diced onion
1 bay leaf, plus 3–4 extra to decorate
3 thyme sprigs, on the stem
40 thin slices pancetta or lardo for lining the terrine
1 egg
100 ml (3½ fl oz) cream
50 ml (1¾ fl oz) cognac or Armagnac
18 g (¾ oz) plain (all-purpose) flour
850 g (1 lb 14 oz) minced (ground) coarse fatty pork
10 g (¼ oz) finely chopped flat-leaf (Italian) parsley
200 g (7 oz) duck livers, cleaned and roughly chopped
½ teaspoon Spice mix (see below)
½ teaspoon freshly ground black pepper
2½ teaspoons fine salt
⅛ teaspoon curing salt for cooked goods
70 g (2½ oz) toasted pistachios

Spice mix

4 g (⅛ oz) ground cloves
4 g (⅛ oz) ground nutmeg
3 g (⅛ oz) ground ginger
3 g (⅛ oz) ground coriander
5 g (⅛ oz) ground cinnamon
10 g (¼ oz) white pepper

Equipment

Terrine mould

Mix the spices for the spice mix and store in an airtight jar for future use. This recipe makes much more than you need for this terrine.

Heat the duck fat in a sauté pan over a low heat and fry the onion with the bay leaf and thyme until completely soft but not coloured. Set aside to cool completely.

Line a 1.5 litre (51 fl oz/6 cups)-capacity terrine mould with overlapping slices of pancetta. Leave the slices hanging over the side so you can wrap them around the finished terrine.

Preheat the oven to 150°C (300°F).

Combine the egg, cream, cognac and flour in a bowl and whisk, then push through a fine-mesh sieve to remove any lumps. Combine this with all the remaining ingredients, except the additional bay leaves, in a large mixing bowl. It's important that you really whip the ingredients together using your hands or a stiff spatula, as this is what makes the terrine stick together and not fall apart when sliced. It's also good practice to cook a small piece of the filling and check for seasoning, making adjustments as needed. Pour the finished mix into the lined terrine. Wrap the overhanging pancetta over the top, arrange the bay leaves on top and cover the whole terrine with aluminium foil. Place the terrine in a deep roasting tin and pour in enough water to come halfway up the side of the terrine. Bake until the internal temperature reads 57–59°C (135–138°F) on a cooking thermometer. When the terrine is cooked, remove it from the oven and the water bath and allow to cool until warm.

Before the terrine is fully cooled you need to press and weight it. Cut a piece of thick cardboard the same size as the top of the terrine, then wrap it in foil. Place it on top of the terrine and refrigerate with a heavy pan or oil bottle on top, weighing it down.

The following day, remove the weight and drop the terrine into a shallow tray with boiling water to release it from the sides. Run a thin sharp knife around the edges and gently pop the terrine out. Serve slices with toasted bread and fruit chutney, or with a frisée or chicory salad and sharp mustardy dressing. It can be kept in the fridge for up to 1 week.

See image on page 244.

Sausage meat

A good sausage meat should be part of every cook's repertoire. Whenever I buy commercially produced sausage mix I am disappointed and a bit confused. I don't know what's in it and sometimes it includes fillers and things that you don't want in your food. This recipe gives me control and I can make adjustments as I like. I prefer to make the mix at home, but putting it into casings is a different story. This is pretty challenging, even for me, and takes some very specific pieces of equipment, so I have skipped teaching you how to make sausages from the sausage meat. The loose mix is great to put in pastas or brown up and serve on sliced broccoli shoots and kale, or even on pizzas. Speak to your butcher about getting you a coarse grind of pork with 25–30 per cent fat content, or if you're feeling ambitious, mince it yourself.

As for the recipe, I've indicated salt as a percentage of the weight of the meat, so you can scale the recipe up or down. Keep in mind that sausage is meant to be heavily seasoned; it is not a burger patty. After that, the seasonings can be amended to whatever you want. Use red wine instead of white wine, add hot chilli flakes, leave the garlic out, add in dried herbs – whatever you think.

There are two crucial steps to making good sausage meat. One relates to the mixing. You need to literally punch and bash and mix the meat to extract a particular protein that binds the meat together. The meat can then stick to itself, creating a good textured sausage and not a crumbly, dry one. I explain this same lesson in the terrine recipe opposite. The other is that everything must be kept cold, cold, cold. If it's a bit warm, I like to mix the sausage meat in a bowl on top of another bowl of ice. If you've minced the meat yourself, you would put all the mincer parts in the freezer before using them, so that even in the mincing process the meat stays cold.

Makes approx. 1 kg (2 lb 3 oz)

1 kg (2 lb 3 oz) minced (ground) coarse fatty pork
1.8% salt (in this case, 18 g/¾ oz)
2 g (⅛ oz) caster (superfine) sugar
3 g (⅛ oz) coarse black pepper
3 g (⅛ oz) toasted fennel seeds, crushed
50 ml (1¾ fl oz) cold white wine
50 ml (1¾ fl oz) cold water
10 g (¼ oz) garlic cloves, crushed

Mix all the ingredients together using clean hands and be sure to keep everything very cold. Punch the meat like you were in a fight with it and mix until you can hold a small piece in your hand, turn your hand over and the meat stays stuck to your hand. The sausage meat can be frozen or stored in the fridge for up to 3 days. Use as desired.

See image on page 245.

Equipment

Meat mincer (optional)

Meat

Left   Pork, duck and pistachio terrine (page 242)
Bottom   Sausage meat (page 243)

Pickles

There are basically two kinds of pickles: vinegar pickles or lacto-fermented pickles, such as sauerkraut. Lacto-fermented pickles require a bit of safety knowledge because a few things can go seriously wrong – this is why I have chosen to focus on vinegar pickles, but there are great books out there about making ferments at home. The basic premise behind pickles is preservation. Nowadays, we have fresh produce available all year long and we make pickles because we like the flavour, but at one point this was a way to keep fresh vegetables through the dreary winter months when fresh produce became scarce. In the restaurant, sometimes we get a glut of onions, cucumbers or cabbage, all of which we preserve because we won't be able to use it at once. These pickles are pretty easy to make and can add a really special pop of acidity to any dish.

Quick vinegar pickles

Many vinegar pickles do not require cooking the vegetables. You simply place the vegetable or fruit in the vinegar brine and wait – quite a while. Usually, I'm not willing to wait that long, so to speed things up you can 'quick' pickle things. All that means is you are cooking the vegetable in the brine before cooling and storing. It means you can have pickles in less than an hour, which works for me.

Once you have the basic brine recipe, the only question you need to ask is do I want to cook the vegetable in the brine or just pour hot brine over it? This really depends on the thickness and density of the vegetable. If I were, for example, pickling whole carrots, I would cook them in the simmering brine for a couple of minutes before cooling them. However, if I was pickling carrot ribbons, I would simply pour the brine over the top. On the flip side, though, if I'm trying to pickle something delicate such as onion slices, I would probably drop them into the simmering brine for about 20 seconds, then pull them out and allow everything to cool before putting them back together. You need to be the judge. If you're not sure, cook it in the brine until it's softened but still crunchy and allow everything to cool before putting it back together. It's a pretty failsafe way to make sure you don't get a soggy, limp pickle.

Basic brine

To pickle approx. 250 g (9 oz) vegetables

180 ml (6 fl oz) rice-wine
    vinegar
1 tablespoon salt
2 tablespoons honey
1 bay leaf
½ teaspoon black
    peppercorns
1 teaspoon yellow mustard
    seeds
1 garlic clove
1 small dried chilli (optional)

Combine all the ingredients in a saucepan with 100 ml (3½ fl oz) water and bring to a simmer. Simmer for 3 minutes, then cook your vegetables in the brine, depending on their size. Before you decide whether to pickle in brine or pour the hot brine over the top, consider the size of your vegetables. For anything sliced, such as carrots and onions, a pour is the way to go. If you want to pickle 'whole' form vegetables, such as carrots or turnips, or perhaps a dense vegetable such as fennel cut into wedges, you will need to cook them for a few minutes in the hot brine so that they tenderise slightly before removing from the heat. When cooking the vegetables, a good rule of thumb is 2 minutes at a gentle simmer, but the best way to know is to take some out and taste it. If it has softened slightly, pull it out of the brine to cool. If it still feels quite raw, give it another minute or two.

Once done, transfer the vegetables and brine to sterilised glass jars (see Note) or other containers. The pickles will keep for up to 1 month in a sterilised jar in the fridge.

Note

To sterilise your jars, wash the jars and lids in hot, soapy water, then rinse well. Place them on a baking tray and heat in a 120°C (250°F) oven for 10–15 minutes. Remove and allow to cool before handling.

Equipment

Jars for storage

What to cook

Putting menus together can be tricky, but once you figure out a few formulas, it can be the most fun part of cooking for others. There are things to consider, such as the balance of heavy and light dishes; how many people you are cooking for; where you are cooking and what equipment you have; the time of year and therefore what is good at the market; how you want the day or night to feel ... Here are a few suggestions for a range of scenarios.

In spring

Asparagus with brown butter, egg yolk, lemon and young pecorino 74

Marinated and grilled rack of lamb 191

Potato, green garlic and sorrel gratin 67

Peas and broad beans with tarragon, mustard and horseradish 78

Strawberry and brown sugar galette 208

In summer

Tomato salad with sumac onions, tahini yoghurt and wild fennel 27

Zucchini with mint, lemon and bottarga 30

Grilled côte de boeuf rested in rosemary and thyme 190

Charred Romano beans with buttermilk herb dressing and crispy shallots 75

Slow-roasted, crispy sweet potatoes 61

Blueberry frozen yoghurt 216

In autumn

Fig and goat's curd salad with smoky paprika vinaigrette 27

Greens with garlic, turmeric, fenugreek and breadcrumbs 85

Mussels with sausage, capsicum and fregola sarda 131

A simple apple galette 213

In winter

Citrus with Meyer lemon dressing and shaved fennel 40

Radicchio with bagna cauda and walnut oil 34

Pappardelle with chilli braised beef, red wine, vinegar, egg yolk and breadcrumbs 102–3

Chocolate miso tart 204

When you want to go vegetarian

Celeriac schnitzel with salsa verde 53

Radish with preserved lemon, feta, mint and sesame 45

Mom's flan with poached cherries 211

When you don't know what to cook

Everyday roasted chicken and broth 12

Almond and cherry custard ice cream 217

When you have time

Homemade ricotta with white wine–braised artichokes, carrots and green garlic 70/238

Ribollita with borlotti beans and cavolo nero 99

Fougasse 234

Cape gooseberry clafoutis 201

When you crave something different

Fragrant and sour fish curry with steamed jasmine rice 156

Pork and garlic chive dumplings with mandarin, chilli and soy 132

When all you want is pasta

Rigatoni with fresh tomatoes, butter and basil 105

For an occasion

Oysters with coriander, lime and white pepper mignonette 139

Bacon and chicken liver parfait 241

Whole roasted pork rack with caramelised apples and mustard 197

Castelfranco with warm chestnut, thyme and prosciutto 37

Fresh corn polenta with chilli and garlic oil 108

Citrus and chocolate mousse trifle 221

For a crowd

Tomato and fried crouton salad with tonnato and capers 28

Porchetta roasted pork shoulder 194

Potato rolls 231

Cucumbers with mustard vinaigrette and dill 30

Iceberg with dried oregano dressing and creamy sheep's milk cheese 34

Slow-roasted, crispy sweet potatoes 61

Pineapple and ginger upside-down cake 203

A special winter meal

Celeriac and Jerusalem artichoke soup with kale and chilli garlic oil 57

Poached whole chicken with winter vegetables and black truffle stuffing 170

Grilled broccoli shoots with anchovy butter and salsa verde 81

Lime curd tart with toasted meringue 206

Index

A

abalone, pipis and chorizo, Arroz negro with 123
A simple apple galette 213–4
A very green soup 86
Aioli 15
    Squid with sweet red capsicums, basil and aioli 153
almond
    Almond and cherry custard ice cream 217
    Braised chicken legs and wings with almonds, olives, raisins and preserved lemon 180
    Buckwheat, brown butter, almond and apple cake 223
    Pasta fredda with almonds and chilli salsa verde 105
    Spaghetti with cauliflower, anchovies, currants and almonds 104
anchovy
    Grilled broccoli shoots with anchovy butter and salsa verde 81
    Grilled chicory with celery, anchovy, parmesan dressing and breadcrumbs 39
    Radicchio with bagna cauda and walnut oil 34
    Salsa verde 17
    Spaghetti with cauliflower, anchovies, currants and almonds 104
apple
    Apple peel glaze 213
    A simple apple galette 213–4
    Buckwheat, brown butter, almond and apple cake 223
    Custard apple and kaffir lime ice cream 217
    Whole roasted pork rack with caramelised apples and mustard 197
    Wilted spinach with fennel, apple and pistachio butter 42
Arroz negro with abalone, pipis and chorizo 123
artichoke
    Celeriac and Jerusalem artichoke soup with kale and chilli garlic oil 57
    Roasted fennel and Jerusalem artichoke with hazelnuts and grapefruit 45
    White wine–braised artichokes, carrots and green garlic 70
asparagus
    Asparagus with brown butter, egg yolk, lemon and young pecorino 74
    Triangoli with asparagus and ricotta 122

B

Baba ghanoush with roasted spring onions, beetroot and green olive 33
Bacon and chicken liver parfait 241
Barley risotto with pumpkin, sage, roasted radicchio and balsamic 100
Basic brine 247
beans
    Charred Romano beans with buttermilk and herb dressing and crispy shallots 75
    Chicken al mattone with white bean purée, lemon, brown butter and capers 178
    Cooking fresh-shelling beans 115

    Pappardelle with borlotti beans, pancetta and rosemary 114
    Ribollita with borlotti beans and cavolo nero 99
    Slow-roasted lamb shoulder with white beans and harissa 182–3
    White bean purée 178
Béchamel 126
beef
    Celeriac, walnut, pear and bresaola 38
    Grilled côte de boeuf rested in rosemary and thyme 190
    Grilled flanken-style short ribs with lemon and olive oil 186
    Lasagne bolognese 125–7
    Pappardelle with chilli-braised beef, red wine, vinegar, egg yolk and breadcrumbs 102–3
    Poached beef short ribs with horseradish and breadcrumb salsa verde 171
    Ragu 102
    Whole grilled beef tenderloin with caramelised onions, treviso and gorgonzola dolce 192
beetroot
    Baba ghanoush with roasted spring onions, beetroot and green olive 33
    Beetroot and persimmon salad with feta, honey, pistachio and Aleppo 25
    Carrot and beetroot curry 82
black truffle stuffing, Poached whole chicken with winter vegetables and 170
Blueberry frozen yoghurt 216
bottarga, Zucchini with mint, lemon and 30
Braised chicken legs and wings with almonds, olives, raisins and preserved lemon 180
bread 230
    Breadcrumbs 14
    Focaccia 233
    Fougasse 234–5
    Greens with garlic, turmeric, fenugreek and breadcrumbs 85
    Grilled chicory with celery, anchovy, parmesan dressing and breadcrumbs 39
    Grilled lamb leg spiedini with flatbreads and harissa-ish oil 189
    Horseradish and breadcrumb salsa verde 171
    Pappardelle with chilli-braised beef, red wine, vinegar, egg yolk and breadcrumbs 102–3
    Poached beef short ribs with horseradish and breadcrumb salsa verde 171
    Poolish 234
    Potato rolls 231
    Tomato and fried crouton salad with tonnato and capers 28
    Yoghurt and spelt flatbreads 232
bresaola, Celeriac, walnut, pear and 38
brine, Basic 247
broad beans with tarragon, mustard and horseradish, Peas and 78
broccoli shoots with anchovy butter and salsa verde, Grilled 81
broth
    Everyday roasted chicken and broth 12
    Rich poultry broth 13
brussels sprouts with sour cream and kumquat and chilli relish, Roasted 61
Buckwheat, brown butter, almond and apple cake 223

butter 11
    Asparagus with brown butter, egg yolk, lemon and young pecorino 74
    Buckwheat, brown butter, almond and apple cake 223
    Chicken al mattone with white bean purée, lemon, brown butter and capers 178
    Grilled broccoli shoots with anchovy butter and salsa verde 81
    Oven-roasted prawns with nasturtium and miso butter 149
    Pot-roasted mud crab with lemon, garlic, chilli, butter and fine noodles 144
    Rigatoni with fresh tomatoes, butter and basil 105
    Steamed cod with leek and seaweed butter 152
    Whole roasted John Dory with brown butter, lemon, capers and nori 147
    Wilted spinach with fennel, apple and pistachio butter 42
buttermilk
    Buttermilk-marinated chicken with roasted grapes and za'atar 176
    Charred Romano beans with buttermilk and herb dressing and crispy shallots 75

C

cake
    Buckwheat, brown butter, almond and apple cake 223
    Pineapple and ginger upside-down cake 203
    Sponge cake 221
camembert with oven-roasted mushrooms and spring onions, Warm 81
Cape gooseberry clafoutis 201
capers
    Chicken al mattone with white bean purée, lemon, brown butter and capers 178
    Whole roasted John Dory with brown butter, lemon, capers and nori 147
capsicum (bell pepper)
    Mussels with sausage, capsicum and fregola sarda 131
    Squid with sweet red capsicums, basil and aioli 153
    Tomato, red capsicum and carrot soup with squash blossoms and basil 73
Caramel 68
carnitas with pineapple and jalapeño salsa, Pork 185
carrot
    Carrot and beetroot curry 82
    Mandarin and Seville orange–braised duck legs with carrots 174
    Poached whole chicken with winter vegetables and black truffle stuffing 170
    Tomato, red capsicum and carrot soup with squash blossoms and basil 73
    White wine–braised artichokes, carrots and green garlic 70
carpaccio with yuzu kosho, orange and fennel, Snapper 142
Casarecce with pesto Trapanese 109

Castelfranco with warm chestnut, thyme and
  prosciutto 37
cauliflower
  Cauliflower and smoked cheese gratin 64
  Spaghetti with cauliflower, anchovies,
    currants and almonds 104
cavolo nero, Ribollita with borlotti beans
  and 99
celeriac
  Celeriac and Jerusalem artichoke soup
    with kale and chilli garlic oil 57
  Celeriac schnitzel with salsa verde 53
  Celeriac, walnut, pear and bresaola 38
  Poached whole chicken with winter
    vegetables and black truffle stuffing 170
celery, anchovy, parmesan dressing and
  breadcrumbs, Grilled chicory with 39
Chardonnay and honey vinaigrette, and how to
  dress a salad 16
Charred Romano beans with buttermilk and
  herb dressing and crispy shallots 75
cheese (*see also* feta; gorgonzola)
  Asparagus with brown butter, egg yolk,
    lemon and young pecorino 74
  Beetroot and persimmon salad with feta,
    honey, pistachio and Aleppo 25
  Cauliflower and smoked cheese gratin 64
  Fig and goat's curd salad with smoky
    paprika vinaigrette 27
  Gorgonzola sauce 192
  Greens and onion galette with crème
    fraîche and Comté 55–6
  Grilled chicory with celery, anchovy,
    parmesan dressing and breadcrumbs 39
  Iceberg with dried oregano dressing and
    creamy sheep's milk cheese 34
  Persimmon, witlof, pomegranate and
    gorgonzola dolce 38
  Radish with preserved lemon, feta, mint
    and sesame 45
  Ricotta 238
  Tomato, onion and cheddar tart 88
  Triangoli with asparagus and ricotta 122
  Verjus-roasted quince with gorgonzola
    dolce and fresh walnuts 91
  Warm camembert with oven-roasted
    mushrooms and spring onions 81
  Whole grilled beef tenderloin with
    caramelised onions, treviso and
    gorgonzola dolce 192
  Whole roasted pumpkin stuffed with wild
    mushrooms and gruyère 59
cheddar tart, Tomato, onion and 88
cherry
  Almond and cherry custard ice cream 217
  Mom's flan with poached cherries 211
  Poached cherries 211
  Sage salt and black pepper duck breasts
    with cherries 172–3
chestnut, thyme and prosciutto, Castelfranco
  with warm 37
chicken
  Bacon and chicken liver parfait 241
  Braised chicken legs and wings with almonds,
    olives, raisins and preserved lemon 180
  Buttermilk-marinated chicken with roasted
    grapes and za'atar 176

Chicken al mattone with white bean purée,
  lemon, brown butter and capers 178
Everyday roasted chicken and broth 12
Fennel braised in chicken fat 91
Pici with chicken liver and marsala ragu 111
Poached whole chicken with winter
  vegetables and black truffle stuffing 170
Rich poultry broth 13
chickpeas, rosemary and roasted garlic
  yoghurt, Socca with 118
chicory
  Grilled chicory with celery, anchovy, parmesan
    dressing and breadcrumbs 39
chilli
  Celeriac and Jerusalem artichoke soup
    with kale and chilli garlic oil 57
  Chilli oil 79
  Fresh corn polenta with chilli and garlic
    oil 108
  Mandarin and chilli paste 133
  Pappardelle with chilli-braised beef, red wine,
    vinegar, egg yolk and breadcrumbs 102–3
  Pasta fredda with almonds and chilli salsa
    verde 105
  Pork and garlic chive dumplings with
    mandarin, chilli and soy 132–3
  Pork carnitas with pineapple and jalapeño
    salsa 185
  Pot-roasted mud crab with lemon, garlic,
    chilli, butter and fine noodles 144
  Roasted brussels sprouts with sour cream
    and kumquat and chilli relish 61
  Steamed eggplant with chilli and pork
    mince 79
chocolate
  Chocolate miso tart 204
  Chocolate mousse 221–2
  Chocolate torte with baked plums 215
  Citrus and chocolate mousse trifle 221–2
chorizo, Arroz negro with abalone, pipis and 123
citrus
  Citrus and chocolate mousse trifle 221–2
  Citrus with Meyer lemon dressing and
    shaved fennel 40
clafoutis, Cape gooseberry 201
clams
  Clams with sorrel, tarragon and green
    garlic 154
  Spaghetti with clams, parsley and spinach 101
cod with leek and seaweed butter, Steamed
  152
Comté, Greens and onion galette with crème
  fraîche and 55–6
Cookie dough 208
corn
  Corn and soffrito with fish sauce 73
  Fresh corn polenta with chilli and garlic
    oil 108
crab with lemon, garlic, chilli, butter and fine
  noodles, Pot-roasted mud 144
cream 11
Crème fraîche 239
crudo and citrus ponzu, Fish 140
crumble, Strawberry and rhubarb 204
Crumble topping 204
Cucumbers with mustard vinaigrette and dill 30
curd tart with toasted meringue, Lime 206–7

curry
  Carrot and beetroot curry 82
  Curry paste 156–7
  Fragrant and sour fish curry 156–7
Custard apple and kaffir lime ice cream 217
custard
  Almond and cherry custard ice cream 217
  Custard 221–2

D

dough
  Cookie dough 208
  Flaky dough 227
dressing
  Charred Romano beans with buttermilk
    herb dressing and crispy shallots 75
  Citrus with Meyer lemon dressing and
    shaved fennel 40
  Grilled chicory with celery, anchovy, parmesan
    dressing and breadcrumbs 39
  Iceberg with dried oregano dressing and
    creamy sheep's milk cheese 34
duck
  Mandarin and Seville orange–braised duck
    legs with carrots 174
  Pork, duck and pistachio terrine 242
  Sage salt and black pepper duck breasts
    with cherries 172–3
dumplings with mandarin, chilli and soy, Pork
  and garlic chive 132–3

E

eggs
  Asparagus with brown butter, egg yolk,
    lemon and young pecorino 74
  Custard 221–2
  Lime curd tart with toasted meringue
    206–7
  Meringue 207
  Pappardelle with chilli-braised beef,
    red wine, vinegar, egg yolk and
    breadcrumbs 102–3
eggplant (aubergine)
  Baba ghanoush with roasted spring onions,
    beetroot and green olive 33
  Steamed eggplant with chilli and pork
    mince 79
escarole with prosciutto, balsamic and
  hazelnuts, Grilled 60
Everyday roasted chicken and broth 12

F

Farmers' markets 46
fennel
  Citrus with Meyer lemon dressing and
    shaved fennel 40
  Fennel braised in chicken fat 91
  Roasted fennel and Jerusalem artichoke
    with hazelnuts and grapefruit 45
  Snapper carpaccio with yuzu kosho,
    orange and fennel 142

Tomato salad with sumac onions, tahini yoghurt and wild fennel 27
Wilted spinach with fennel, apple and pistachio butter 42

feta
Beetroot and persimmon salad with feta, honey, pistachio and Aleppo 25
Radish with preserved lemon, feta, mint and sesame 45

fig
Fig and goat's curd salad with smoky paprika vinaigrette 27
Pork neck braised with figs, lemon and oregano 184

fish (see also anchovy)
Corn and soffrito with fish sauce 73
Fish crudo and citrus ponzu 140
Fragrant and sour fish curry 156–7
Radicchio with bagna cauda and walnut oil 34
Slow-cooked ocean trout on fig leaves with kohlrabi and tomato salsa 148
Snapper carpaccio with yuzu kosho, orange and fennel 142
Steamed cod with leek and seaweed butter 152
Tomato and fried crouton salad with tonnato and capers 28
Tuna steaks with gribiche 158
Whole roasted John Dory with brown butter, lemon, capers and nori 147
Zucchini with mint, lemon and bottarga 30
Flaky dough 227
flan with poached cherries, Mom's 211

flatbread
Grilled lamb leg spiedini with flatbreads and harissa-ish oil 189
Yoghurt and spelt flatbreads 232
Focaccia 233
Fougasse 234–5
Fragrant and sour fish curry 156–7
fregola sarda, Mussels with sausage, capsicum and 131
Fresh corn polenta with chilli and garlic oil 108
Fresh pici 110

G

galette
A simple apple galette 213–4
Greens and onion galette with crème fraîche and Comté 55–6
Strawberry and brown sugar galette 208

garlic
Celeriac and Jerusalem artichoke soup with kale and chilli garlic oil 57
Clams with sorrel, tarragon and green garlic 154
Fresh corn polenta with chilli and garlic oil 108
Greens with garlic, turmeric, fenugreek and breadcrumbs 85
Nettle and green garlic risotto with crispy speck 128
Pork and garlic chive dumplings with mandarin, chilli and soy 132–3

Potato, green garlic and sorrel gratin 67
Pot-roasted mud crab with lemon, garlic, chilli, butter and fine noodles 144
Socca with chickpeas, rosemary and roasted garlic yoghurt 118
White wine–braised artichokes, carrots and green garlic 70
ginger upside-down cake, Pineapple and 203
glaze, Apple peel 213
goat's curd salad with smoky paprika vinaigrette, Fig and 27

gorgonzola
Persimmon, witlof, pomegranate and gorgonzola dolce 38
Verjus-roasted quince with gorgonzola dolce and fresh walnuts 91
Whole grilled beef tenderloin with caramelised onions, treviso and gorgonzola dolce 192
grapefruit, Roasted fennel and Jerusalem artichoke with hazelnuts and 45
grapes and za'taar, Buttermilk-marinated chicken with roasted 176

gratin
Cauliflower and smoked cheese gratin 64
Potato, green garlic and sorrel gratin 67
Green pasta with zucchini, sage and peas 116
Greens and onion galette with crème fraîche and Comté 55–6
Greens with garlic, turmeric, fenugreek and breadcrumbs 85
gribiche, Tuna steaks with 158
Grilled broccoli shoots with anchovy butter and salsa verde 81
Grilled chicory with celery, anchovy, parmesan dressing and breadcrumbs 39
Grilled côte de boeuf rested in rosemary and thyme 190
Grilled escarole with prosciutto, balsamic and hazelnuts 60
Grilled flanken-style short ribs with lemon and olive oil 186
Grilled lamb leg spiedini with flatbreads and harissa-ish oil 189
gruyère, Whole roasted pumpkin stuffed with wild mushrooms and 59

H

harissa
Grilled lamb leg spiedini with flatbreads and harissa-ish oil 189
Slow-roasted lamb shoulder with white beans and harissa 182–3

hazelnut
Grilled escarole with prosciutto, balsamic and hazelnuts 60
Pencil leeks with hazelnut picada and citrus zest 60
Roasted fennel and Jerusalem artichoke with hazelnuts and grapefruit 45

honey
Beetroot and persimmon salad with feta, honey, pistachio and Aleppo 25
Chardonnay and honey vinaigrette, and how to dress a salad 16

Horseradish and breadcrumb salsa verde 171
how to dress a salad, Chardonnay and honey vinaigrette, and 16

I

Iceberg with dried oregano dressing and creamy sheep's milk cheese 34
Ice creams 216
Almond and cherry custard ice cream 217
Blueberry frozen yoghurt 216
Custard apple and kaffir lime ice cream 217

J

jalapeño salsa, Pork carnitas with pineapple and 185
John Dory with brown butter, lemon, capers and nori, Whole roasted 147

K

kaffir lime ice cream, Custard apple and 217
kale and chilli garlic oil, Celeriac and Jerusalem artichoke soup with 57
kitchen tools 10
kohlrabi and tomato salsa, Slow-cooked ocean trout on fig leaves with 148
kumquat and chilli relish, Roasted brussels sprouts with sour cream and 61

L

lamb
Grilled lamb leg spiedini with flatbreads and harissa-ish oil 189
Marinated and grilled rack of lamb 191
Slow-roasted lamb shoulder with white beans and harissa 182–3
Lasagne bolognese 125–7

leek
Pencil leeks with hazelnut picada and citrus zest 60
Steamed cod with leek and seaweed butter 152

lemon
Asparagus with brown butter, egg yolk, lemon and young pecorino 74
Chicken al mattone with white bean purée, lemon, brown butter and capers 178
Citrus with Meyer lemon dressing and shaved fennel 40
Grilled flanken-style short ribs with lemon and olive oil 186
Pork neck braised with figs, lemon and oregano 184
Pot-roasted mud crab with lemon, garlic, chilli, butter and fine noodles 144
Radish with preserved lemon, feta, mint and sesame 45
Whole roasted John Dory with brown butter, lemon, capers and nori 147

lime
Custard apple and kaffir lime ice cream 217
Lime curd 207
Lime curd tart with toasted meringue 206–7
Oysters with coriander, lime and white pepper mignonette 139
Linguine with mussels and nduja 119
liver
Bacon and chicken liver parfait 241
Pici with chicken liver and marsala ragu 111

M

mandarin
Mandarin and chilli paste 133
Mandarin and Seville orange–braised duck legs with carrots 174
Pork and garlic chive, dumplings with mandarin, chilli and soy 132–3
Marinated and grilled rack of lamb 191
Meringue 207
meringue, Lime curd tart with toasted 206–7
mignonette, Oysters with coriander, lime and white pepper 139
mint and sesame, Radish with preserved lemon, feta, 45
miso
Chocolate miso tart 204
Oven-roasted prawns with nasturtium and miso butter 149
Mom's flan with poached cherries 211
mousse
Chocolate mousse 221–2
Citrus and chocolate mousse trifle 221–2
mud crab with lemon, garlic, chilli, butter and fine noodles, Pot-roasted 144
mushrooms
Warm camembert with oven-roasted mushrooms and spring onions 81
Whole roasted pumpkin stuffed with wild mushrooms and gruyère 59
mussels
Linguine with mussels and nduja 119
Mussels with sausage, capsicum and fregola sarda 131
mustard
Cucumbers with mustard vinaigrette and dill 30
Peas and broad beans with tarragon, mustard and horseradish 78
Whole roasted pork rack with caramelised apples and mustard 197

N

nasturtium and miso butter, Oven-roasted prawns with 149
Nettle and green garlic risotto with crispy speck 128
nduja, Linguine with mussels and 119
noodles, Pot-roasted mud crab with lemon, garlic, chilli, butter and fine 144
nori, Whole roasted John Dory with brown butter, lemon, capers and 147

nut (see also almond; hazelnut; pistachio; walnut)
Beetroot and persimmon salad with feta, honey, pistachio and Aleppo 25
Braised chicken legs and wings with almonds, olives, raisins and preserved lemon 180
Castelfranco with warm chestnut, thyme and prosciutto 37
Celeriac, walnut, pear and bresaola 38
Grilled escarole with prosciutto, balsamic and hazelnuts 60
Pencil leeks with hazelnut picada and citrus zest 60
Pork, duck and pistachio terrine 242
Radicchio with bagna cauda and walnut oil 34
Roasted fennel and Jerusalem artichoke with hazelnuts and grapefruit 45
Verjus-roasted quince with gorgonzola dolce and fresh walnuts 91
Wilted spinach with fennel, apple and pistachio butter 42

O

oil
Celeriac and Jerusalem artichoke soup with kale and chilli garlic oil 57
Chilli oil 79
Fresh corn polenta with chilli and garlic oil 108
Grilled lamb leg spiedini with flatbreads and harissa-ish oil 189
Radicchio with bagna cauda and walnut oil 34
olives
Baba ghanoush with roasted spring onions, beetroot and green olive 33
Braised chicken legs and wings with almonds, olives, raisins and preserved lemon 180
onion
Baba ghanoush with roasted spring onions, beetroot and green olive 33
Greens and onion galette with crème fraîche and Comté 55–6
Tomato, onion and cheddar tart 88
Tomato salad with sumac onions, tahini yoghurt and wild fennel 27
Warm camembert with oven-roasted mushrooms and spring onions 81
Whole grilled beef tenderloin with caramelised onions, treviso and gorgonzola dolce 192
orange
Citrus and chocolate mousse trifle 221–2
Citrus with Meyer lemon dressing and shaved fennel 40
Mandarin and Seville orange–braised duck legs with carrots 174
Snapper carpaccio with yuzu kosho, orange and fennel 142
Oven-roasted prawns with nasturtium and miso butter 149
ovens 11
Oysters with coriander, lime and white pepper mignonette 139

P

pancetta and rosemary, Pappardelle with borlotti beans, 114
Pappardelle with borlotti beans, pancetta and rosemary 114
Pappardelle with chilli-braised beef, red wine, vinegar, egg yolk and breadcrumbs 102–3
parfait, Bacon and chicken liver 241
parmesan dressing and breadcrumbs, Grilled chicory with celery, anchovy, 39
pasta 96–7
Arroz negro with abalone, pipis and chorizo 123
Casarecce with pesto Trapanese 109
Fresh pici 110
Green pasta with zucchini, sage and peas 116
Lasagne bolognese 125–7
Linguine with mussels and nduja 119
Mussels with sausage, capsicum and fregola sarda 131
Pappardelle with borlotti beans, pancetta and rosemary 114
Pappardelle with chilli-braised beef, red wine, vinegar, egg yolk and breadcrumbs 102–3
Pasta dough 102, 116
Pasta fredda with almonds and chilli salsa verde 105
Pici with chicken liver and marsala ragu 111
Pot-roasted mud crab with lemon, garlic, chilli, butter and fine noodles 144
Ribollita with borlotti beans and cavolo nero 99
Rigatoni with fresh tomatoes, butter and basil 105
Spaghetti with cauliflower, anchovies, currants and almonds 104
Spaghetti with clams, parsley and spinach 101
Triangoli with asparagus and ricotta 122
pastry 88, 226
Chocolate miso tart 204
Flaky dough 227
Greens and onion galette with crème fraîche and Comté 55–6
Lime curd tart with toasted meringue 206–7
Pâté sucrée (sweet pastry) 228–9
Strawberry and brown sugar galette 208
Tomato, onion and cheddar tart 88
Witlof tarte tatin 68
Pâté sucrée (sweet pastry) 228–9
peas
A very green soup 86
Green pasta with zucchini, sage and peas 116
Peas and broad beans with tarragon, mustard and horseradish 78
pear and bresaola, Celeriac, walnut, 38
pecorino, Asparagus with brown butter, egg yolk, lemon and young 74
Pencil leeks with hazelnut picada and citrus zest 60
persimmon
Beetroot and persimmon salad with feta, honey, pistachio and Aleppo 25
Persimmon, witlof, pomegranate and gorgonzola dolce 38
pesto Trapanese, Casarecce with 109
pici, Fresh 110
Pici with chicken liver and marsala ragu 111

pickles, Quick vinegar 247
pineapple
    Pineapple and ginger upside-down cake 203
    Pork carnitas with pineapple and jalapeño salsa 185
pipis and chorizo, Arroz negro with abalone, 123
pistachio
    Beetroot and persimmon salad with feta, honey, pistachio and Aleppo 25
    Pork, duck and pistachio terrine 242
    Wilted spinach with fennel, apple and pistachio butter 42
Pistou 86
plums, Chocolate torte with baked 215
Poached beef short ribs with horseradish and breadcrumb salsa verde 171
Poached whole chicken with winter vegetables and black truffle stuffing 170
polenta with chilli and garlic oil, Fresh corn 108
pomegranate and gorgonzola dolce, Persimmon, witlof, 38
Ponzu 140
ponzu, Fish, crudo and citrus 140
Poolish 234
Porchetta roasted pork shoulder 194
pork
    Arroz negro with abalone, pipis and chorizo 123
    Bacon and chicken liver parfait 241
    Castelfranco with warm chestnut, thyme and prosciutto 37
    Grilled escarole with prosciutto, balsamic and hazelnuts 60
    Linguine with mussels and nduja 119
    Mussels with sausage, capsicum and fregola sarda 131
    Nettle and green garlic risotto with crispy speck 128
    Pappardelle with borlotti beans, pancetta and rosemary 114
    Porchetta roasted pork shoulder 194
    Pork and garlic chive dumplings with mandarin, chilli and soy 132–3
    Pork carnitas with pineapple and jalapeño salsa 185
    Pork, duck and pistachio terrine 242
    Pork neck braised with figs, lemon and oregano 184
    Sausage meat 243
    Steamed eggplant with chilli and pork mince 79
    Whole roasted pork rack with caramelised apples and mustard 197
potato
    Potato, green garlic and sorrel gratin 67
    Potato rolls 231
    Slow-roasted, crispy sweet potatoes 61
Pot-roasted mud crab with lemon, garlic, chilli, butter and fine noodles 144
Poultry and meat 166–8
    Resting 167
    Salting 167
    Temperatures 166

prawns with nasturtium and miso butter, Oven-roasted 149
prosciutto
    Castelfranco with warm chestnut, thyme and prosciutto 37
    Grilled escarole with prosciutto, balsamic and hazelnuts 60
pumpkin
    Barley risotto with pumpkin, sage, roasted radicchio and balsamic 100
    Whole roasted pumpkin stuffed with wild mushrooms and gruyère 59
purée, White bean 178

Q

Quick vinegar pickles 247
quince with gorgonzola dolce and fresh walnuts, Verjus-roasted 91

R

rack of lamb, Marinated and grilled 191
radicchio
    Barley risotto with pumpkin, sage, roasted radicchio and balsamic 100
    Radicchio with bagna cauda and walnut oil 34
Radish with preserved lemon, feta, mint and sesame 45
Ragu 102
ragu, Pici with chicken liver and marsala 111
raisins and preserved lemon, Braised chicken legs and wings with almonds, olives, 180
relish, Roasted brussels sprouts with sour cream and kumquat and chilli 61
rhubarb crumble, Strawberry and 204
Ribollita with borlotti beans and cavolo nero 99
ribs with horseradish and breadcrumb salsa verde, Poached beef short 171
rice
    Arroz negro with abalone, pipis and chorizo 123
    Nettle and green garlic risotto with crispy speck 128
Rich poultry broth 13
Ricotta 238
ricotta, Triangoli with asparagus and 122
Rigatoni with fresh tomatoes, butter and basil 105
risotto with crispy speck, Nettle and green garlic 128
risotto with pumpkin, sage, roasted radicchio and balsamic, Barley 99
Roasted brussels sprouts with sour cream and kumquat and chilli relish 61
Roasted fennel and Jerusalem artichoke with hazelnuts and grapefruit 45
rolls, Potato 231
Romesco 183

S

Sage salt and black pepper duck breasts with cherries 172–3
salad
    Baba ghanoush with roasted spring onions, beetroot and green olive 33
    Beetroot and persimmon salad with feta, honey, pistachio and Aleppo 25
    Castelfranco with warm chestnut, thyme and prosciutto 37
    Celeriac, walnut, pear and bresaola 38
    Citrus with Meyer lemon dressing and shaved fennel 40
    Cucumbers with mustard vinaigrette and dill 30
    Fig and goat's curd salad with smoky paprika vinaigrette 27
    Grilled chicory with celery, anchovy, parmesan dressing and breadcrumbs 39
    Iceberg with dried oregano dressing and creamy sheep's milk cheese 34
    Persimmon, witlof, pomegranate and gorgonzola dolce 38
    Radicchio with bagna cauda and walnut oil 34
    Radish with preserved lemon, feta, mint and sesame 45
    Roasted fennel and Jerusalem artichoke with hazelnuts and grapefruit 45
    Tomato and fried crouton salad with tonnato and capers 28
    Tomato salad with sumac onions, tahini yoghurt and wild fennel 27
    Wilted spinach with fennel, apple and pistachio butter 42
    Zucchini with mint, lemon and bottarga 30
salsa
    Pork carnitas with pineapple and jalapeño salsa 185
    Seared scallops with sautéed witlof and Meyer lemon salsa 161
    Slow-cooked ocean trout on fig leaves with kohlrabi and tomato salsa 148
Salsa verde 17
    Celeriac schnitzel with salsa verde 53
    Grilled broccoli shoots with anchovy butter and salsa verde 81
    Pasta fredda with almonds and chilli salsa verde 105
    Poached beef short ribs with horseradish and breadcrumb salsa verde 171
salt 10–11
sauce
    Aioli 15
    Béchamel 126
    Gorgonzola sauce 192
    Gribiche 158
    Ponzu 140
    Romesco 183
    Tomato sauce 126
Sausage meat 243
scallops with sautéed witlof and Meyer lemon salsa, Seared 161
schnitzel with salsa verde, Celeriac 53
seafood (*see also* clams; mussels) 136
    Arroz negro with abalone, pipis and chorizo 123

Clams with sorrel, tarragon and green garlic 154
Linguine with mussels and nduja 119
Mussels with sausage, capsicum and fregola sarda 131
Oven-roasted prawns with nasturtium and miso butter 149
Oysters with coriander, lime and white pepper mignonette 139
Seared scallops with sautéed witlof and Meyer lemon salsa 161
Spaghetti with clams, parsley and spinach 101
Squid with sweet red capsicums, basil and aioli 153
Seared scallops with sautéed witlof and Meyer lemon salsa 161
seaweed butter, Steamed cod with leek and 152
sesame, Radish with preserved lemon, feta, mint and 45
shallots, Charred Romano beans with buttermilk and herb dressing and crispy 75
Slow-cooked ocean trout on fig leaves with kohlrabi and tomato salsa 148
Slow-roasted, crispy sweet potatoes 61
Slow-roasted lamb shoulder with white beans and harissa 182–3
Snapper carpaccio with yuzu kosho, orange and fennel 142
Socca 118
Socca with chickpeas, rosemary and roasted garlic yoghurt 118
sorrel
Clams with sorrel, tarragon and green garlic 154
Potato, green garlic and sorrel gratin 67
soup
A very green soup 86
Celeriac and Jerusalem artichoke soup with kale and chilli garlic oil 57
Ribollita with borlotti beans and cavolo nero 99
Tomato, red capsicum and carrot soup with squash blossoms and basil 73
Spaghetti with cauliflower, anchovies, currants and almonds 104
Spaghetti with clams, parsley and spinach 101
speck, Nettle and green garlic risotto with crispy 128
spelt flatbreads, Yoghurt and 232
spiedini with flatbreads and harissa-ish oil, Grilled lamb leg 189
spinach
A very green soup 86
Spaghetti with clams, parsley and spinach 101
Wilted spinach with fennel, apple and pistachio butter 42
Sponge cake 221
squash blossoms and basil, Tomato, red capsicum and carrot soup with 73
Squid with sweet red capsicums, basil and aioli 153
Steamed cod with leek and seaweed butter 152
Steamed eggplant with chilli and pork mince 79
strawberry
Strawberry and brown sugar galette 208
Strawberry and rhubarb crumble 204
stuffing, Poached whole chicken with winter vegetables and black truffle 170

T
tahini yoghurt and wild fennel, Tomato salad with sumac onions, 27
tart
Chocolate miso tart 204
Lime curd tart with toasted meringue 206–7
Tomato, onion and cheddar 88
Witlof tarte tatin 68
terrine, Pork, duck and pistachio 242
tomato
Rigatoni with fresh tomatoes, butter and basil 105
Slow-cooked ocean trout on fig leaves with kohlrabi and tomato salsa 148
Tomato and fried crouton salad with tonnato and capers 28
Tomato, onion and cheddar tart 88
Tomato, red capsicum and carrot soup with squash blossoms and basil 73
Tomato salad with sumac onions, tahini yoghurt and wild fennel 27
Tomato sauce 126
tonnato and capers, Tomato and fried crouton salad with 28
torte with baked plums, Chocolate 215
treviso, Whole grilled beef tenderloin with caramelised onions, treviso and gorgonzola dolce 192
Triangoli with asparagus and ricotta 122
trifle, Citrus and chocolate mousse 221–2
trout on fig leaves with kohlrabi and tomato salsa, Slow-cooked ocean 148
Tuna steaks with gribiche 158

V
Verjus-roasted quince with gorgonzola dolce and fresh walnuts 91
vinaigrette
Chardonnay and honey vinaigrette, and how to dress a salad 16
Cucumbers with mustard vinaigrette and dill 30
Fig and goat's curd salad with smoky paprika vinaigrette 27

W
walnut
Celeriac, walnut, pear and bresaola 38
Radicchio with bagna cauda and walnut oil 34
Verjus-roasted quince with gorgonzola dolce and fresh walnuts 91
Warm camembert with oven-roasted mushrooms and spring onions 81
White wine–braised artichokes, carrots and green garlic 70
Whole grilled beef tenderloin with caramelised onions, treviso and gorgonzola dolce 192
Whole roasted pork rack with caramelised apples and mustard 197
Whole roasted pumpkin stuffed with wild mushrooms and gruyère 59
Wilted spinach with fennel, apple and pistachio butter 42

witlof
Persimmon, witlof, pomegranate and gorgonzola dolce 38
Seared scallops with sautéed witlof and Meyer lemon salsa 161
Witlof tarte tatin 68
Women in the kitchen 162

Y
yoghurt 237
Blueberry frozen yoghurt 216
Roasted garlic yoghurt 118
Socca with chickpeas, rosemary and roasted garlic yoghurt 118
Tomato salad with sumac onions, tahini yoghurt and wild fennel 27
Yoghurt and spelt flatbreads 232

Z
za'atar, Buttermilk-marinated chicken with roasted grapes and 176
zucchini (courgette)
A very green soup 86
Green pasta with zucchini, sage and peas 116
Zucchini with mint, lemon and bottarga 30

Thank you

To Jane Willson for believing in me and championing this book. I am forever grateful for the opportunity.

To Anna Collett for keeping me on deadline and dealing with my thousands of edits. Your kindness in an unknown process made everything so much easier. Thank you also to Andrea O'Connor for your attention to detail during the copy-edit.

To Justin and Bettina Hemmes, and everyone at Merivale, who built the world's most beautiful kitchen at Fred's and who also took a risk on giving me the reigns. Because of Fred's, my world has changed.

Thanks to Benito Martin and Jess Johnson, who photographed and styled these incredible images. Those days with you all were some of the most fun and exciting of my career. Let's do it again please!

To Evi O, your energy and incredible design style have made the most beautiful book come together. I feel so grateful to have worked with you on this.

To Georgia Lahiff and Madeleine Jeffreys for helping me create such beautiful food. Your touch, positivity, support and excellent cooking made these images what they are and I could not have done it without you.

To my partner, Dan Sharp. Thank you for tasting everything I tested and re-tested, and for saying it was delicious even when it wasn't. I love you.

To my friend Georgie Neal, your drive to find the best produce and support our local farms is inspiring. Your eye for beauty, flavour and aesthetics has changed the way I look at things and I am forever grateful for your help on this project and your friendship in life.

To my team at Fred's, especially Hussein Sarhan, Pia Papenfuss, Saavni Krishnan and Helise Heggen. Your support and talent gives me the freedom to do things like this. I am so thankful and lucky to work with all of you.

To all my previous teachers, especially Alice Waters, Amy Dencler, David Tanis, Jean-Pierre Moulle, Jerome Waag, Mary Jo Thoresen and Amaryll Schwertner, as well as the countless chefs that took the time to show me something. I often wonder if you realise the impact your small acts of kindness and the sharing of knowledge has had on me and so many others.

To David Prior, your ability to connect people has literally altered the course of my life. I am so thankful for your friendship.

To Frank Roberts, who pretty much taught me everything I know about running a business. Who would have thought one little email could change someone's life? Thank you for believing in me.

To Ben Greeno for always pushing me to be better. Your mentorship and support have been my saving grace in a chaotic world. When the work becomes a bit too much, you always know what to say. Thank you for always looking out for me – it means more than you know.

To my dear friends Deirdre Ryan, Jessica Roberts, Karen Taylor, Stella Agostino, Glen Choy and Libby Travers – you each have played a pivotal role in my life and you also make it more fun. Thank you for helping me through hard times and for always bringing me joy and wine!

To Judy Stewart, you are an inspiration and I am lucky to know you. Thanks for pushing me to write a book.

To the farmers who supplied all the beauty and nourishment in these pages, especially Olivier and Falani Sofo, Erika Watson and Hayden Druce, Fabrice Rolando, Elle Brown and Dylan Abdoo and Phil Lavers. I am so thankful to know those of you that do things the right way, even if it means the hard way. Please don't stop doing what you do – we all need you!

To Grant and Laura Hilliard of Feather & Bone. Not just because you have the best butcher shop in Australia, but because the friendship and trust we have built over the years continuously reminds me that supporting good people is good for everyone.

Lastly and MOSTLY, to my mom, dad, Christie, Marty, Manny, Charlie and Mia. More important than cooking and food, you all have taught me about love and what it means to be family. I am so thankful we are in this together.

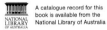 A catalogue record for this
book is available from the
National Library of Australia

Always Add Lemon
ISBN 978 1 74379 543 9

10 9 8 7 6 5 4 3 2 1

Publishing Director: Jane Willson
Project Editor: Anna Collett
Editor: Andrea O'Connor
Design Manager: Jessica Lowe
Designer: Evi O. Studio | Evi O. & Nicole Ho
Photographer: Benito Martin
Stylist: Jessica Johnson
Home Economists: Georgia Lahiff, Madeleine Jeffreys
Production Manager: Todd Rechner
Production Coordinator: Mietta Yans

Colour reproduction by Splitting Image Colour Studio
Printed in China by Leo Paper Products LTD.

If I ever find myself getting too cheffy about things, I remind myself to cook like a grandma, because that's what everyone loves.